A REPUBLIC IN TIME

A REPUBLIC IN TIME

Temporality and
Social Imagination
in Nineteenth-
Century America

THOMAS M. ALLEN

The University of
North Carolina Press

Chapel Hill

© 2008 The University of North Carolina Press

Set in Bulmer, Didot, and Madrone types
by Tseng Information Systems, Inc.
Manufactured in the United States of America

The paper in this book meets the guidelines for permanence
and durability of the Committee on Production Guidelines for
Book Longevity of the Council on Library Resources.

Library of Congress Cataloging-in-Publication Data
Allen, Thomas M., 1967-
A republic in time : temporality and social imagination in nineteenth-
century America / Thomas M. Allen.
    p. cm.
Includes bibliographical references and index.
ISBN 978-0-8078-3179-3 (cloth : alk. paper) —
ISBN 978-0-8078-5865-3 (pbk. : alk. paper)
1. United States—Intellectual life—1783-1865. 2. United States—
Social conditions—To 1865. 3. United States—Politics and government
—1783-1865. 4. Space and time—Social aspects—United States—
History—19th century. 5. Space and time—Political aspects—United
States—History—19th century. 6. Nationalism—United States—
History—19th century. 7. Democracy—United States—History—19th
century. 8. Material culture—United States—History—19th century.
9. American literature—19th century—History and criticism.
10. Space and time in literature. I. Title.
E165.A43 2008
973.3—dc22   2007023207

cloth   12 11 10 09 08   5 4 3 2 1
paper   12 11 10 09 08   5 4 3 2 1

For Susan

CONTENTS

Acknowledgments xi

Introduction: Time and Modern Nationhood 1

Chapter 1. The Future Republic 17

Chapter 2. Material Time 59

Chapter 3. Clockwork Nation 114

Chapter 4. Time in the Land 146

Chapter 5. Emerson's Deep Democracy 186

Conclusion: The Ends of Time 217

Notes 225

Bibliography 251

Index 267

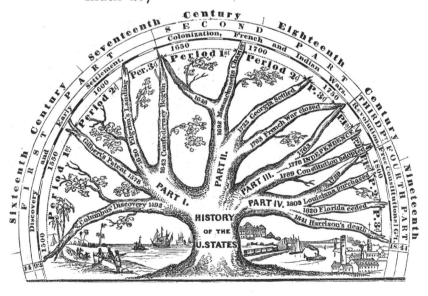

ILLUSTRATIONS

1.1. "The Temple of Time," frontispiece to Emma Willard's *Universal History in Perspective* 33

1.2. Frontispiece to Emma Willard's *Abridged History of the United States, or, Republic of America* 35

1.3. Title page of Emma Willard's *Abridged History of the United States, or, Republic of America* 45

1.4. Thomas Cole, *The Course of Empire: The Consummation of Empire* 49

1.5. Thomas Cole, *The Course of Empire: Destruction* 50

1.6. Thomas Jefferson, architectural drawing of a Tuscan monopteros 57

2.1. John Lewis Krimmel, *Quilting Frolic* 68

2.2. William Sidney Mount, *Rustic Dance after a Sleigh Ride* 69

2.3. Lilly Martin Spencer, *Listening to Father's Watch* 71

2.4. James Wady, dial plate of tall clock 72

2.5. Jean-Baptiste Dubuc, George Washington mantle clock 76

2.6. Louis Mallet, neoclassical mantle clock 77

2.7. John Paul, tall clock, detail of cabinet 79

2.8. Simon Willard, calendar shelf clock, detail of interior of lower cabinet 82

2.9. Simon Willard, patent timepiece ("banjo clock") 84

2.10. Simon Willard, lighthouse alarm clock 87

2.11. Simon Willard, lighthouse alarm clock, detail view from side 89

2.12. Eli Terry, pillar-and-scroll shelf clock 92

2.13. Label of Silas Hoadley "Franklin" clock 95

2.14. John Ehninger, *Yankee Peddler* 97

2.15. Francis William Edmonds, *The Speculator* 99

2.16. Francis William Edmonds, *Taking the Census* 100

2.17. Chauncey Jerome, Gothic revival shelf clock 109

3.1. Frontispiece to E. A. Howland's *The American Economical Housekeeper* 121

3.2. James Goodwyn Clonney, *Mother's Watch* 138

4.1. Frederic Edwin Church, *The Icebergs* 155

4.2. Frontispiece to second American edition of Robert Bakewell's *Introduction to Geology* 160

4.3. Edward Hitchcock and Orra White Hitchcock, topographical cross-section of Massachusetts geology 166

4.4. Orra White Hitchcock, *Sugar Loaf Mountain, Deerfield* 168

4.5. Thomas Cole, *The Subsiding of the Waters of the Deluge* 174

4.6. Thomas Cole, *The Course of Empire: The Savage State* 176

4.7. Thomas Cole, *The Course of Empire: Desolation* 177

4.8. The Temple of Jupiter Serapis, illustration from James D. Dana's *Manual of Geology* 179

ACKNOWLEDGMENTS

My interest in questions of time was first sparked when I came across David Levin's book *History as Romantic Art* in the stacks of Memorial Library at the University of Wisconsin. I have returned to that elegant volume many times since then. During my years in Madison, Bruce Burgett, Glen Van der Ploeg, Kate Anderson, Keiko Nitta, Amy Kort, James Sedgwick, and Travis Koplow all offered valuable advice on this project in its early stages. John McGuigan, Amy Feinstein, and Warren Oberman kept me from going crazy at various times. Dale Bauer dazzled in class, extended the range of bibliographical references in the margins, expressed a certain degree of bemusement in the hallway, and incited furious bouts of scrivening through example. The late Sargent Bush Jr. set a standard for scholarship that every graduate student tried to meet, despite knowing that we could never come close to his accomplishments. I used to look forward to showing him my first book.

In subsequent years, as the project took shape, Suzanne Jones, Peter Lurie, Ilka Saal, Matt Basso, Kathy Hewett-Smith, Abigail Cheever, Tong Lam, Andy Lewis, Woody Holton, Doug Winiarski, and Erling Sjovold provided a stimulating and supportive intellectual environment. I owe a special debt to Ed Larkin and John Marx, who not only read and offered incisive comments on this manuscript but also provided a great deal of inspiration through their own excellent scholarship. I could not have asked for better colleagues. Maurice Lee, Carlene Stephens, Anne Raine, Janice Fiamengo, Ian Dennis, and Robert Stacey also read and helped me to improve various parts of this manuscript, as did the two anonymous peer reviewers for the University of North Carolina Press. Dana Nelson, Donald Pease, and Priscilla Wald all offered terrific responses on conference panels. I have to thank David Rampton for thinking enough of my work to bring me to the peaceable kingdom of Ottawa. Alexis McCrossen deserves special thanks for her indefatigable support and enthusiasm for this project over many years. Of course, this book would not exist without the support of my editor, Sian Hunter, who shepherded it to publication with skill and professionalism.

To produce a book featuring this many images, I have of course had to rely upon the generosity of many librarians, curators, and collectors, especially Nancy Dyer at the National Association of Watch and Clock Collectors Library in Columbia, Pennsylvania; Audrey Johnson at the Library of Virginia; Jeanette Robichaud at Old Sturbridge Village; Jim Orr at the Henry Ford Museum; Peter Nelson at the Amherst College Archives and Special Collections; and Susan Newton at Winterthur. Antique clock experts John Delaney and Paul Foley went far beyond any reasonable definition of courtesy in supplying me with beautiful photographs of a significant clock. Art historian Nick Clark resolved a small crisis by pointing me to the location of an important painting at a critical moment. University of Ottawa students Nikki Pratt and Leah Brisco came through with some timely aid to enable me to get the manuscript finished at last.

The National Endowment for the Humanities supported this work in two ways. First, my participation in the NEH Summer Institute "Ralph Waldo Emerson at 200: Literature, Philosophy, Democracy" was crucial to developing the ideas in Chapter 5. I must thank especially the institute organizer, Russell Goodman. Second, an NEH residential fellowship at the Winterthur Museum and Library was essential to completing the material culture component of the book. At Winterthur, Gretchen Buggeln was astonishingly generous as director of research programs. Gretchen did everything from discoursing on the nuances of art historical method to teaching me how to use the slide scanner. Staff members Pat Elliott, Katherine Hunt, and Charles Hummel also gave me a great deal of their time and expertise. I was lucky to be at Winterthur with a cohort of wonderful visiting scholars, including Anthony Light, Paula Mohr, Melissa Duffes, Kerry Dean Carso, David Hancock, and Michael Epp. It would not have been the same without that community. I also benefited from a Batten Fellowship at the International Center for Jefferson Studies, Monticello. Andrew O'Shaughnessy made me feel welcome and allowed me to present a version of these ideas in a colloquy with some most learned Jeffersonians. A portion of Chapter 2 of this book was published in the *Journal of American Studies* as "Clockwork Nation: Modern Time, Moral Perfectionism, and American Identity in Catharine Beecher and Henry Thoreau"; I thank Cambridge University Press for permission to reprint that material here.

On a more personal note, my parents, Michael and Margaret Allen, provided important financial and moral support for my pursuit of an academic career, and my brother Jonathan never let on that he thought it was weird that I was still a student at the age of thirty. Maurice and Eileen Redding offered a quiet, sunny office space and the world's best child care. I never could have finished my degree, let alone written a book, without the guidance and encouragement of Gordon Hutner, who was first my teacher, then my adviser, and finally my friend. Most of all, I have to thank Susan Redding for keeping faith in this endeavor across all the years, and for remaining supportive through all the evenings and weekends of work; and thanks to Henry Trane for pulling daddy away from the computer once in a while.

A REPUBLIC IN TIME

INTRODUCTION

Time and Modern Nationhood

In an 1835 article for the *North American Review* inspired by
that year's *American Almanac*, William O. B. Peabody argues
that the precision of time measurement provides an index of
the progress of civilization, represented by "the steps of discovery, from the first helpless attempts at dividing time" to
the accurate calendars and clocks of the nineteenth century.
Peabody's essay sketches a history of timekeeping, emphasizing how technical improvements led to greater accuracy in
measuring natural units of time, such as years and days, and
also to the development of artificial units, such as hours and
minutes. "It is surprising to see what a vast amount of talent
the necessity of establishing measures of time has called into
exertion," Peabody remarks, indicating that time is not only
an aspect of nature but also a product and sign of human ingenuity. The "entirely modern" result of this process is the
clock, the standard of timekeeping in Peabody's own age and
an item whose mass production (beginning in 1807) was one
of the first achievements of American industrialization. The
history of timekeeping, Peabody finds, leaves one with "a profound impression of the reach of human power."[1] How the
people of a particular moment experience time, Peabody suggests, signifies where that moment and its people are located
in a continuum of historical time. In his faith in progress and
the power of civilization, especially American civilization,
Peabody had, of course, the company of many of the young
nation's leading citizens and opinion makers. Early to mid-
nineteenth-century periodicals and public lectures reveal a
widespread sense that the American nation was a particularly
modern place, and that what was often called "the present
age" possessed historically unique characteristics.[2] Peabody's
1835 essay articulates an especially important way of thinking

about the modernity of that civilization: in terms of the measurement, employment, and mastery of time.

Although Peabody celebrates the increasing accuracy of mechanical timekeeping, he does not, as we might expect, distinguish clock time from other forms of time reckoning rooted in nature or religion. Instead, Peabody employs his review of an almanac—a work traditionally devoted to tracking natural time—as an occasion for thinking about the intersections and reciprocal influences between various conceptions of time. In Peabody's discussion, the temporal rhythms of nature reflect God's design of the cosmos. "It is said," Peabody notes, "in the account of creation, that the heavenly bodies were intended to measure times, seasons, days, and years." Peabody attributes the importance of the seven-day week to the observation of the Sabbath and explains how the "division of the year into months, is suggested by the changes of the moon."[3] Mechanical timekeeping derives, in part, from this design but also adds to it new, more secular and less natural temporal measures. In the story Peabody tells, the hours of the day made familiar on nineteenth-century clock dials reflect what was initially a partitioning of the natural periods of day and night in the practices of medieval monks; this religious division of natural time morphed into the more rigid forms of mechanical timekeeping. Minutes and seconds, Peabody goes on to note, have no basis in nature at all. Peabody's review essay thus reveals the complexity of time as Americans experienced it in this period. Clock time was, to be sure, understood as significantly different from natural and religious time, but it was also deeply intertwined with those other temporal modes. While Peabody does describe the clock as the most "modern" form of timekeeper, for Peabody clocks produce a form of time that is largely—but not entirely—a manifestation of natural and religious temporal modes.

To a great extent, Peabody's linking of these different forms of time seems provoked by the content of the almanac itself, which includes an introductory essay on the difference between apparent solar time (marked by the sun's passage across the sky) and mean solar time (the time told by clocks), along with a variety of other materials both correlating and contrasting clock time with nature and religion.[4] However, almanacs had included such materials since the eighteenth century. What makes the *American Almanac* different from its eighteenth-century predecessors is its nationalist idiom. The almanac features a variety of demographic information testifying to the growth of the United States. A table of latitude and longitude locates important cities in a nationalized space and time by recording their distances from Washington, D.C., not only in miles but also in hours, minutes, and seconds of difference in local time. Furthermore, a note to this table makes clear the inherent connection between the measurement of space and time: "The Longitude of those [places] marked with a †, was recently determined by the Editor by chronometers, by comparing the place in question with Washington, the University of Virginia, Philadelphia, or Boston, the position of which is supposed to be correctly ascertained."[5] Through these precise chronometrical observations, the *American Almanac* situates an expanding American population within national time and space. As if to reinforce the importance of accurate time measurement to the establishment of a coherent national identity, the volume reviewed by Peabody includes a brief essay titled "The Punctuality of General Washington"—thus Americans reading the almanac would find themselves aligned with both the first president and the capital city bearing his name through precise chronometry.

However, such endorsements of the power and importance of mechanically measured time share space in the almanac with more traditional calendar pages showing the phases of the moon and the rising and setting of the sun, along with notations of historical events important to the American nation situated within this more natural temporal context. The natural time of the cycles of the sun and moon is then linked once again to the clock through the use of mean time, rather than apparent solar time, to indicate the times of the rising and setting of these heavenly bodies. Taking his cue from the heterogeneous temporal modes represented in the contents of the almanac itself, then, Peabody imagines a complex layering of different forms of temporal experience—technological, natural, and religious—all of which he treats as pertinent to the modern moment. The fact that almanacs had long included such information, but that both Peabody and the almanac's editors shape this material into a nationalist idiom, is precisely what makes this material remarkable. In a particular historical moment, it became possible to make use of long-available materials for new purposes: the creation of narrative representations of national identity within time. If writers such as Peabody and the almanac's editors defined national identity through time, then the heterogeneity of time itself provided opportunities for diverse agents with different interests to produce competing accounts of American national identity. America's manifold temporal cultures were like pieces of a puzzle that might be assembled into a variety of different pictures. That is to say, rather than simply recording how all or some Americans experienced time in this period, narratives such as these give time particular forms—they produce versions of temporality—in order to found particular accounts of American nationhood.

A Republic in Time explores the diverse temporal modes of national emergence by focusing upon such narrative accounts of national identity within time. In the category of narrative I include not only traditional literary narratives but also images that can be read as texts and objects such as clocks that are susceptible to analysis through material culture approaches. While recognizing that different types of artifacts of cultural history each have their own distinct ways of producing meaning, I consider them all within the general rubric of narrative in order to indicate that my primary interest is in how they tell stories about time, and especially how they provide accounts of national identity within time. The fact that these accounts rarely agree with one another makes up a large part of their interest. For every writer who saw the clock as central to modern life, another emphasized the approach of the millennium, or the continuing importance of nature. For every clock that celebrated the triumph of technology, another evoked a powerful sense of historicity in its design. The most interesting of such narratives, from the pens of writers such as Catharine Beecher, Henry Thoreau, and Ralph Waldo Emerson, and from the shops of artisans such as Simon Willard and Eli Terry, combine these different forms of temporality, creating out of America's heterogeneous temporal cultures a vision of America as a nation in time that is, itself, heterogeneous.

In making time central to their accounts of American nationhood, these narratives form part of the long and important tradition in Western political and social theory that sees modern nationality as emerging out of particular forms of temporality. However, in making time heterogeneous, they give us cause to rethink one of the basic premises of this tradition as it has been codified in the twentieth century: that time, as experienced in the modern world, is essentially homogeneous, and thus constitutes a homogenizing force in the formation of modern national states. The complex cultural history of temporal experience in America—in which time could be, at once, both natural and artificial, both millennial and secular—allows us to see that time has been, and remains, a medium for addressing the apparent contradictions of modern national identity not by eliminating them but rather by making it possible to imagine nationality as an ongoing negotiation, in narrative, of heterogeneous temporal modes.

Although much contemporary political rhetoric invites us to imagine that nations, as we now know them, have always existed, nations are in fact a relatively recent historical phenomenon. The oldest nations trace their cultural origins back to the medieval or ancient worlds, but the forms of state organization and concepts of citizenship and belonging that characterize modern nations did not begin to emerge until the seventeenth century at the earliest.[6] J. G. A. Pocock has shown how central time has been to this emergence. Pocock demonstrates that the "civic humanist" thought of post-Renaissance political philosophers (influenced by, but quite different from, certain branches of classical political theory) depended upon a recognition of the importance of secular history. Medieval philosophers, according to Pocock, saw secular time as of little import. Eternity was what mattered, and events transpiring within time were of interest only insofar as they reflected God's providence: "History . . . acquired meaning through subordination to eschatology."[7] In Christian theology, as exemplified by Augustine, eternity is not an infinite quantity of time but rather the absence of time and change. The development of republican civic humanism, with its emphasis on the virtuous subordination of individual interests to those of the political body, was a response to the new level of importance Renaissance Europe assigned to events transpiring within time. The temporal world was no longer perceived as simply an interlude between the Fall and salvation. Time still might be, as medieval Christians had thought, the realm of chaotic Fortune, but in the Renaissance that chaos began to matter. Hence, Pocock argues, the republic emerged as a stabilizing force, a bulwark against a ceaseless tide of chaotic temporal change.[8]

Pocock's analysis provides a powerful insight into what political thinkers in the modern era have wanted nations to do. Rather than simply treating the modern national state as an effect or outcome of certain historical trends, Pocock shows that the nation as we now know it was created, both in theory and in practice, in order to solve certain problems — problems, most fundamentally, of temporality. While Pocock focuses on republican political theory, temporality has also been essential to Lockean liberalism. "In the beginning, all the world was America," John Locke wrote in the second of his *Two Treatises of Government* (section 49).[9] In grounding his theory of contractual politics upon an imagined American state of nature, Locke suggests that America represents both the universal beginning of historical time as well as an ideal, empty container for the template of future, modern nationhood, in that he is making an argument about what future governments ought to look like. Locke's hypothetical "American" nation-state would develop within time, both in the sense that the economic and social relations between individuals would multiply organically so as to create a shared history for the people, and in the sense that within this historical time the people would invent a government for themselves. The rights of individuals—the core of liberal political theory—derive from the nation's status as a temporal invention, a contract made (and potentially unmade) within time. Hence, in liberal thought as well as republican, a secular sense of time as a medium of meaningful human activity has been essential.[10]

Locke's use of America as a model for this process illustrates the special role that the New World has played in thinking about time and modern nationhood. While Locke's *Two Treatises* were written almost 100 years before the American Revolution, their treatment of the New World as a kind of pristine laboratory for thought experiments about the nature of political society ramified into a powerful influence on revolutionary politics, represented most strikingly in Thomas Jefferson's appropriation of a Lockean vocabulary in the Declaration of Independence.[11] Precisely because New World nations constituted themselves within the span of history—within time as human beings had known it—they staged the process of nation formation in an exemplary way for an audience across the Atlantic. Benedict Anderson has pointed out the "unselfconscious provincialism" of the assumption that modern nationhood must have begun in Europe and described how the New World "creoles" (individuals of European descent not born in Europe) became the source of the first successful modern nationalist movements. "The close of the era of successful national liberation movements in the Americas," Anderson observes, "coincided rather closely with the age of nationalism in Europe." Hence, European nationalists "were able to work from models provided by" predecessors in both North and South America.[12] Underlying the creation of these models was the emergence of New World print cultures centered on the commercial activities of particular regions. These print cultures led to political communities organized horizontally, within secular time, rather than vertically through historical or messianic time. The "empty, homogeneous time" (a phrase from Walter Benjamin that becomes central to Anderson's argument) of commerce, first coalescing in the Americas precisely because of the relative lack of overdetermining caste traditions, provided the basis for modern nationhood. As clock time was spread through the space of the nation via trade and print culture, Anderson proposes, it created a shared "simultaneity" of experience that linked individuals together in an "imagined community" moving together through time.[13]

As Anthony D. Smith has noted, Anderson's "ideas about the decline of large-scale sacred communities and the emergence of linear time, which lie at the heart of his modernism," have unfortunately received far less attention from scholars than has his celebrated concept of "imagined communities" fostered by print culture.[14] Indeed, the same point can be made more generally: the quite sweeping analysis of large-scale shifts in temporal perception that underlies much influential political theory has received little scrutiny. Both Anderson and Pocock argue that modern nationalism requires the invention of a stable and, crucially, empty temporal container within which national affiliation can express itself. For both theorists, time must therefore be homogeneous; that is, it must not be filled with competing cultural imperatives pulling individuals away from their national affiliations. For Pocock, this value-free, homogeneous time is secular; the escape from the religious saturation of time with chiliastic significance is the principal requirement for the emergence of national political imagination. For Anderson, homogeneous time is mechanical. The abstract rationality of the clock, in Anderson's view, works to drive all other meanings out of time. Clock time supersedes modes of temporal experience based in religion, nature, or other "premodern" cultural traditions. Both of these accounts make rational, value-free temporal structures central to modern nationhood.

In so doing, they mirror a more general theory of modernity characterized by social homogeneity and rationalism. Ernest Gellner, perhaps the most important theorist of nationalism, has described the basic qualities of modern society as "anonymity, mobility, atomisation" and argued that "homogeneity of culture is *the* political bond" in the modern world. Gellner contrasts this anonymous, mobile, and homogeneous culture with a premodern agrarian society that "encourages cultural differentiation within itself."[15] In this respect, the clock provides an apt symbol of modernity, since it seems to lead inevitably toward the homogenization of temporal experience. A most prestigious body of social theory and economic history has linked this temporal homogenization to the kinds of cultural homogeneity that Gellner describes as fundamental to the modern nation. As early as 1903, Georg Simmel argued that the clock was central to regulating the networks of capitalist economic exchange that constitute the central feature of modern social life. "[I]f all the clocks and watches in Berlin would suddenly go wrong in different ways, even if only by one hour," Simmel wrote, "all economic life and communication in the city would be disrupted for a long time. . . . Thus, the technique of metropolitan life is unimaginable without the most punctual integration of all activities and mutual relations into a stable and impersonal time schedule."[16]

The theory of clock time's importance to modern economic and social life was later adopted by Lewis Mumford in his influential studies of technology; as Mumford sees it, "the clock, not the steam engine, is the key machine of the modern industrial age."[17] This position became conventional wisdom following the publication of E. P. Thompson's seminal 1967 essay "Time, Work-Discipline, and Industrial Capitalism." The introduction of mechanical clocks into factories in England, Thompson argues, resulted in a "restructuring of working habits" and a concomitant change in the "inward notation of time" that led individuals to accept the Industrial Revolution's basic premises of quantifiable wage labor and systematic production.[18] According to Thompson's successors, historians such as David Landes, the relationship between clocks and other forms of modernization has been recursive; advances in technology have made it possible to measure time more accurately, and this greater accuracy has in turn facilitated greater productivity, more efficient transportation networks (think of railroad timetables), and the punctuality so important to modern business.[19] The result of such temporal modernization, this very diverse group of thinkers agrees, has been a world made over not only economically but also socially and culturally to suit first the exchange networks of mercantile capitalism and later the clockwork rationality of the free market.[20] In Mumford's rather poetic formulation, the clock "marks a perfection toward which other machines aspire."[21]

Of course, no one would deny that modern nations are, in fact, heterogeneous in many respects, including in the people's experience of time. The consensus view that emerged over the course of the twentieth century understood temporal homogeneity to be an ideal worked toward by both capitalist modes of production and the bureaucratic activities of modern nation-states. According to the consensus view, these homogenizing activities marginalized, but never completely erased, alternate temporalities. This consensus is (perhaps unintentionally) epitomized in Homi Bhabha's argument that the time of the modern nation is "double," both performative and pedagogical. National pedagogy, both the activities of the official bureaucracy and the even more crucial work of cultural and economic institutions, cultivates homogeneous national time within the consciousness of the people. Meanwhile, Bhabha theorizes, the people themselves resist state authority by asserting the traditions of particular local, regional, or protonational cultures. Bhabha celebrates the temporal heterogeneity thus enacted as a form of resistance to national authority, but in the same gesture consigns the "performative" temporality of the people to a state of perpetual, albeit internal, exile from the time of the modern nation.[22] In this respect, Bhabha reproduces the consensus account of national time. Theorists from Simmel to Thompson to Anderson have been well aware of the existence of multiple forms of temporal experience, but they have defined temporal modes other than homogeneous clock time as atavistic and irrelevant in the modern world. Bhabha's theory attempts to reclaim such alternate temporal modes as sites of resistance, but in so doing it reproduces the account of these temporalities as marginal to modern nationhood.

This same problematic gesture reappears in the even more recent work of Donald Pease, who, in an important essay celebrating the antinationalist perspective of C. L. R. James, refers to "the continuist and homogeneous time reproduced within U.S. literature and history"—a mechanism, Pease argues, "through which the state assimilated persons to the national geography." In contrast to this homogeneous national time, Pease identifies in James the "interruptive temporalities," "syncopated times," and "disjointed temporality" that would make possible a "transnational social movement" of individuals who could "[refuse] to conform to a state's monocultural taxonomy and could not be integrated within a nationalizing telos."[23] In the introduction to the prominent essay collection *The Futures of American Studies*, published two years after Pease's article on James first appeared, Pease and Robyn Wiegman would then employ the same rhetoric of temporal subversion to describe the work of themselves and their academic peers, portraying the "New Americanists" featured in the volume as contesting a "national mythos" that generates "an imaginary homogeneity out of discrepant life worlds" by producing "what Benedict Anderson called the empty homogeneous time of the imagined national community." In contrast to this official national homogenizing practice, Pease and Wiegman argue, the New Americanists enable a more progressive politics by eliciting the heterogenous insurgent time present in the "anti-imperial discourses" upon which New Americanist scholarship focuses.[24] Clearly the concept of homogeneous national time is one that still carries great weight, albeit negatively construed, among American studies scholars. Simmel and Thompson had also been critical of the power of homogeneous time to discipline individuals and subsume them within totalizing nationalism, but they had viewed resistance to this homogenizing power as largely futile. Bhabha and Pease are more optimistic about the ability of individuals and local groups to resist totalizing national time. However, in defining heterogenous time as inherently antinational, transnational, or postnational, they join the earlier theorists in assuming that national time must necessarily be homogeneous.

Even as major recent theorists such as these have continued to describe the dominant or hegemonic time of the nation as homogeneous, this position has been implicitly (though not directly) challenged by emerging work in fields such as social history and sociology. Scholars in these fields have produced a steadily growing body of evidence to illustrate how time in the modern world is actually "a kind of web, spun from ideas about nature, religion, civil authority, and mechanical timepieces," as Carlene Stephens aptly puts it.[25] While the majority of these scholars have not concerned themselves directly with theoretical definitions of national time, their work has implicitly called into question the assumptions about time that underlie influential theories of nationalism. For example, in a magisterial study of timekeeping in Europe, Gerhard Dohrn–van Rossum argues against "widespread distortions in the discussions about modernization processes in Europe" based upon misrepresentations of the social, cultural, and economic history of the clock.[26] In the American context, social historians such as Stephens, Paul Hensley, Alexis McCrossen, Martin Bruegel, Mark M. Smith, and Michael O'Malley have demonstrated empirically that changes in time consciousness cannot be explained as a story of progress from a more primitive to a more rational organization of time.[27] These historians have gathered the evidence to prove that Americans continued to think of time in terms of religion and nature even as mechanical timepieces became increasingly important beginning in the nineteenth century.

Most importantly, the more progressive scholars working in this area have shown that the homogeneity of time that supposedly results from the centrality of such instruments as clocks, watches, and calendars to modern life is only possible if technologies produce time by themselves. As McCrossen points out, "Simply because the technology existed to synchronize personal and public timepieces, does not mean that timepieces were correctly set, or that time discipline was perfectly internalized."[28] Once we begin to ask what people did with technologies of time, and why they wanted such technologies, the homogeneity of modern national time begins to shatter into myriad fragments of heterogeneous, local, and transient temporal cultures. The sociologist Norbert Elias has employed such insights to produce a striking revision of Simmel's way of thinking about metropolitan time. In the modern world, Elias argues, "chains of interdependencies between people became not only longer, but also more differentiated; their web became more complex and the accurate timing of all relationships became more pressing, and in fact indispensable, as a means of regulating them."[29] As these lines indicate, Elias focuses his analysis upon "timing" as an activity, rather than "time" as an object. Instead of assuming, as Simmel did, that the syncronization of activities via a shared network of strictly regulated time must result in a flattening out of political differences, Elias posits that such a network actually lends itself to the creation of a more complex and differentiated world of human interactions. "Timing" is the activity through which diverse individuals and local groups can create heterogeneous national cultures. The shared network or web of timing activities links people together, but because timing is an active process, the network as a whole is constructed out of the very diverse uses individuals make of time. Temporal heterogeneity thus becomes central to the experience of modern collective belonging. The crucial point that must be made in regard to recent theorizing about nationalism in American studies is that these heterogeneous temporalities are not marginal or resistant to the nation, nor do they represent forms of collective affiliation that will emerge after the demise of the nation. Rather, they are themselves the threads out of which the fabric of national belonging has long been woven.

Thus far, there have been very few studies that draw connections between political theory and the newly developed scholarly insights into the complexity of modern temporal experience. That is, while some social historians and sociologists employ nationalist descriptors such as "American," most of the scholars doing interesting work on time have simply not been concerned with rethinking theories of nationalism. Meanwhile, political theorists and scholars in American studies who have focused on creating theoretical accounts of nationalism have paid scant attention to the scholarship on time. In this work, I seek to put these bodies of knowledge in dialogue with one another, to create new knowledge by drawing connections as well as by offering my own analysis of heretofore understudied temporal artifacts. The brief survey I have offered of the existing scholarship on time, modernity, and nationhood is intended both to illustrate how important these three terms are to one another and to point toward the need for new scholarship focusing specifically on the nationalist aspects of time. A better model of the relationship between time and the nation would attend to the recursive and dynamic interactions between these two terms. Such a model would dispense with the notion of time as a transhistorical phenomenon, an aspect of nature or product of technology existing outside of human society, and treat time as a historical artifact produced by human beings acting within specific historical circumstances. To employ Elias's terminology, we need to know how individuals have employed diverse forms of *timing* to create the imagined communities of modern nations.

A Republic in Time does not attempt to explain how all, or even many, nations have existed within time, but rather to explore the unique cultural, social, intellectual, political, and material conditions within which Americans struggled to define their particular nation within time. The writers, artists, tradespeople, and others I discuss in this book are rarely systematic. Sometimes they do not even intend to comment on political or social issues. Certainly most of them would never have imagined that they had much to do with one another. Nevertheless, all of the figures discussed in these chapters made substantial contributions to America's sense of itself as a nation in time. Hence, the term "theory" is not precisely appropriate to the ideas I study here; a looser rubric such as "social imagination" better reflects the lack of formal rigor that characterizes these materials. Social theory implies a systematic attempt to make sense of the behavior and beliefs of human beings in groups. Likewise, political theory seeks axioms, the underlying principles of specific forms of government or national life. I prefer to use the term "social imagination" to identify the practices through which the works of these thinkers and makers engage questions of social and political theory in ways that are highly unsystematic, but nevertheless are most revealing and important.

Chapter 1 sets the stage for these considerations of time and American national identity by investigating the relationship between time and space through a reconfiguration of the classic problem of republic and empire. The idea that Americans looked to the possibility of unlimited westward expansion as a salve for the problem of imperial corruption has long been one of American studies' most cherished theses. As Drew McCoy notes in *The Elusive Republic*, the Louisiana Purchase presented Jeffersonian Republicans with a seemingly insoluble dilemma: how could America be, as Jefferson put it, an "empire for liberty"? However, McCoy also paradoxically argues that the apparently limitless space of the West promised resolution to the very problem it created: "In addition to resolving the Mississippi crisis, the Louisiana Purchase was important to the Jeffersonians precisely because it promised to preserve the fundamentally agricultural, and hence republican, character of American society for centuries to come. In simplest terms, the Purchase guaranteed that the American empire would be able to continue to expand across space, rather than be forced to develop through time."[30] This argument does not really resolve the problem posed: if empire and republic were antithetical terms for nationhood, then how could the imperial occupation of space preserve the republican character of the nation? The contradictory nature of the spatial solution has only been perpetuated in recent revisionary work in this area, which has decried the violence and oppression of westward expansion even while continuing to characterize

American nationalism in terms of an effort to escape time by conquering space.

In this book, I reformulate the issue by looking at how a diverse array of American historical thinkers imagined America as an empire extending through time rather than across space. Without denying the historical importance of westward expansion, I focus on how the cultural conflicts that such expansion provoked were resolved through temporal narratives that imaginatively deflected the exercise of American power into the future. As an empire of time rather than space, the creators of such narratives hoped, America would both dominate world history, determining the fates of other nations, and avoid the unjust exercise of power that republican political theory abhorred. In contrast to the traditional interpretation, then, I propose that many significant American national theorists sought to escape the political paradoxes of space by conquering time.

From this ground, subsequent chapters proceed to map out particular sections of the heterogeneous temporal geography that constituted the most significant territory of the American nation. Chapters 2 and 3 focus upon clocks and watches, not as producers of a distinctly mechanistic form of temporality but rather as loci for richly layered temporal experience: mechanical, natural, historical, and religious. Chapter 2 primarily takes a material culture approach to the history of clock and watch design, decoration, marketing, and consumption in the first half of the nineteenth century. During this crucial period of American nation formation, mechanical timepieces of many different designs carried into American homes a variety of temporal signatures, from the neoclassical to the Gothic, from the pastoral to the technophilic. I analyze these timepieces themselves as material objects, as well as the representation of such objects in media such as advertisements and genre paintings. The traditional theory of clock time's centrality to modern nationhood relied upon a form of technological determinism rejected by most contemporary historians and philosophers of technology. For example, Bruno Latour argues that the meaning of a technology is neither contained within the technology itself nor determined by the human being making use of that technology, but emerges out of the interaction between the two. Latour writes of human and nonhuman agents (devices, machines, processes) acting in tandem, so that technologies neither produce outcomes by themselves nor simply "mediate" human actions. Rather, human beings and machines each possess unique capacities for action that produce new possibilities when combined. Obviously only human actors possess the will to make decisions, to initiate action, but the possession of a particular device can shape what a human being wants to do—in ways that are, themselves, contingent upon that human being's position in history.[31] Hence, the emergence of new ways of measuring and thinking about time has the potential to result in many different forms of collaboration between human beings and the nonhuman world: technology, nature, and the numinous realm of religion.

Chapter 3 turns the focus toward literary narratives, demonstrating how writers such as Sarah Hale, Catharine Beecher, and Henry Thoreau employed the idea of clock time to imagine different forms of capitalist market exchange and modern national identity. Beecher, for example, makes the process of redeeming the quantified time of commerce central to her vision of a national market for Christian salvation. Thoreau, in turn, imagines an inexhaustible natural market that rescues commerce from Beecher's feminized domesticity and delivers it to what Thoreau portrays as the robust masculinity of a clock time consonant with nature. Central to the argument I make in this chapter is an analysis of mechanical time as a commodity in a specifically Marxist sense. As a reified and fetishized object of consumption, mechanical time makes it possible to internalize the abstract logic of the market itself. Through the process of identity formation that accompanies the consumption of commodities within capitalism, a new process of production emerges that transforms the market itself. Hence, the consumption of mechanical time becomes a complement to the production of clocks and watches themselves. Together, Chapters 2 and 3 illustrate how, at each end of the production-consumption cycle, creative activity takes place that perpetually revises the nature of time, prompting, in turn, new versions of national narrative.

Chapters 4 and 5 also form a pair, in this case focusing on the revolutions in natural time that took place in the nineteenth century. Chapter 4 examines how the expansion of the temporal scale in the nineteenth century by major developments in natural history, especially geology, shaped American thinking about history and nationhood. Between about 1750 and 1860, a series of naturalists and science writers including Comte de Buffon, James Hutton, John Playfair, Charles Lyell, Louis Agassiz, and Charles Darwin revolutionized the Western world's understanding of time by expanding the scale of the earth's history from thousands to millions of years. This shift was brought about by major theoretical and methodological developments in the sciences of geology and biology, developments that were disseminated through the literate public by books and reviews written for an intelligent lay audience. The impact of this expansion of the temporal scale was immense, providing the basis for important American theories of national identity from the natural theology of Edward Hitchcock to the dynamic theory of history of Henry Adams.

Chapter 5 is the only chapter that focuses on the ideas of a single individual, Ralph Waldo Emerson. Emerson's importance to American political philosophy has only grown in importance in recent years, both for defenders of liberal democracy such as George Kateb and for radical critics such as Cornel West. It is a token of the tremendous vitality of Emerson's thought that contemporary political theorists have used Emerson not simply to explore the history of American democracy but more often to ground their own contemporary arguments about what direction American political philosophy ought to take in the present and future. Many of our most important thinkers have made him central to the possibility of a revitalized democratic politics. A recent outpouring of work on Emerson and natural history has made it possible now to consider how Emerson's thinking about time shaped his ideas about democratic nationhood. In contrast to the natural theologians discussed in Chapter 4, Emerson perceived deep time as entropic and antihumanist. This discovery liberated Emerson from both the telos of romantic historiography and the oppressive, utilitarian rationalism of the market, enabling him to imagine a new form of historical time more appropriate to the needs of a democratic nation, reformulating human identity and social relations within the "perpetual inchoation" of nature.[32] Natural theology reconciled the history of the earth with religious traditions and hence made the modern nineteenth century compatible with the past. In contrast, Emerson perceived that a new kind of nation required new ways of thinking about history, a project that rested, ultimately, upon new ways of thinking about time itself.

Throughout this investigation, one of my fundamental assumptions is that writing and making, along with reading, seeing, employing, and even hearing, are actions lending historical significance to ideas about time. The artifacts employed in everyday life are the material expression of systems of belief that link individuals to the social matrix. As Louis Althusser observes, ideas only enter history insofar as they are concretized in the form of practices, institutions, or materials. Hence, when I refer to such abstract concepts as "time consciousness" or "modernity," what I wish to call attention to is the way in which such ideas may be perceived through the practices of the people of the nineteenth century. In general, I focus on literary and material representations of time as artifacts of the way that people inscribed beliefs about time into their daily lives and, in so doing, continuously produced time for themselves. It is fruitful to allow the central terms of my analysis — time, modernity, history, and nationhood — to define themselves inductively through their expression in cultural artifacts. To borrow a phrase from Susan Strasser, such artifacts are "representations that produce reality as well as recording it."[33] Because the production and consumption of such artifacts were themselves media through which ideas about time and nation were produced and consumed, each articulation of the temporal theme contributes new meanings to that theme. The historical evidence about the nature of time cannot simply be gathered together and synthesized into a coherent picture of how nineteenth-century Americans defined time, because they did not define it; they practiced it. And each practical act of time challenges any consensus about the nature of time and nationhood.

Different kinds of artifacts of these practices reveal different sorts of information. Jules Prown cautions that material objects "are disappointing as communicators of historical fact; they tell us something, but facts are transmitted better by verbal documents." Material objects are, however, "excellent and special indexes of culture, concretions of the realities of belief of other people in other times and places, ready and able to be reexperienced and interpreted today."[34] Other media, such as literary narratives and paintings, carry their own blindnesses and special opportunities for insight. By combining analysis of diverse materials, I hope to make use of the strengths of each while mitigating their weaknesses. By itself, the design and operation of a single clock, for example, cannot tell us anything about the nature of time for its maker or its owner. However, when considered in the context of many timepieces, this clock becomes part of a pattern. Juxtaposing this object with literary narratives about the employment of clock time may make its significance, formerly mysterious, suddenly much more clear. And finally, placing clock time within the many other temporal modes — natural, historical, religious — circulating within the culture brings out its historical significance in a way that could never be understood through a narrow focus on objects in isolation from culture. Through study of these different genres and kinds of cultural artifacts, I explore the various modes of national belonging that specific acts of producing time made possible.

1

THE FUTURE REPUBLIC

Six years before coining the phrase "manifest destiny," John O'Sullivan wrote an article for his *Democratic Review* entitled "The Great Nation of Futurity." In contrast to his more famous 1845 editorial in support of the annexation of Texas, the 1839 article emphasizes America's place in time rather than space. "American patriotism is not of soil," O'Sullivan proclaims. "We are not aborigines, nor of ancestry, for we are of all nations."[1] Rather than an "aboriginal" attachment to a particular land, O'Sullivan declares, the true affiliation of Americans is to the future: "The expansive future is our arena, and for our history. We are entering on its untrodden space."[2] In making "untrodden space" the vehicle of a metaphor in which "the expansive future" is the tenor, O'Sullivan's figurative language implicitly renders time the more important term. To be sure, at other points in this 1839 essay O'Sullivan is less eager to dismiss the importance of space to American national development, but he always insists that time is at least equally important. Indeed, the headiest imagery of the 1839 essay emerges as O'Sullivan links these two terms together to describe how Americans will build an exemplary "temple" of mythic dimensions across both time and space:

> The far-reaching, the boundless future will be the era of American greatness. In its magnificent domain of space and time, the nation of many nations is destined to manifest to mankind the excellence of divine principles; to establish on earth the noblest temple ever dedicated to the worship of the Most High—the Sacred and the True. Its floor shall be a hemisphere—its roof the firmament of the star-studded heavens, and its congregation an Union of many Republics, comprising hundreds of happy millions, call-

ing, owning no man master, but governed by God's natural and moral law of equality, the law of brotherhood.[3]

O'Sullivan's temple of continental expanse recalls Jefferson's vision of a confederation of small republics stretching ever farther westward to meet the needs of an expanding population.[4] Rather than focusing exclusively on the spatial dimension of the Jeffersonian vision, however, O'Sullivan emphasizes the temporal dimension of national expansion that was equally important to Jefferson himself. In "The Great Nation of Futurity," Jefferson's confederation becomes a "congregation" that stretches into the future as much as it does into the West. O'Sullivan thus reproduces, in the context of Young America and Jacksonian democracy, Jefferson's own formative appeal to the possibility of national development through time.

O'Sullivan's celebration of the importance of time to American national identity, and concomitant diminution of the importance of "soil," may seem surprising given the preeminent role assigned to the land by a long tradition of American studies scholarship. The most canonical works in the field have interpreted the development of the American nation in the nineteenth century in terms of expansion through space, the impulse to heed what Henry Nash Smith describes as the "pull of a vacant continent drawing population Westward."[5] Revisionist scholars have disagreed with Smith's description of North America as "vacant," calling attention to the presence of indigenous peoples as well as immigrants and creoles from a variety of cultural and national origins. However, the revisionists have, for the most part, maintained the focus on territorial expansion as the crucial issue in American national development. From Frederick Jackson Turner's "frontier thesis" to the "myth and symbol" school, and on through the "new Americanists" and the subsequent proliferation of critical subfields of American studies, the land itself, whether viewed as integral or crisscrossed by borders, vacant or inhabited, has been at the center of scholarly attention in discussions of American national development.[6]

Despite what this tradition of scholarship would lead us to assume, however, the focus on temporality evident in the metaphors employed in "The Great Nation of Futurity" is equally central to American nationalist writing. These metaphors participate in a tropic economy of time and space that has operated throughout American history, a nationalist rhetoric that produces the United States as a republic whose real territory is more temporal than spatial. This tradition has flourished alongside the body of writings producing the spatial rhetoric to which scholars have paid more attention. Although it would be quixotic to attempt to trace a direct line of descent for a way of thinking that has surfaced in wide-ranging contexts, Jefferson stands out among the Revolutionary generation for the especially rich language of temporality developed in his writings. In an 1823 letter to James Monroe, for example, in response to Monroe's queries regarding American efforts to define the New World as its own political sphere and exclude European influence from that sphere, Jefferson wrote: "The question presented by the letters you have sent me, is the most momentous which has ever been offered to my contemplation since that of Independence. That made us a nation, this sets our compass and points the course which we are to steer through the ocean of time opening on us."[7] In this letter, as in many of his other writings, Jefferson makes clear that he imagined the American Republic growing and developing through time. In Jefferson's imagination, as in O'Sullivan's, space often serves primarily as a metaphor for time—here, national space not as land at all, but as an ocean awaiting a project of national exploration.

In this chapter, I trace this temporal dimension of American nationalism through a variety of different areas of cultural production, including journalism (O'Sullivan), political theory (Jefferson), narratives in prose and verse (William Gilmore Simms, George Bancroft, and William Cullen Bryant), painting (Thomas Cole), and education reform (Emma Willard). Focusing in depth upon any one of these areas would be a valuable scholarly endeavor, but the purpose of the present study is different. In order to illustrate the wide-ranging provenance and elastic vitality of the idea of the future republic, I have sought to illustrate how otherwise dissimilar individuals, such as Willard and O'Sullivan, Jefferson and Bryant, all imagined elements of an American dominion over time. It would be reductive to assert that all of these thinkers held the same ideas about time and nationalism. What I seek to show in this chapter is the range of different ways in which different figures made time the medium for nationalist thought, in order to resolve the same fundamental contradictions in the nation's self-conception. I begin with O'Sullivan and Jefferson precisely because they have been most closely associated with the idea of American expansion through space. While acknowledging that both O'Sullivan and Jefferson did envision the United States expanding across space, I show that these two key figures were, in fact, equally preoccupied with expansion and development through time. The chapter then goes on to analyze the work of other important purveyors of ideas about nationalism who were, if anything, far more interested in time than space. Finally, at the end of the chapter I return to Jefferson in order to suggest another representative aspect of his ideas about temporality; not only did they provide the foundation for a fertile, creative way of imagining the nation, they also, most significantly, never achieved any closure to the problem of republican nationalism that they set out to solve. The Republic could never be achieved in any given present moment, because the nation would always be riven with present contradictions to its republican character. Hence, Jeffersonian ideas about time perpetuated themselves by creating the need for further theorizing, since they deflected the fulfillment of American nationalism into an endlessly retreating future. Those thinkers after Jefferson who also embraced the vision of an American dominion over time found themselves gazing toward a distant horizon, the temporal analogue of the "new, yet unapproachable America" Emerson claimed to have glimpsed in the West. "And what a future it opens!" Emerson exclaimed with longing.

Against Time

Scholars in the mainstream of American studies scholarship from the mid-twentieth century to the present have largely ignored this tradition of temporal nationalism in order to produce a particular account of the relation of the American nation to its own history. Because the national development of the United States was exclusively spatial, the argument has gone, Americans have lacked a sense of historical change. Mainstream American culture has been immersed in an ideological belief in its own transcendence of history. Two important books of the last twenty years exemplify this position. Myra Jehlen's *American Incarnation* (1986) argues that Americans, committed to an ideology of liberal individualism, rejected the "modern sense of history in Europe," a sense of history that was "ongoingly mutable" and filled with "further possibilities," and opted instead for a "translation of time into space."[8] In Jehlen's view, Americans saw themselves as posthistorical, having transcended the need for change within time by achieving the ideal form of the modern nation. All that remained, then, was for this posthistorical, unchanging nation to expand across the space of the West, already having reached the end of history.

Almost twenty years later, David Noble would make a very similar argument about time and space in *Death of a Nation* (2002). As a reflective, retrospective work from the hand of a historian who has long been one of our most esteemed scholars, *Death of a Nation* is uniquely informative about where we have come in these ongoing debates over the nature of time and space in American cultural history. While Noble has much to say that is new in this book, he echoes Jehlen in his remarks on temporality, arguing that Americans transformed a European attention to historical time into a preoccupation with space, creating a "paradigmatic assumption that Europe represented time and America (the United States) represented timeless space."[9] Like Jehlen, Noble characterizes this set of beliefs as ideological — a mystification of the real processes of historical development taking place even as Americans denied that time was a medium of change in the New World. While Jehlen extends the major part of her analysis only through the middle of the nineteenth century, Noble portrays Americans of that period as initiating the evasion of history whose legacy he traces through mid-twentieth-century American studies scholarship. Noble's heroes are those few Americans, usually members of marginalized or subjugated groups, who have, intermittently, awakened from ideology and into an awareness of historical change. Both Noble and Jehlen are revisionists in the sense that they disavow the exceptionalist theories of America's transcendence of history that they describe. Nevertheless, they both conclude that by the early nineteenth century the majority of Americans, especially the most politically empowered groups of Americans, believed themselves to have reached the end of history, to have achieved a state in which space, rather than time, was the only medium of national development.

While agreeing with most of what Jehlen and Noble have to say about the often pernicious politics of liberal individualism and American exceptionalism, I would posit that these exemplary scholars are too quick to dismiss the complexity, richness, and importance of American thinking about time in the crucial period of nation formation extending from the late eighteenth century to the middle of the nineteenth century. I cite these books because they are representative of how the field of American studies has treated the cultural history of ideas about time over the long period flagged by their dates of publication, 1986 and 2002. American studies scholarship of the 1980s and 1990s maintained the premise of America's belief in its own transcendence of history that had been promoted by midcentury American studies scholarship, but it reversed the values of those earlier critics and made what had been perceived as a positive attribute of American culture into a negative.

Along with *Death of a Nation*, most of the "postnational" American studies scholarship of the twenty-first century has, thus far, perpetuated the assumption that American nationality is linked to a North American space shrouded in a mystified conception of innocent time. Recent work in American studies has sought to move beyond the paradigm of nationhood by investigating "transnational" or "postnational" spaces such the "border-lands" of the Southwest, the "Black Atlantic," and the Pacific Rim. John Carlos Rowe argues that American studies must focus both research and pedagogical activity upon the "contact zone" (a phrase he borrows from Mary Louise Pratt), defined as "the liminal region or border zone in which different cultures meet."[10] Donald Pease, perhaps the leading figure in creating these new postnational paradigms for American studies, has called for the invention of a radical political "imaginary" that would account for the experiences of "deterritorialized and extraterritorial peoples."[11] Pease's proposed new direction for American studies is meritorious, but his linkage of the terms and concepts of "postnational" and "extraterritorial" reveals how postnational American studies continues to assume that American nationalism is inherently territorial—the movement beyond the nation is also a movement away from a particular territory.[12] By linking the nation to the land in this way, the scholars endeavoring to create a postnational American studies have continued to work within the framework created by the myth and symbol school. One might say that the importance of an integral land to American nationalism has itself become American studies' most enduring myth.

The Paradox of Expansion

In this chapter I shall argue that it was precisely America's lack of territorial integrity at inception, its problematic relationship to the space of North America from the very moment of national emergence, that produced the appeal of the elusive temporal horizon of national wholeness. The notion of national space created an unresolvable contradiction in the nation's self-conception. As Lawrence Buell has pointed out, Americans in the early national period faced an ambiguous political situation in which they could just as readily perceive themselves as a people recently liberated from imperial domination or as the agents of a nascent empire colonizing North America.[13] Though the term "empire" was sometimes employed as a label for any large or powerful nation, it was often used in antithesis to the ideal of the Republic. Hence, Americans habitually identified their own nation in opposition to empire, even as they also became aware that they were, in some sense, a successor to the Old World empires they read about in history books. J. G. A. Pocock writes that as Americans colonized the trans-Appalachian West they began to perceive "an evident paradox in the discovery that imperial conquests, which had rendered them secure against foreign and aboriginal enemies, now faced them with the threat of corruption by their own government." This recognition prompted a crisis of national self-identity: "Were not Americans," Pocock asks, "even in their own eyes, a system of colonies extending an empire, and not a republic at all?"[14] According to the romantic theories of nationhood that prevailed in the late eighteenth and nineteenth centuries, expansion was a necessary ingredient of national viability. A failure to grow would represent stagnation; increase in population, commerce, and power were all necessary if the nation were to thrive. However, it was not clear to Americans how national expansion could take place without the unjust conquest of territories inhabited by other peoples. Hence, the idea of occupying additional territory was both seductive and repellent, both an affirmation that the Republic was thriving and an ominous sign of its growing corruption. Though Thomas Jefferson referred to the West as a potential "Empire of liberty," he also wrote that if there were "one principle more deeply rooted than any other in the mind of every American, it is that we should have nothing to do with conquest."[15] Americans from Jefferson's generation through O'Sullivan's wrestled with the problem of how a republic could grow without becoming a tyrannical empire. "The Great Nation of Futurity" attempts to resolve this problem by making time the medium for an effusive nationalism, in which the future itself would become American territory. The viability of the young Republic lay in this process of expansion through time. Hence, it was the very effort to resolve the paradox implicit in an "empire of liberty" that set the stage for the translation of political affiliation away from space and toward time, toward a utopian horizon in the future where the nation's contradictions would resolve themselves into a coherent republic.

In pursuing this argument, I do not wish to rehearse all of the many claims that have been made since the 1970s regarding the existence and nature of an American empire.[16] There have been, by now, so many studies of "United States imperialism" that it has become an academic truism to hold that Americans of the nineteenth century almost universally wanted to extend an empire across North America, Latin America, the Pacific, Asia, and perhaps even Antarctica. Nor, to be clear, does my argument deny that many Americans celebrated the expansion of the nation across space. My purpose, rather, is to shift the focus of our understanding of nationhood away from a preoccupation with this process of spatial expansion and toward a recognition of the equally important role of temporality in imaginative constructions of the nation. I touch upon the subject of empire merely to build upon the relatively uncontroversial notion that Americans of the early republican period were, themselves, conscious of a certain paradoxical tension as the former colonial provinces began to acquire subject territories of their own.[17] If some Americans aspired to conquer territory, others were equally eager to avoid such conquests in order to forestall the possibility that the exercise of unjust hegemony might make the United States an empire, might begin to corrupt the nation's traditions of liberty or threaten the Republic with tyranny. Thus, the expansion through space, though quite real and important, was always fraught with tensions that many important figures sought to resolve or displace through a concomitant focus upon time.

Jefferson expressed this fear of imperial corruption when he wrote, in 1797, that "a mind devoted to the preservation of our republican government in the true form and spirit in which it was established" found itself "oppressed with apprehensions that fraud will at length effect what force could not, and that what with currents and countercurrents, we shall in the end be driven back to the land from which we launched 20. years ago."[18] The Jeffersonian antipathy to tyranny, even or especially when practiced by the United States, became a major chord in American political writing of the nineteenth century. "It may be that, even in our day," the popular historical novelist William Gilmore Simms speculated in an 1854 lecture, "we shall behold the banner of our civilization planted in mastery upon the ruined shrines of the luxurious Asiatic." Simms then went on to render a negative judgment upon the potential American empire that he invited audiences in Washington, Richmond, Petersburg, and Charleston to imagine. "The result of all this achievement," he told these audiences, "as well in our case as in that of England, is to exaggerate in the national estimate—as it did with the Assyrian, the Roman and the Macedonian,—the merit of mere material acquisition." Here Simms cautioned against the acquisition of empire because of the danger that excessive power would lead to corruption, a hubristic exaggeration of national self-worth, and eventually national decline. Simms summed this point up bluntly: "Here was the simple secret of Roman and Assyrian overthrow. They had but a single aim—acquisition—the spread of their empire—the seizure of foreign realms."[19] In the popular poem "The Rise of the West," poet Henry Rowe Schoolcraft put this American abhorrence of empire into historical perspective, calling for a new political paradigm in the New World:

> But ah, forbid, whate'er my country's end,
> One freeborn hand should tyrant power defend,
> Forbid, whate'er its pathway may afford,

Her triumphs should be triumphs of the sword.
Dire, bloody feats, that elder states have tried,
Rose, glittered, triumphed, tottered, sunk and died.
Ah, rather let her spirit and increase,
Shine in the glorious energies of peace.[20]

For Jefferson, contraction into the nation's original geographical space would represent historical regression, a loss of twenty years of national time to the corruption of public virtue that paradoxically accompanied the waxing of national power. Simms perceived this danger of national collapse paradoxically growing even as the United States gained dominion over greater and greater expanses of territory. Schoolcraft's poem presents the more optimistic counterpoint, the possibility of escaping from the historical pattern that seemed to have repeated itself inevitably throughout European history. O'Sullivan also echoes Jefferson's aversion to conquest when he boasts that Americans have never engaged in wars of expansion, never "suffered themselves to be led on by wicked ambition to depopulate the land, to spread desolation far and wide, that a human being might be placed on a seat of supremacy."[21] The creation of new states in the West required the conquest of territory that most Americans were, *pace* Smith, well aware was hardly "vacant." Even in the 1845 article in which O'Sullivan writes of America's "manifest destiny," he still acknowledges the legitimacy of Mexican sovereignty and warns against so much as the appearance of unjust conquest of territory from Mexico, advocating instead that Texas and California be allowed to achieve independence "without the agency of our government, without responsibility of our people—in the natural flow of events, the spontaneous working of principles." Eventually, O'Sullivan thought, these newly independent states would join the Union—though in the case of California, this process might take some time: "Unless the projected rail-road across the continent to the Pacific be carried into effect, perhaps they may not," O'Sullivan muses regarding the chances that an independent California would become a state of the Union, "though even in that case, the day is not distant when the Empires of the Atlantic and Pacific would again flow together into one, as soon as their inland border should approach each other." Indeed, O'Sullivan explicitly casts the process of annexation—whether of Texas and California or Oregon—as anti-imperial, a rejection of the "bayonets and canon, not only of France and England, but of Europe entire," a process reliant upon nature rather than force of arms.[22] O'Sullivan's vigorous struggle to naturalize the process of territorial expansion through a rhetoric that quickly becomes riddled with contradictions speaks to the depth of the irony Americans perceived in their relationship to national space.

The recognition of the paradox of expansion through space propelled the nationalist imaginations of writers such as O'Sullivan toward time — an abstract "space" that could, unlike the land of the North American continent, legitimately be described as "untrodden," as O'Sullivan proclaims in the 1839 article. Wai Chee Dimock has argued that Manifest Destiny required a "representational form for its agency," and that this form was the allegory of personification, a human body growing to incorporate more territory.[23] Without disputing the cogency of Dimock's analysis of how expansion through space was allegorized, I would submit that throughout American history much of the rhetoric of national expansion has made space, itself, a tropic medium for explorations of time, the "representational form" through which Americans make tangible the pursuit of a more abstract but also more ideologically palatable quest: the colonization of future time.

The Importance of Ideological Time

Of course, the annexation of Texas was, in fact, effected by military force, and with the military victory over Mexico came more territory in the Southwest. Hence, O'Sullivan's rhetoric seems to present a contradiction. He disavows the legitimacy of military conquest yet still calls for American appropriation of foreign territory. Consequently, we might view temporal rhetoric such as O'Sullivan's simply as an evasion of the actual extension of American dominion through space via the coercive exercise of economic, political, and military power. To some extent, O'Sullivan's essay does strive to make it possible for his readers to imagine that their nation is not doing what it is, in fact, doing: conquering territory and subjugating or driving out the inhabitants of that territory. In this sense, O'Sullivan's essay encourages a collective forgetting of the injustices that make national expansion possible. However, political theory of the last two decades has elucidated the great importance of such representational constructions of the nation. Benedict Anderson's famous concept of "imagined communities" depends upon the shared acts of imagination made possible by print culture; indeed, Anderson points out that forgetting can often be as important as remembering in the creation of shared national identity. Influenced by constructivist theories such as Anderson's, Simon During defines the activity of nationalism as "the battery of discursive and representational practices which define, legitimate, or valorize a specific nation-state or individuals as members of that state."[24]

Looked at in this way, the nation does not exist prior to nationalism. Rather, when different actors create representations of the nation, they intervene into a dialogue whose effect is a continuously evolving narrative of national identity. These narratives possess as much reality, in a historical sense, as the material history of the people and territory of the nation.

Such a formulation certainly seems appropriate to the early years of the American nation, when individuals experienced a dense array of allegiances to local, state, and regional communities, all of which competed with nationality as potential modes of political affiliation. Americans strove to define national identity both in relation to these more local political formations and in relation to existing models provided by European nations. The American difference from these European models, the status of the United States as the first modern democracy, made the need for narrative accounts of its identity all the greater. However, Anthony Smith cautions that theories treating nationality purely as an effect of representational practices risk instrumentalizing the process of representing the nation and dehistoricizing the origins and boundaries of those representations. "Constructing the nation always misses the central point about historical nations," Smith argues, "their powerfully felt and willed presence, the feeling shared among so many people of belonging to a transgenerational community of history and destiny."[25] Smith reminds us that individuals have never been able simply to imagine the nation in whatever form they wished; expressions of national identity must necessarily work within parameters established by the existing cultural dialogue about nationhood. Hence, an essay such as O'Sullivan's "The Great Nation of Futurity" enters into a conversation about national time that had been central to the "transgenerational community" inhabiting the space of North America since before the nation's inception. Social historians such as David Hackett Fisher, Michael Kammen, and others have shown how important historical memory was to the sense of collective belonging of the American people, despite, or perhaps because of, their geographical and cultural diversity. O'Sullivan's representation of the nation as a republic extending through time speaks to this need for historical texture, but it is also bounded in its possibilities by the historical and national imaginaries already present among the people.

Above, I described the project of colonizing time as "more ideologically palatable" than the colonization of space. I agree with scholars such as Jehlen, Noble, and Pease, who have characterized American attitudes toward time as ideological, but I challenge the view that Americans have therefore treated time as unreal. Instead, an analysis of American temporal rhetoric as ideological should reveal that American time has been at once both real and unreal. Marx and Marxist theorists such as Althusser describe ideology as the inversion of reality, the reversed image seen in a mirror or a *camera obscura*. The ideological is neither the real itself nor wholly imaginary. To say that the ideological has nothing to do with reality would be as misguided as conflating ideology with reality itself. Hence, we ought to take seriously the ideological notion proposed by narratives of national expansion through time, the notion that American nationality is not composed simply of occupying the space of North America in the present moment. The more profound dimension of national belonging extends into the past and, crucially, into the future, the territory that is, in O'Sullivan's words, "for our history"—the plural pronoun "our" inviting readers to participate imaginatively in a shared, collective experience of future time where ideology could play out its vital antiphonies to the material reality of American history.

What has been missing, then, from scholarly accounts of American national development is serious attention to the complexities of ideological representations of time. Just as the politics of westward expansion were tied to the processes of representation through which the landscape of North America acquired meaning, so too did the Jeffersonian vision of a temporal empire that O'Sullivan and other writers put forward involve cultural constructions of time. This chapter begins to explore such constructions by looking broadly at how Americans thought about the historical time in which they understood their nation to be situated, and how these ideas shaped, in turn, the contours of American nationalism.

What Was American History?

History is, itself, a historical concept, constructed differently in different times and places. In drawing some connections between American conceptions of history in the nineteenth century and the recent debates about historicity that have been central to the reshaping of American studies as an academic discipline, I do not wish to collapse these differences. American attitudes toward history in the nineteenth century developed out of efforts to adapt European paradigms to the unique situation of the American people. The scholars who became the preeminent historians of the period, such as George Bancroft and William Prescott, were steeped in the late neoclassical philosophy of thinkers such as Edmund Burke and Hugh Blair. Students in American colleges were required to memorize texts such as Blair's *Lectures*

28 : *The Future Republic*

on Rhetoric and Belles Lettres (possibly the most widely used textbook in American colleges and universities during the early part of the century). But this neoclassicism was strongly modified by the romantic historiography of writers such as Johann Gottfried Herder, Johann Gottlieb Fichte, and Thomas Carlyle.[26] Poets and novelists such as William Wordsworth, Lord Byron, and Sir Walter Scott, whose work American intellectuals devoured, were also perceived to a large extent as historians.[27] The lionization of Scott, in particular, paved the way for historical fiction to take its place as a serious type of history writing.[28] Distinctions between nonfiction and fictional history writing, even between historical narratives in prose and verse, were muted rather than sharp. Attention to precise detail was less important than capturing the spirit and moral lesson of an event. In the era of the "romantic historians," to use David Levin's term, the perspective now known as "presentism," and considered a grave sin, was usually considered a virtue.[29] Far from cultivating a detached, objective attitude, most historical writers sought to achieve in their writing the qualities that Levin describes as "vitality," "color," and "embodiment," because "no history could be valuable unless it brought the Past to life upon the printed page."[30] Or, as William Ellery Channing said, "What avails it that a man has studied ever so minutely the histories of Greece and Rome, if the great ideas of freedom, and beauty, and valor, and spiritual energy, have not been kindled by these records into living fires in his soul?"[31] Although historians such as Bancroft and Prescott were certainly well versed in the primary source materials they used, vibrant narrative was as important to their work as scrupulous attention to details of fact. In a favorable review of Prescott's *Conquest of Mexico* (1843), Simms wrote that for "the lover of romance" the scenes depicted would provide "the very material which his passionate nature most desires."[32] A striking narrative such as Prescott's would bring readers closer to what Simms and other Americans saw as the most valuable historical truth: the moral lesson to be learned. While antiquarian versions of local history had been the dominant form of historical writing in the late eighteenth century—as the young nation began to cohere and acquire more of a sense of truly national, rather than local, identity—its invented traditions were codified in these romantic historical narratives that emphasized expansion through time and the power to shape the future.

Neither the reading nor the writing of this new national history was exclusively the province of highly educated male intellectuals. Lecturers, popular periodicals, and inexpensive editions of historical novels brought history to the masses, and public monuments and inexpensive prints made historical art available to the emerging middle and working classes. Emma Willard, Lydia Maria Child, Catharine Sedgwick, and the dozens of other women who wrote history and historical fiction and verse, while denied access to university education and historical archives, learned their history through solitary and group readings of European and American authors. Girls whose families possessed sufficient financial resources attended private academies in which they studied famous male authors or history texts distilled from the works of such authors. Bruce Harvey notes that history textbooks were among the most important of the "discursive and institutional spaces where U.S. nationhood and temporal concerns most expressly or palpably came into conjunction," resulting in a "national canon of memory" available to the growing numbers of Americans able to attend school.[33] Lydia Sigourney describes how, at her Hartford academy, teacher and students "like a band of sisters . . . traced in the afternoon, by the guidance of Rollin, the progress of ancient times, or the fall of buried empires." After the readings, students were encouraged to "express their own opinions of heroes, or other distinguished personages."[34] Through such readings and discussions, Americans learned to bring the past to life and to understand America as a nation that occupied time more than it did space, a position in world history more than a position on the map. In an 1851 textbook, author Jesse Olney described a "Golden Future" for America, declaring that in "these United States, the great Republic of the World, lies the grand and imposing theatre of the future progress of the race. We are to work out, not our destiny alone, but that of the whole world."[35] For a nation so geographically far flung, and with such little infrastructure in the early decades that travel between states was tedious, difficult, and often dangerous, the romance of history offered a compelling vision of national wholeness and union.

Along with Olney, the period's many educational activists strove to create a literate culture of Americans steeped in world history and in the new national history. One of this movement's seminal documents was Emma Willard's 1819 manifesto, *An Address to the Public, Particularly the Members of the Legislature of New York, Proposing a Plan for Improving Female Education.* Willard, born in Connecticut in 1787, had been teaching professionally since 1804. She published the 1819 *Address*, in part, out of a sense of despair at the inadequate educational opportunities available to women. The *Address* calls for the establishment of women's schools that would provide an education equivalent to that which young men received in the colleges from which female students were barred. But significantly, the *Address* makes its case by appealing not to women's particular interests in the present but rather to what Willard represents as the nation's universal interests in the future, proposing through women's education to strengthen and perpetuate the vitality of American civic life in response to the threat of national decline: "An opinion too generally prevails, that our present form of government, though good, cannot be permanent. Other republics have failed, and the historian and philosopher have told us, that nations are like individuals; that at their birth, they receive the seeds of their decline and dissolution." Willard calls this organic metaphor for nationhood a "false analogy" and goes on to write that the "existence of nations cannot, in strictness, be compared with the duration of animate life; for by the operation of physical causes, this, after a certain length of time, must cease: but the existence of nations, is prolonged by the succession of one generation to another, and there is no physical cause, to prevent this succession's going on, in a peaceable manner, under a good government, till the end of time."[36] The mechanism for the perpetuation of national virtue into the future was maternal education, a nineteenth-century revival of the work of republican motherhood that had been so important to the Revolutionary generation.[37] Because the nation was a multigenerational entity, pedagogy, especially the moral pedagogy best effected by women, was key to its vitality. Hence, reformers such as Willard collectively embarked on a national pedagogical project to, in essence, teach Americans what they were and render them suitable citizens of the American future.

Beyond establishing elite academies, these reformers brought historical education to the less privileged by disseminating textbooks and skilled teachers to America's common schools. Willard created an impressive pedagogical infrastructure that spread her ideas about national development through all levels of American society. As Anne Firor Scott explains, within two years of publishing her 1819 *Address*, Willard had founded the Troy Female Seminary, through the agency of which she "aimed to impress her cultural values on the developing society through the agency of well-trained women teachers who would go out, not only nearby but also to the growing South and West, and wherever possible, found schools modeled upon the original."[38] Teachers trained at the Troy Female Seminary founded, or took charge of and transformed, schools in Georgia, South Carolina, Maryland, Virginia, Pennsylvania, Ohio, and other places. Willard also disseminated her ideas by authoring a large number of textbooks used in the schools her alumni founded and in other schools as well, including schools for boys.[39] The most important of these texts were her widely used *History of the United States, or, Republic of America* (1831 and many subsequent editions), and *Universal History in Perspective* (1835 and many subsequent editions; "universal history" was the nineteenth-century term for world history). The *History of the United States* was available in a more expensive edition for private academies and a less expensive, abridged edition for common schools, thus uniting disparate classes of Americans in the study of a common historical narrative, producing America's imagined community within shared historical time.

Willard's textbooks include both geographical and chronographical charts, but her introductions for teachers emphasize the use of the chronographs much more than the maps. Her *Universal History in Perspective* begins with an illustration of the "Temple of Time" (Illustration 1.1), a classical temple with columns on each side representing centuries and "empires" mapped out on the floor, and also includes a larger foldout "Historical Chart."[40] Both of these illustrations depict the imperial occupation of time. The *North American Review* gave special praise to this feature when it noticed the textbook: "First, we have the chronographical picture of nations, in which are represented the different empires, and the most remarkable persons who have flourished in them, together with the dates of the most important events both before and after Christ. As they present themselves to the eye, they cannot fail to make an impression upon the mind of the scholar, and thus assist him essentially in the accomplishment of his task."[41] In this "chronograph," the longest enduring "empires" receive the most space, thus making space into a metaphor for the real national topos, time. Near the front of the "Historic Chart" one finds a relatively new nation, or perhaps "empire," named "Republic of America." The narrative text of the *Universal History* is divided into three sections: ancient, middle, and modern history. The middle period ends with the fall of Constantinople in 1453, representing the end of the last vestiges of the Roman Empire. The modern period begins with Columbus's discovery of America, which Willard describes as "the most important event recorded in profane history."[42] The implications of this organization are clear: America, here figured as a unified "Republic," is heir to, or will actually supersede, the greatest previous "empire," Rome; and, crucially, the nature of these successive empires is best understood temporally, rather than geographically. By situating the United States in such a world historical context, educators and textbook authors such as Willard self-consciously set about propagating national narratives through time, claiming the future as American territory.

ILLUSTRATION 1.1. *"The Temple of Time," frontispiece to Emma Willard's* Universal History in Perspective *(The Library of Virginia)*

The Malthusian Equation

Willard's form of historical pedagogy reflects the widespread belief that it was population growth over time, the increase of the people from generation to generation, that was the motive power of national development. As population density increased on the eastern seaboard, the same pressures that had always been a major cause of immigration to the New World caused more and more young Americans and new immigrants to begin crossing the Appalachians in search of land and opportunity. It is not a coincidence, then, that early in the nineteenth century the figurative language of American nationalism began to turn upon images of proliferation, fecundity, and generation. For example, the frontispiece to Willard's *Abridged History of the United States* (first published in 1843) depicts U.S. history as a stout tree with many branches (Illustration 1.2). The composition alludes to clock time because the chronology of history, whose events are represented in the small outer branches of the tree, moves clockwise around the circular form of the tree as a whole. However, the tree's trunk is rooted in a bucolic landscape that can be seen in the background of the picture, and there is no indication of a progression away from a natural conception of national time. Indeed, it is most important to see that in this illustration it is not the nation itself that is represented by the tree, but rather national *history*. The tree is not labeled "The United States" but instead "History of the United States," a significant difference. Thus time itself is imagined as an organic thing, a medium of growth, development, and fecundity.[43]

These sorts of images were perfectly compatible with the romantic theories that depicted national development through the trope of organic growth. Tellingly, the very sentence in which O'Sullivan first employs the phrase "manifest destiny" cites the growth of population as the fundamental rationale and justification for America's territorial expansion. Complaining of "other nations" that have "undertaken to intrude themselves" between the United States and Texas, O'Sullivan writes of "our manifest destiny to overspread the continent allotted by Providence for the free development of our yearly multiplying millions."[44] The most important word in this sentence is not "manifest" or even "destiny," but "yearly." It is the temporal vector of ever-increasing population that comprises the essence of national growth. Expansion across space is a derivative of this population growth across time.

The temporal dimension implicit in population growth was well known to Willard, O'Sullivan, and their contemporaries from the natural science

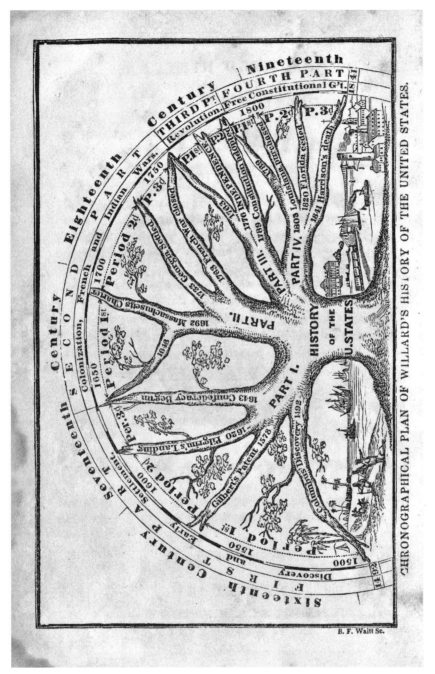

Text visible within the illustration:

Nineteenth Century
Eighteenth Century
Seventeenth Century
Sixteenth Century

THIRD P.ᵗ FOURTH PART
Revolution Free Constitutional G.ᵗ
1800
P.1ˢᵗ P.2ᵈ P.3ᵈ

SECOND PART
FIRST PART

Colonization, French and Indian Wars.
Early Settlement.
Discovery and Settlement.

P.3ᵈ
Period 2ᵈ
Period 1ˢᵗ
Per.3ᵈ
Period 2ᵈ
Period 1ˢᵗ

1750
1700
1650
1600
1550
1500

1783 French War Closed
1776 INDEPENDENCE
1789 Constitution formed
1733 Georgia Settled
1692 Massachusetts Charter
1643 Confederacy Began
1620 Pilgrim's Landing
Gilbert's Patent 1578
Columbus's Discovery 1492

PART III.
PART IV.
PART II.
PART I.

1803 Louisiana ceded
1820 Florida ceded
1841 Harrison's death

HISTORY OF THE U. STATES.

CHRONOGRAPHICAL PLAN OF WILLARD'S HISTORY OF THE UNITED STATES.

B. F. Waitt Sc.

ILLUSTRATION 1.2. *Frontispiece to Emma Willard's* Abridged History of the United States, or, Republic of America *(The Library of Virginia)* and political economy of the period—fields of thought notably synthesized in the theories of Thomas Malthus, whose *Essay on Population* (1798) was a necessary text for any educated person in the nineteenth century. "Population, when unchecked," Americans learned from Malthus, "increases in a geometrical ratio. Subsistence increases only in an arithmetical ratio. A slight acquaintance with the numbers will shew the immensity of the first power in comparison of the second."[45] Malthus's vision of change over time was dystopian; he argued that it was impossible for any human society to eliminate poverty, war, disease, and starvation because such tragedies were the natural consequence of population growth that would always outstrip the food supply. Hence, future history could only be characterized by a series of inevitable catastrophes. O'Sullivan's "manifest destiny" and Jefferson's "empire of liberty" both envision western expansion as a way of ameliorating the Malthusian problem, relieving the pressure of population growth upon resources and hence facilitating continued national development into future time. Adding territory to the nation provided a uniquely American way of transforming the temporal vector of the terrible Malthusian equation. Space was important, but its importance lay in its capacity to enable unlimited expansion through time.

Jefferson responded to the ideas of Malthus in detail in an 1804 letter to Jean-Baptiste Say. Jefferson reported to Say that he had just been engaged in "the perusal of Malthus' work on population, a work of sound logic, in which some of the opinions of Adam Smith, as well as of the economists, are ably examined." Jefferson was most interested in the implications of Malthus's theory for America's future history. Malthus had predicted that America would inevitably succumb to the same population pressures that plagued the Old World. Despite his general admiration for Malthus's work, Jefferson disagreed vigorously with the Englishman's conclusions regarding America. He observed that important "differences of circumstance between this and the old countries of Europe," particularly the fixed quantity of available food in Europe versus its relative abundance in America, would lead to different political results. While in Europe "supernumerary births . . . add only to your mortality," in America "the immense extent of uncultivated and fertile lands enables every one who will labor to marry young, and to raise a family of any size." Furthermore, Jefferson argued, the unlimited potential food supply in America meant that, unlike in Europe, where many laborers were necessarily employed in manufactures, American laborers would be best employed entirely in agriculture. In this way, Jefferson concluded, Americans would produce enough surplus food to "nourish the now perishing births of Europe, who in return would manufacture and send us in exchange our clothes and other comforts." The political benefits of this agricultural economy would be to "the moral and physical preference of the agricultural, over the manufacturing, man."[46] Altogether, then, Jefferson thought that the unique geographical situation of the United States would forestall indefinitely the dire Malthusian consequences of population increase over time that seemed so inevitable in Europe. Drew McCoy notes that Jefferson's "brimming confidence" regarding this issue in 1804 can be attributed mostly to the recent acquisition of the Louisiana Territory, for it was the accession of unlimited amounts of potential farmland to the nation that Jefferson thought important to the future health of the Republic.[47]

McCoy and other scholars have concluded from Jefferson's many expressions of admiration for the benefits of agricultural labor that Jefferson's ideal nation would not move through time at all; according to this influential interpretation, Jefferson hoped that the United States would remain permanently in temporal stasis, with farms expanding ever westward in place of population increase, and concomitant Malthusian economic and political crises, on the eastern seaboard. McCoy applies a similar line of analysis to other founders as well, characterizing the Revolutionary generation as widely antipathetic to the notion of change within time. For example, after describing how James Madison urged that the Constitution be crafted in order to accommodate future changes to the Republic, McCoy concludes that behind these plans lay Madison's fear of and resistance to change: "It was wise to anticipate and provide for future changes; it was even wiser to forestall their development for as long as possible." McCoy contextualizes Madison's thoughts on the Constitution with his other writings to show that the very activity of planning for change could coexist with a fervent desire that such change would never really occur. McCoy sums up the anxiety he sees in Madison's thoughts about the national future with the statement that "Madison's republic was in a race against time."[48]

McCoy's deservedly influential analysis certainly captures one aspect of the thought of both Jefferson and Madison. However, his brilliant portrayal of the common threads linking the Revolutionary generation together comes at the expense of the very real and important differences in the way that the members of that generation thought about time, space, and nationhood. As Michael Lienesch observes, by the mid-1780s "McCoy's 'Jeffersonians' were dividing themselves rapidly into competing intellectual camps, each with different definitions of development."[49] While Madison might have recognized the likelihood of temporal change and striven to avoid it, Jefferson in contrast embraced the notion of change and contingency as salient aspects of national development within time.

Throughout his life, Jefferson wrote many times about political and social change as a natural and healthy component of the relations between succeeding generations. In fact, it is precisely the inevitability that Malthus ascribed to the temporal vector of his equation that was most off-putting to Jefferson. Jefferson agreed with Malthus's theory in regard to Europe, but he disagreed with the universal application of the theory. For Malthus, change over time always brought the same results. For Jefferson, time was a medium of contingencies and novel discoveries. "We can no longer say there is nothing new under the sun," Jefferson crowed to Joseph Priestley in 1801. "For this whole chapter in the history of man is new."[50] Each generation, Jefferson insisted, created its own political and cultural world, and just as his own generation had made a revolution, so too would future generations make revolutions of their own.[51] Years after leaving the presidency, when he had begun to grow more fearful and pessimistic about the prospects of the United States, Jefferson still insisted on this basic premise of generational change, writing to Samuel Kercheval in 1816:

> Each generation is as independent of the one preceding, as that was of all which had gone before. It has then, like them, a right to choose for itself the form of government it believes most promotive of its own happiness; consequently, to accommodate to the circumstances in which it finds itself, that received from its predecessors; and it is for the peace and good of mankind, that a solemn opportunity of doing this every nineteen or twenty years, should be provided by the constitution; so that it may be handed on, with periodical repairs, from generation to generation, to the end of time, if anything human can so long endure.[52]

We can contrast Jefferson's portrayal of healthy intergenerational change with the anxious desire to preserve the status quo that McCoy so aptly limns in Madison's writings. In the model of generational succession Jefferson proposes to Kercheval, change occurs within the context of a common political affiliation that persists. The Constitution is "handed on"; changes in the form of government amount to "repairs" to the national imaginary signified by that document.[53] In predicting that each future generation would make such changes in response to "the circumstances in which it finds itself," Jefferson acknowledges the historical contingencies that might shape the nation, contingencies that are unpredictable until they arise. Finally, in imagining the Constitution enduring "to the end of time," Jefferson posits that this flexibility of response to time's fortunes would allow the nation to remain viable indefinitely. In other words, it is precisely the historicity of the nation, the embeddedness of the American people in the mutability of time, that makes the nation eternal.

Far from expanding into the West in order to avoid developing through time, then, Jefferson's ideal republic would occupy only as much space as necessary in order to facilitate development through time. Of course, such spatial expansion would still constitute a threat to the republican character of the nation, since it smacked, as we have seen, of conquest and tyranny. There is no real resolution to this paradox; what is worth noting is the particular way in which Jefferson employed his transgenerational rhetoric to render western settlement benign. In an 1803 letter to John C. Breckenridge on the subject of the Louisiana Purchase, Jefferson wrote:

> When I view the Atlantic States, procuring for those on the Eastern waters of the Missipi friendly instead of hostile neighbors on it's Western waters, I do not view it as an Englishman would the procuring future blessings for the French nation, with whom he has no relations of blood or affection. The future inhabitants of the Atlantic and Missipi States will be our sons.... [I]f they see their interest in separation, why should we take side with our Atlantic rather than our Missipi descendents? It is the elder and the younger son differing. God bless them both, & keep them in union, if it be for their good, but separate them, if it be better.[54]

Jefferson's model of national growth through time rejects the hierarchical relationship between colony and metropole that had been one of the greatest sources of American complaint about the British Empire. Instead, Jefferson envisions a growing population producing a network of politically equal realms. This idea was important enough that Jefferson repeated it almost verbatim in a letter to Priestley in 1804, declaring that the question of whether the United States would "remain in one confederacy, or form into Atlantic and Mississippi confederacies, I believe not very important to the happiness of either part." If the western states were to separate and form a discrete government for themselves they "will be as much our children & descendents as those of the eastern, and I feel myself as much identified with that country, in future time, as with this; and did I now foresee a separation at some future day, yet I should feel the duty & the desire to promote the western interests as much as zealously as the eastern, doing all the good for both portions of our future family which should fall within my power."[55] The repeated use of the word "future" in the letter to Priestley brings the temporal dimension of this vision of egalitarian empire to the fore. An empire of liberty would descend through time by changing and even fragmenting, taking on forms that could not be anticipated in the present. Most importantly, in the empire of liberty there would be no essential connection between the people and their land. The descendents of the current generation of Americans might set up their future republics anywhere. When any space becomes suitable for American development, then no space is of any special importance. National continuity is defined by the intergenerational transmission of principles of liberty. As in O'Sullivan's metaphor of the temple of continental expanse, space would provide the foundation for Jefferson's empire of liberty, but the true development of the nation would take place through time — and along routes different from those prescribed in the Malthusian equation.

In order to serve as a medium for multiple possible futures, time needed to be rich and variegated. In Jefferson's view, the pressure of population must have different effects upon space and time. Space should remain a blank, undifferentiated, fungible; as Philip Fisher has argued, Jefferson's vision of egalitarian democracy required that American space be Cartesian, "identical from point to point," and this powerful idea (with help from the Land Ordinance of 1785) influenced generations of Americans to come.[56] But the temporal world that was layered onto that flat, undifferentiated land was, in Jeffersonian theory, three dimensional and textured. Almost at the end of his life, Jefferson created an image of how he thought expanding population had shaped the relationship between time and space in North America. Employing the conceit of the imperial prospect that had been a prominent feature of the eighteenth-century literature of his youth, Jefferson imagined himself surveying a swelling population forming bands of national time as it spread across the continent:

> Let a philosophic observer commence a journey from the savages of the Rocky Mountains, eastwardly towards our seacoast. These he would observe in the earliest stage of association living under no law but that of nature, subsisting and covering themselves with the flesh and skins of wild beasts. He would next find those on our frontiers in the pastoral state, raising domestic animals to supply the defects of hunting. Then succeed our own semi-barbarous citizens, the pioneers of the advance of civilization, and so in his progress he would meet the gradual shades of improving man until he would reach his, as yet, most improved state in

our seaport towns. This, in fact, is equivalent to a survey, in time, of the progress of man from the infancy of creation to the present day.

Jefferson's prospect captures historical change spatially, freezing a moment of ever-changing time through the spatial metaphor. It is significant that Jefferson begins his prospect at the Rocky Mountains, for, as Fisher explains, geographical diversity was antithetical to Jefferson's concept of national union. Hence, his prospect surveys the Great Plains and makes no mention of what differences of climate and geography do exist between the East Coast and the Rockies. In contrast, time is highly differentiated, the medium for heterogeneous forms of economic and social organization. As we have seen, Jeffersonian time could also contain diverse modes of political affiliation, as long as the fundamental principles of liberty were retained.

This letter was written in response to a proposal for a small utopian community sent to Jefferson by William Ludlow. In his response, Jefferson expressed agreement with Ludlow that small communities were best suited to republican government. Jefferson thought that seventy families, the number Ludlow mentioned, could form a kind of family, in which liberty and order would go hand in hand. The greatest threat to the long-term success of Ludlow's community, Jefferson thought, was population growth: "Some regulators of the family you still must have, and it remains to be seen at what period of your increasing population your simple regulations will cease to preserve order, peace, and justice." Here Jefferson equates political complexity with corruption. As more "regulators" become necessary to govern an increasingly large society, danger arises of a class of purely political, rather than productive, citizens. Population growth would cause social and political change. In Ludlow's seventy families, Jefferson saw a microcosm of the United States. The vitality of the people had rendered national time heterogeneous. All across the continent, they were making new things under the sun, propelling the nation into the future. "And where this progress will stop," Jefferson wrote to Ludlow, "no one can say."[57]

The Progress of Virtue

The particular stages of historical development incorporated into Jefferson's vision of heterogeneous bands of national time were drawn from the stadialist model of historical progress and regress. Americans had adapted stadialism from European philosophers of history who sought to find orderly, repeating patterns in human history. Unlike many of the intellectual trends of the Enlightenment, stadialism retained its currency in the Anglo-American world even after the romantic revolution of the early nineteenth century. According to the version of stadialist theory most popular in America, a civilization would ascend from the savage state to the pastoral state (characterized by domestication of animals), and thence to the agricultural state (farming), and finally to a commercial and manufacturing state. In an 1845 essay for the *American Review* entitled "Society and Civilization," John Quincy Adams neatly precised this theory when he described "four different modes, by which, in different ages and in divers regions, men have been associated together in numbers. 1. As Hunters. 2. As Shepherds. 3. As Tillers of the ground, and 4. As civilized, or inhabitants of cities. The progress of human society is in this order."[58] Although Jefferson notes that the bands of time he pictured in his 1824 letter blended in "gradual shades," the different stages of progress he identifies clearly correspond with those named by Adams. Neither of these two men took the sequence farther than the civilized stage, but, according to classic stadialism, after the climax, the civilization would inevitably grow wealthy and corrupt, the virtue of its citizens compromised by luxury and avarice at home and the unjust exercise of power abroad, and decline into tyranny and weakness (the distressing eventuality to which Willard's *Address* alludes), ultimately to be overthrown by barbarians.[59]

The case of the Roman republic and empire was exemplary in this theory, but Americans also liked to point to the excesses of British imperial power as the latest example of a powerful nation grown corrupt. As a power on the rise, George Bancroft wrote in his *History of the United States*, England had "exulted in its conquests," to be sure, and enjoyed "the glory of extended dominion in the confident expectation of a boundless increase of wealth," but its success had been "due to its having taken the lead in the good old struggle for liberty." Once England's power and wealth had corrupted it, then the empire had abandoned "the nobler policy of liberty to find its defenders where it could" and, "wilfully, and as it were fatally blind to what would follow," embarked upon a "policy of conquest and exclusion" across the globe.[60] Americans saw their own revolution as a historical rebuke to such abuses of power and hoped that their nation would avoid the scripted narrative that Old World empires such as Rome and England had always followed.

While Bancroft was a widely read and popular historian, these ideas were spread even farther through popular lectures and through their incorporation into textbooks. The possibility of American "decline and dissolution" that Willard voiced in her *Address* and repeatedly in her history textbooks, for example, was directly connected to the problem of empire as constructed in the stadialist model. As both a revolutionary rebuke to imperial corruption and a potential new empire in its own right, the United States occupied uncertain historical ground. Building political consensus by celebrating the United States as a newer, better empire inevitably created a sense of apprehension that success and power might lead to the corruption that had doomed previous empires. Throughout her history texts, Willard shies away from dealing directly with the problem of the exercise of American power to conquer space. At times, she even describes negative consequences of some territorial acquisitions, as when she comments with disapproval of the acquisition of Florida from Spain that "the addition of this peninsula, which completes the ocean boundary of the United States" led almost immediately to "a bloody war following this increase of territory." Similar remarks throughout her texts suggest that Willard herself sometimes viewed the acquisition of territory, especially territory already occupied by people who would have to be subjugated by force, as a possible threat to American liberty. For the most part, despite occasional bursts of enthusiasm, she is simply indifferent to expansion through space, writing at the end of the 1855 edition of her *History of the United States* that "our Republic is powerful and influential, especially with the lesser Republics of our own Continent. To lead onward in a career of liberty and public virtue, is the only leadership of nations, which the truly sagacious American covets for his country. Compared with this, conquest by war is but an antiquated vulgarity; the one bringing security as well as honor, the other tending, as with ancient Rome, to decay and dissolution."[61] As this passage reveals, Willard's true interest lay not in celebrating the American conquest of space but rather in shaping and disseminating a particular rhetoric of nationhood that would perpetuate American virtue and liberty at home while also influencing the development of foreign nations. In carrying out this project, Willard substitutes pedagogy for space, making American national identity into something teachable, a universal idea to be disseminated across time rather than a particular government to be imposed upon others through force of arms.

Willard's pedagogy was thus devoted to cultivating a utopian American empire of time with specifically progressive qualities that would differentiate it from the corrupt Roman Empire. These uniquely American qualities are portrayed in a drawing on the title page of Willard's *Abridged History of the United States*. The drawing depicts three women within "the chain of union," each link of which bears the name of one of the original thirteen states (Illustration 1.3). A motto inscribed across the picture reads, "Liberty peace and safety within the chain of union, without — violence and fraud." The nation as a whole thus replicates a feminized domestic sanctuary from the violence and fraud of the world.

As this illustration makes clear, there is an important gendered component to Willard's theory of national identity. Nina Baym points out that Willard's history texts focus primarily upon episodes of politics, war, and conquest; that is, all traditionally masculine endeavors. This was, of course, inevitable, given that Willard compiled the information in her textbooks from published secondary sources that focused upon such matters; she could hardly have begun conducting original research projects on social history. However, Willard's chain of union makes national identity explicitly female. As she wrote in the 1819 *Address*, history provides many examples of nations

> whose legislatures have sought to improve their various vegetable productions, and their breeds of useful brutes; but none whose public councils have made it an object of their deliberations, to improve the character of their women. Yet, though history lifts not her finger to such an one, anticipation does. She points to a nation, which having thrown off the shackles of authority and precedent, shrinks not from schemes of improvement, because other nations have never attempted them; but which, in its pride of independence, would rather lead than follow in the march of human improvement; a nation wise and magnanimous to plan, enterprising to undertake, and rich in resources to execute. Does not every American exult that this country is his own? And who knows how great and good a race of men may yet arise from the forming hand of mothers, enlightened by the bounty of that beloved country, — to defend her liberties, — to plan her future improvement, — and to raise her unparalleled glory?[62]

What would save American space, then, from following the corruption and decline of the Roman Empire was the potential of maternal nationalist pedagogy to transform space into time. In a poem accompanying the illustration of the "chain of union," Willard writes, "In Union's Chain, within its spell / Freedom and Peace and Safety dwell." The "spell" of union might be taken to represent this ideological project of unleashing the temporal energy latent in the land of North America, still in its primitive state before the beginning of historical time. When the land is made political through the establishment of the new nation, it enters time and moves toward the romantic *telos* — the wholeness of a future utopia in which the "united states" would constitute

ABRIDGED HISTORY

OF THE

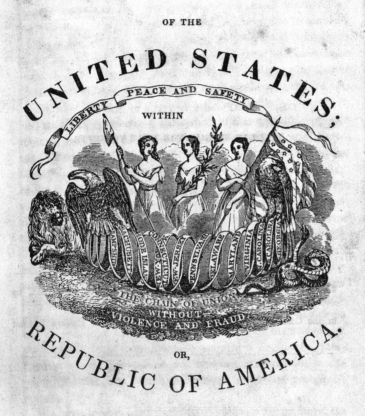

UNITED STATES;

WITHIN

LIBERTY PEACE AND SAFETY

THE CHAIN OF UNION WITHOUT VIOLENCE AND FRAUD

OR,

REPUBLIC OF AMERICA.

BY EMMA WILLARD.

IMPROVED EDITION.

NEW YORK:
PUBLISHED BY A. S. BARNES & CO.
No. 51 JOHN STREET.
1846.

ILLUSTRATION 1.3. *Title page of Emma Willard's* Abridged History of the United States, or, Republic of America *(The Library of Virginia)* one republic, propelled into the future by a maternal nationalist pedagogy producing virtuous citizens and staving off the kinds of corruption located outside the chain of union.

Related to this problem of empire was apprehension over the consequences for national virtue of the development of commerce—first, the mercantile system of the late eighteenth century, and later the rise of free-market capitalism in the nineteenth century. McCoy explains that by the late eighteenth century, the benefits and perils of commerce had become the subject of hot debate throughout Europe; Americans devoured British and Continental tracts warning, in McCoy's gloss, that "commerce always had the power to corrupt, as well as to polish manners and morals."[63] As the United States developed into a liberal, commercial, and eventually market-oriented society, Pocock notes, the persistence of Jeffersonian ideals of civic humanism resulted in "tensions between individual self-awareness on the one hand and consciousness of society, property, and history on the other." Hence, as American political, military, and economic power increased over the first decades of the nineteenth century, public debate over the legitimate exercise of this power also amplified. Willard's textbooks combined the dangers of both commerce and empire into omnibus warnings against corruption that echoed what she had written in the *Address* in 1819. In the *Universal History in Perspective*, she averred that "the course of history, which we have pursued, has shown to us, that with virtue a nation may continue prosperous and happy; but when the people become corrupt, then ensues anarchy."[64] In 1855 she concluded her *Last Periods of Universal History* with the following ominous warning to young Americans:

> If, as we believe, they are wrong, who teach that it is the inevitable destiny of our republic to fall into anarchy and thence pass to despotism; no less do they err, who treat with levity every suggestion that such is our danger. Has the Ruler of Nations given assurance, that he will set aside the order of his providence in our behalf? Has he given us a license to commit, with impunity, offences for which he has filled other nations with blood?[65]

The interrogative form of Willard's lesson indicates the degree of contingency that Americans ascribed to history. Eschewing the notion of an "inevitable destiny," Willard warns that the American future might take either the more positive or the more negative of the courses she describes. This historical contingency turns upon the possibility of corruption, and hence, for students and teachers employing Willard's textbook, the "individual self-awareness" to which Pocock refers becomes linked to the historical destiny of the nation as a whole.

Contingent Stadialism

Both of these lamentable trends could fall under the rubric of Simms's well-chosen word, "acquisition." The acquisition of alien territory through unjust means was the national equivalent of the acquisition of excessive wealth by individuals; both were sources of corruption. Simms's use of Rome as a historical exemplar of both of these dangers is typical of stadialist thought. For Americans from the Revolutionary era through the mid-nineteenth century, the touchstone for the distinction between republic and empire was ancient Rome, a political entity that, as Edward Gibbon had famously elucidated, morphed from a republic into an empire and then fell victim to its own corruption—both the unjust exercise of power and the decline in virtue linked to excessive wealth. Baym notes that for many Americans, "Rome stood for history itself—history as hope, history as horror and obstacle. . . . The supplanting of republican Rome by the Roman Empire provided a storehouse of data for understanding the dynamics of history."[66] Russel Nye argues that it was the necessity of a post-Revolutionary alternative to "the Anglo-Saxon heritage" of England that led the United States to look to antiquity for "symbols it might adapt to its own uses," including the Roman eagle, the design of the Great Seal, the neoclassical elements of public architecture, and the classical poses and garb of the figures in national monuments such as Horatio Greenough's Washington. "Without a nationalistic tradition of its own," Nye observes, "the United States drew heavily on classicism for the forms and symbols it needed to affirm its sense of nationality."[67] In its ambiguity, this adopted national tradition reflected precisely those feelings Americans held toward their erstwhile mother country. Even after the Revolution, England was still perceived by many Americans as the bastion of traditions of liberty that had merely been vitiated by a corrupt tyrant. How telling, then, that Americans turned away from England and toward a historical empire infamous for representing precisely that same hazard. In their choice of a national symbolism, Americans revealed their preoccupation with the historical dynamics of empire.

Because it embodied not merely the hopes but also the fears of Americans for the possible future course of their own nation, the Roman touchstone provided important analogies for warnings against the perils of empire such as those voiced by Simms. Such warnings proliferated in the nineteenth century. In "The Rise of the West," Schoolcraft explicitly calls upon Americans to depart from the insufficient models provided by ancient republics:

> Greece built her temples, Rome in purple shone,
> Be man our temple, and the mind our throne,
> So shall the West, her brightest crown receive,
> And shine with jewels, kings could never give.[68]

Only by avoiding both pagan worship (that is, cultural corruption) and the imperial decadence signified by the color purple (political corruption) can Americans receive a more valuable form of wealth: national virtue and the perpetuation of the Republic. Bancroft's essay "The Decline of the Roman People" (1834) issues a more specific warning. Bancroft follows Gibbon in tracing the decline of Rome from republic to empire and finally to conquest by barbarians. Bancroft's own contribution to the well-known story is to condemn the turpitude resulting from the institution of slavery in Rome. His readers could hardly have failed to notice the similarities between Bancroft's condemnation of slavery in the ancient empire and the kinds of criticisms of American slavery mounted in abolitionist tracts. Bancroft's piece describes the Roman slaveholder as "the competitor of the free laborer"; warns that in a slaveholding society such as that of ancient Rome "the slave population will perpetually gain in relative numbers" because men of the slaveholding class "preferred the dissoluteness of indulgence to marriage"; laments that "idleness and treachery and theft, are the vices of slavery"; and, echoing an especially sensational charge made often by American abolitionists, grieves that female slaves "had no defence against the avarice or rage of a master." In conclusion, Bancroft writes that slavery in ancient Rome "had destroyed the democracy, had destroyed the aristocracy, had destroyed the empire; and at last it left the traces of its ruinous power deeply furrowed on the face of nature herself."[69] Free labor, the sanctity of marriage, and the chastity of women were concerns much more germane to nineteenth-century Americans than they would ever have been to ancient Romans. Bancroft's essay is really a warning to his fellow citizens, veiled in a Roman allegory.

While not specifically identified as Roman, the neoclassical iconography of Thomas Cole's lauded series of paintings *The Course of Empire* (1833–36) is clearly intended to evoke the Roman touchstone. The series traces the supposed course of civilization through individual paintings titled *The Savage State*, *The Arcadian or Pastoral State*, *The Consummation of Empire* (Illustration 1.4), *Destruction* (Illustration 1.5), and *Desolation*. As Stephen

ILLUSTRATION 1.4. *Thomas Cole,* The Course of Empire: The Consummation of Empire, *1835–36. Oil on canvas, 51¼ × 76 inches (Collection of the New-York Historical Society)*

Daniels notes, "In upholding the spectacle of classical history for American eyes, Cole seemed to challenge those who believed in unlimited, upward progress."[70] Daniels reveals that Cole himself compared the city depicted in *The Consummation of Empire* to New York; hence, New York becomes a modern Rome, the capital of an empire. The image also brings the Malthusian population problem into the stadialist model, for as Andrew Wilton and Tim Barringer have pointed out, the "excessive population, crowding every balcony and parapet" would have evoked to viewers "the millenarian population theories of Thomas Malthus."[71] The series omits the agricultural stage, raising the question of how the masses of people depicted are able to feed themselves, and *The Consummation of Empire* depicts a society already characterized by wealth, luxury, and power, significantly located in a seaboard city with ships in the harbor. As George Dekker observes, "In omitting the agricultural stage, Cole was also bypassing the society which Jefferson and other stadialists believed most favorable to republican government."[72] In this way, *The Course of Empire* reflects the characteristic ante-

ILLUSTRATION 1.5. *Thomas Cole,* The Course of Empire: Destruction, *1836.*
Oil on canvas, 39¼ × 63¼ inches (Collection of the New-York Historical Society)

bellum concern with the possibility that America had already progressed
beyond its republican origins, that through its very success it had paved the
way for its own destruction.

It is curious, then, to find Cole employing the same stadialist paradigm
to describe American history in more optimistic terms in one of his essays,
where he invites readers to imagine that "in looking over the yet uncultivated
scene, the mind's eye may see far into the futurity. Where the wolf roams, the
plough shall glisten; on the gray crag shall rise temple and tower—mighty
deeds shall be done in the now pathless wilderness; and poets yet unborn
shall sanctify the soil."[73] Cole's reference to the "plough" introduces into
American history the agricultural stage so pointedly omitted from *The
Course of Empire.* While Cole also mentions the "temple and tower" that appear in *The Course of Empire,* in the essay the plough seems to characterize
American history.

Together, then, the essay and the series of paintings point toward an
ambiguous political situation. Rather than providing an allegory with a de-
terminate meaning, Cole's work questions the stability of American politi-

cal institutions in time. Dekker interprets the omission of the agricultural stage in *The Course of Empire* as an indication that Cole thought America's republican character was already fatally compromised, that the passage of time had already destroyed the conditions necessary for liberty. However, given that Cole himself identifies American history with the development of agriculture in his essay, it seems more reasonable to view the omission not as rendering a verdict but as posing a question: simply, whether history would follow its Old World script in North America. The nation depicted in *The Course of Empire* clearly shares certain important similarities with Jacksonian America. However, as an allegory, a mode of representation in which one thing stands for something else without collapsing the distinction between the two, *The Course of Empire* leaves America itself distinct from the images rendered on canvas.

This contingent version of stadialism also informs William Cullen Bryant's "The Ages," a verse narrative delivered to the Phi Beta Kappa Society at Harvard in 1821 (Ralph Waldo Emerson was in attendance) and included in his *Poems* issued later that same year.[74] Bryant portrays America as the potential redeemer of a national virtue that has been lost and recovered successively by different peoples over the course of history. Despite its more optimistic conclusion regarding America's national prospects, Bryant's poem dwells upon the possibility of corruption. Throughout the long verse narrative of world history, Bryant equates virtue with republican liberty. For example, Greece holds the spark of virtue for a time,

> when liberty awoke,
> new-born, amid those beautiful vales, and broke
> Sceptre and chain with her fair youthful hands. (15)

But Greece loses the spark of virtue when its "hard hand oppressed / And crushed the helpless" in the creation of empire. The spirit of Greek virtue then flees to Rome, Bryant relates, but here too virtue eventually succumbs to the corrupting influence of power; in the end, "her degenerate children sold the crown / Of earth's wide kingdoms to a line of slaves," words that anticipate Bancroft's later condemnation of Roman slavery, though the relevance of that critique to nineteenth-century America might have been less vivid to an audience in 1821 than it would become by the 1830s. "Guilt reigned," Bryant continues, "and woe with guilt, and plagues came down" to destroy the "degraded race" and its corrupt empire (16). After tracing the history of Christianity, the corruption of the Catholic Church, and the Protestant Reformation, Bryant concludes by describing the arrival of liberty in America, where

> towns shoot up, and fertile realms are tilled . . . the full region leads
> New colonies forth, that toward the Western seas
> Spread, like a rapid flame among the autumnal trees.

The adjective "autumnal" is interesting here, suggesting as it does that North American time was already "old," in some sense, before the youthful civilization of the Americans arrived. Bryant's description of the land as "tilled" indicates the presence of the agricultural activity that Cole had omitted from his series. Since the land was "autumnal," or old, before the American tillers arrived, the stadialist cycle must have already run its course before American history began and has now begun anew. The "autumnal" quality of North America probably alludes directly to the theory that the "mound-builder" civilization had flourished and then perished in North America (a theory that also informs Bryant's poem "The Prairies"), but it also represents a transposed European oldness. Hence, in North America "the free spirit of mankind, at length / Throws its last fetters off" (24). America shall "never fall," Bryant concludes, because its people will keep alive the spirit of virtue and liberty.[75]

On one level, the poem is a simple reproduction of the stadialist *translatio imperii*, the notion that empire had moved farther and farther into the West throughout history and would finally come to rest in America. The last three stanzas of Bishop Berkeley's "On the Prospect of Planting Arts and Learning in America," including the famous line "Westward the course of empire takes its way," encapsulate this view of historical change and progress. Berkeley describes America's future history in terms of a "rise of empire and of arts" that contrasts with European "decay."[76] Bryant's "autumnal" forests of America would also be losing leaves, and hence beginning the process of "decay" that Berkeley had famously attributed to Europe. This Berkeleyan use of the imagery of decay to describe European scenes was commonplace in American literature and provides the context for understanding Bryant's poem. For example, Willard's European travelogue describes for American readers how "Versailles reminded me of what the *grand monarque* himself was in his old age, the decaying monument of an outward splendor, which had dazzled and half destroyed his country. It is grand, yet one sees at a glance, that it is a grandeur, in poverty, and coming decay." As Willard portrays it, landscape and built environment both reflect the state of political institutions. This point of view resonates with the use of such imagery in the political allegories of landscape painters like Cole but also in the work of American poets such as Bryant who relied heavily on nature imagery in their work. In her travelogue, Willard employs her description of Versailles as an occasion to contrast European decay with the youthful vigor of America: "Nature herself, on this last day of autumn, seemed like art, her mistress here, putting off her gay attire;—and in a sombrous mantle of dark, dead green, which my own country never presents, awaiting the final loss of her summer splendors."[77] Berkeley's millennialism lends support to the argument made by Jehlen and Noble that America was perceived as the transcendence of history. Berkeley describes America as "the last" of the great empires, the "fifth act" that would close the drama of history, and as such the American empire would seem to put an end to the stadialist cycle. What is noteworthy about Simms's, Cole's, and Bryant's appropriations of stadialism, then, is how much less confident the Americans seem in this belief than their English predecessor had been. These American works suggest, to the extent that Americans perceived their own national development to take place within the context of the *translatio imperii*, they saw themselves between two possible outcomes. The fantasy of transcending time existed in dialogue with its antithesis: entrapment within a predetermined historical narrative of corruption and decline. American writers worked between these two antitheses, neither beyond time nor wholly entrapped by it. This practice made history an imagined space of national development characterized by mutability and contingency, in which many possible national futures lay open to the nation.

In contrast, then, to the historical determinism usually attributed to Cole and other stadialists, these images and texts situate the American nation within historical time characterized by contingency and change. American artists and writers such as Cole and O'Sullivan were inventing a historical sense even as they worked. Their creative expressions implicitly constituted theories of history. These elements of romantic history appear in different permutations in O'Sullivan's essays, in Bancroft's analysis of the fall of the Roman Empire, and in Cole's *The Course of Empire*. Together, these images and texts make clear that the romantic engagement with the past produced a sense of ambiguity in the present and contingency in the future. Stadialism envisioned history in terms of repeating cycles, and as such it could provide the basis of deterministic narratives of national history. However, American writers and artists who employed the stadialist model usually rejected determinism, instead emphasizing that the question of whether the stadialist cycle would repeat itself in the American case remained open.[78]

Jefferson's Horizon

This sense of uncertainty and possibility returns us to Jefferson's proto-typical formulations of national time. My purpose in locating the origins of so many of the ideas discussed in this chapter in Jefferson's work is not to idealize one of the founding fathers or promote a so-called great man account of history. Rather, I wish to suggest that the major contradictions that structured American thinking about history in the nineteenth century, for writers and artists as diverse as O'Sullivan, Willard, Simms, Cole, and many more, were present at the nation's inception, and that these originary contradictions, though sometimes suppressed, have been woven deeply into the American national fabric. America has propelled itself forward in time as a means of seeking resolution to the irresolvable problems of defining its own relationship to history—and this unresolvability has kept the nation perpetually focused upon the future, the utopian horizon in which the tautological "empire of liberty" might be imagined to achieve coherence. This problem was the great object of Jefferson's lifelong intellectual work. Earlier, I quoted at some length from Jefferson's 1824 letter to Ludlow. Here, I would like to repeat one of the lines quoted earlier, but in fuller context. "I am eighty-one years of age," Jefferson wrote, "born where I now live, in the first range of mountains in the interior of our country. I have observed this march of civilization advancing from the sea-coast, passing over us like a cloud of light, increasing our knowledge and improving our condition, insomuch that we are at this time more advanced in civilization here than the seaports were when I was a boy. And where this progress will stop no one can say."[79]

Jefferson wrote these words not simply in the piedmont of Virginia but at Monticello, the estate that he had carefully designed to reflect his political philosophy. Monticello is nothing less than a nexus of national time. The neoclassical architecture of the main house signifies the continuity of republican principles across the centuries. The play of the seasons is evident in the landscape, especially given the panoramic view that the estate's location provides. As Malcolm Kelsall has demonstrated, the position of the estate on a hill overlooking the countryside was appropriated from English country houses and made tangible the benevolent hegemony that a Whiggish gentleman exercised over the surrounding area. Hence, Jefferson's Monticello linked time to power. Monticello was designed to emblematize benevolent hegemony, not only over space but over time.

The inescapable problem of tyranny was also incorporated into Jefferson's home, in the form of the labor of the enslaved that was shunted to the side of the prospect, at least partly hidden from view, in a fruitless effort to maintain the purity of Monticello's republican iconography. The sounds of industry were, however, quite apparent, for labor on the estate was regulated by a Great Clock that chimed a bell each hour. Clocks were very important to Thomas Jefferson. There was a clock in every public room at Monticello, and bells rang during the day to mark the hours. Jefferson designed the French-made clock that was mounted on a bracket in his sleeping alcove. This piece incorporated two black marble obelisks, between which the mechanical works of the chronometer were suspended. The obelisk is an ancient symbol of empire, an interesting design choice on Jefferson's part. The suspension of the clockworks between the two obelisks creates a layering of different temporalities, ancient and modern, and suggests an interplay between power and time. The Great Clock above the main entrance to Monticello was designed according to Jefferson's specifications by Philadelphia clockmaker Robert Leslie and actually installed in 1793 by Leslie's employee Peter Spruck.[80] This clock also is deeply embedded in Monticello's architecture of power. Because the clock is located directly underneath the front portico, the exterior face would have been invisible to most people on the outside, and thus the bell is actually the only temporal signifier of which those working outside the house would have been aware. Slaves working on the grounds to the sides of the house would never have seen the clock. In this way, the bell functions as a kind of aural panopticon, enacting a temporal hegemony over the landscape that is parallel to the visual hegemony of the prospect.

The physical context of the Great Clock is rich with temporal signifiers. First, the clock itself is differentiated; the outside face has only an hour hand, while the inside face adds a minute hand and a small seconds dial. As many other commentators have noted, Jefferson's decision to include only an hour hand on the clock's exterior dial indicates that those outside the house have a different relationship to time than those inside. What has not often been remarked, however, is the fact that since few would have seen the exterior face, the exclusion of the minute hand on the outside must have been a largely symbolic gesture on Jefferson's part, an effort to sort out the temporal relations on the estate in his own mind. It seems most likely that Jefferson considered the need or ability to keep track of minutes and seconds to be a sign of a higher level of culture.[81] The more refined measurement of time on the inner dial face might be seen as an indication of the higher level of civilization possessed by those inside the house. The relationship between inside and outside might be modeled on that which Jefferson described in his letter to Ludlow, that is, a relationship between primitive and more advanced stages in the progress of society. However, it is also possible that the difference between the inside and the outside clock faces signified not different stages in the movement toward civilization, but different classes within a single stage. In other words, it is possible that Jefferson viewed himself and those working outside the house as members of the same civilization, gentleman and laborer, rather than members of more and less advanced societies on the stadialist spectrum.

Jefferson left no explanation of his thinking in designing the Great Clock this way, but the iconography of the hall itself provides some clues. As Kelsall has noted, the hall combines "republican simplicity" with emblems of national power. "On the ceiling above," Kelsall explains, "there was (probably) displayed then (as now) the American eagle. The national symbol has now acquired a halo of 18 stars (rather than the 13 of 1782) which would date it between 1812 (when Louisiana was admitted to the union) and 1816 (Indiana's admission). It would seem, therefore, to be a triumphalist allusion to the Louisiana purchase by Jefferson and the extent of the 'empire for liberty.'"[82] Kelsall also calls attention to the number of American Indian artifacts displayed in the hall. Just as with the two faces of the clock itself, the meaning of the presence of these native artifacts is ambiguous. In his letter to Ludlow, Jefferson had situated American Indians within the most primitive band of history. Hence, the artifacts might be taken as signs of a common past out of which the refinement of Monticello had itself emerged (after passing through, of course, the agricultural stage represented by the activity outside of the house). However, these artifacts were situated in the context of a selection of natural history specimens. If Indian artifacts were understood to comprise part of the natural history display, then their presence in the Entrance Hall might have represented an enduring, ahistorical difference between savagery and civilization. The room's decor also included emblems of national expansion over the course of time, such as maps of American territory and an engraving of John Trumbull's *Declaration of Independence of the United States of America*. The clock itself is encoded with neoclassical design elements, which of course characterize Monticello as a whole. Hence, the hall exhibits a very complex temporality. The clock would be understood as "modern," in a certain sense, and a sign of technological achievement. It also evokes Enlightenment associations between clockwork and the smoothly functioning machinery of nature, as well as a deistic sense of the "clockmaker god." The presence of the Trumbull print connects this

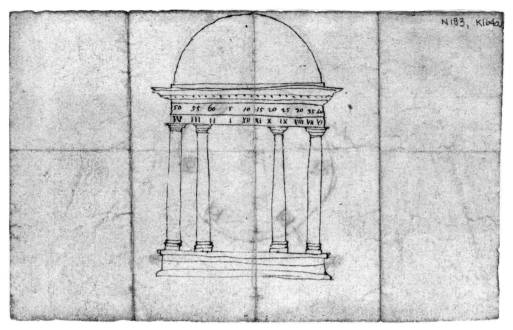

ILLUSTRATION 1.6. *Thomas Jefferson, Tuscan monopteros, recto, 1804 or later. Architectural drawing, 3¾ × 6³⁄₁₆ inches (Coolidge Collection of Thomas Jefferson Manuscripts, Massachusetts Historical Society)*

clockwork cosmos to the American political system. (Jefferson himself had, in his 1801 letter to Priestley, described the federal government and the Constitution as a "clock or watch" that could, if run down, simply be rewound and set working again.)[83] The Great Clock and the Entrance Hall are thus at the center of an estate that juxtaposes all of the major temporal signifiers important to American national identity.

Monticello leaves us one final temporal marker, albeit one that was never built. Indeed, no one can be sure that Jefferson's drawing of a monopteros (or small, round temple with a single ring of columns) was even intended to be a building (Illustration 1.6). A time track—that is, a series of numbers from one to twelve such as one would find on a clock dial—circles the roof of the structure. Hence, this drawing may well have been a shelf clock in the form of a temple (such clocks did exist in the period). However, architectural historian Fiske Kimball notes that a "very similar" structure "still exists on Madison's estate at Montpellier" and concludes that "it would not be surprising if the suggestion or even the actual design of Madison's pavilion had come from Jefferson." Kimball also notes that the monopteros may be the structure described as a "turning Tuscan temple, 10 f. diam. 6 columns. proportions of Pantheon" that Jefferson alludes to in some of his notes for the development of the grounds at Monticello.[84]

It is strange but appropriate that Jefferson would have designed a building in the image of a clock, for in that way the drawing performs, in capsule form, the same work performed by the estate as a whole. In linking clock to temple, Jefferson's drawing links the moments of time in the present to time stretching back to antiquity. In proposing such a structure for his idealized estate, Jefferson connects past and present time to the utopian future. As the philosophical seat of the empire of liberty, Monticello strives to accomplish this same end by pulling all time into itself, indexing and organizing it, and rendering it usable in the construction of the national imaginary. The ongoing presence of slavery at Monticello, the employment of time as an instrument of both liberation and domination, was only the most obvious of the many evidences of the perpetual failure to realize that utopia in each new present moment, of the deferral of the ideal republic into the future. The ghostly monopteros thus perfectly symbolizes a fact of which Jefferson was evidently quite painfully aware: this project of construction can never be completed. Hence, we might find a wistful anticipation of Emerson's 1844 encomium to the "new yet unapproachable America," always awaiting discovery in the next moment, in one of Jefferson's lines to John Adams in 1816: "I like the dreams of the future better than the history of the past."[85]

MATÉRIAL TIME

If Americans set out to colonize time in the nineteenth century, the emergence of mechanical timekeeping as a major cultural force lent new contours to the imagined empire. To a great extent, mechanical time was closely associated with the economic activities of the market. As such, it sometimes posed challenges to the teleological orientation of romantic historicism. Mechanical time could be construed as meaningless, value free, or "empty," to use Walter Benjamin's term, an endless series of present moments leading toward no particular future. However, Americans also experienced and created forms of mechanical time that were neither homogeneous nor distinct from other temporal modes. History, nature, and religion continued to play important roles in American thinking about time, and throughout the nineteenth century Americans continued to understand mechanical time within the context of these other temporal modes. Indeed, clocks and watches were themselves often viewed as traditional and premodern objects. In the eighteenth century, Enlightenment philosophy had made both clocks and watches into symbols for deism and natural theology, and these significations remained strong in the nineteenth century.[1] The mass production of clocks, which began in 1807 in a small Connecticut factory, added new meanings to mechanical time without erasing the old. When American companies began mass-producing affordable pocket watches in the 1850s, these more personal timepieces sent even more ideas about time circulating through the nation. In dialogue, then, with other temporal modes, mechanical time lent the unique characteristics made possible by its particular technologies to rich, multifaceted narrative accounts of the republican empire.

A clock label used by J. J. & W. Beals's "Clock Establishment" of Boston in the late 1840s illustrates the complexity of the connection between mechanical time and nationalism. The label features an engraving depicting rows of shelf and wall clocks in a showroom. This label would have been placed inside the cases of clocks sold, but not made, by the concern.[2] Such labels were a common form of advertising for merchants serving as middlemen in the clock trade. On the showroom's floor lies a pile of boxes, two of which are conspicuously labeled "London" and "Texas." The question immediately raised by the engraving is whether the first box has arrived from London with an imported clock or whether this box will be used to send an American-made clock to England. England had long been a center of clock making, exporting finished timepieces and parts to other European countries, to China, and to colonial or postcolonial locales such as North America.[3] However, in 1842, only a few years before this label was printed, Connecticut clock maker Chauncey Jerome had opened an export trade from the United States to England. Exporting any kind of manufactured goods to England was both an economic and a cultural coup for Americans, as it reversed the traditional relationship between colony and mother country.[4] Hence, in the context of the late 1840s the meaning of the engraving is ambiguous. The box on the floor labeled "London" might indicate that this firm exports American-made clocks to England, or it might indicate that the shop vends English clocks, still possessing much cachet, to American consumers. In either case, the illustration attests not only to the practical value of the timepieces available in the shop but also to their cultural prestige as objects whose production and trade were bound up in America's emerging sense of national identity on a global stage. The Bealses' label makes clocks seem desirable by representing them as commodities circulating in a world market. In other words, clocks are desirable commodities precisely because they allow American consumers to lose their provincial status and become cosmopolitan participants in such a world market.

The clock industry was especially significant to Americans not only because England, the colonial mother country, had such established leadership in that particular field but also because clocks were among the first objects mass-produced in American factories whose proprietors longed to compete with the English. The production method pioneered by Plymouth, Connecticut, clock maker Eli Terry in 1807, using mass-produced, interchangeable parts, became famous around the world as the "American system" of manufacturing.[5] As a result of such Yankee entrepreneurship, clocks, which had been expensive, handcrafted items in the eighteenth century, became affordable commodities available to all levels of American society. By the

1850s, five Connecticut clock factories produced roughly half a million clocks each year, and the clock industry became a source of considerable national pride.[6] "For many years," Jerome boasted in his 1860 autobiography, "I have extensively advertised throughout every part of the civilized world, and in the most conspicuous places, such a city as New Haven Connecticut, U.S.A., and its name is hourly brought to notice wherever American clocks are used, and I know of no more conspicuous or prominent place than the dial of a clock for this purpose."[7] In Jerome's formulation, only those parts of the world that employ clocks are civilized; even more, it seems that only those parts of the world that buy American clocks are civilized. Hence, in this representation clock time becomes the instrument of America's economic, and cultural, expansion. Exporting clocks as commodities renders the rest of the world "civilized" in American terms.

This theme is reinforced by the presence of the box labeled "Texas" in the Bealses' label. Since no clocks were commercially produced in Texas in the 1840s, the meaning of this element of the image is relatively clear. The Bealses' shop must export clocks to Texas, a territory recently conquered from Mexico and a symbol of U.S. expansion to the South and West. Through this trade, Boston assumes the same colonial relationship to Texas that London used to hold to Boston. Thus, the advertisement implies, in the 1840s Boston has succeeded London as an imperial capital, if not literally in a political sense then at least in a cultural and economic sense. However, the precise nature of this succession becomes caught up, once again, in the picture's overall ambiguity. If Boston is now sending American clocks to London, then the succession is in fact a supersession, with Boston replacing London as the center of a world market in clocks, exporting to both London (the old capital) and Texas (the new colonial territory). However, if Boston is still importing English clocks that have maintained their prestige even in the face of American competition, and moving those clocks, or cheaper American-made clocks, further along to Texas, then Boston has not superseded London but simply joined the old capital as a node in the global market. Indeed, if the latter interpretation is correct, then Boston might still be inferior to London, since the trade would flow exclusively from east to west. The engraving thus testifies to America's uncertain sense of the meaning of its own national emergence, to its effort to formulate a coherent identity both in relation to models provided by Old World nations and as a qualitatively new form of political entity, self-consciously modern and forward-looking, taking shape in the temporal space of a New World.

But what was the nature of this temporal space—what was time? It seems clear that the clocks celebrated by the Bealses and by Jerome served not only as particular commodities—instances of America's growing economic power—but also as general signs of the modernity of American civilization. If the commerce in clocks between London, Boston, and Texas signified a temporal movement toward the *telos* of empire, then the employment of those same clocks determined the nature of time in the present moment of that movement. Hence, time was not merely a vertical continuum along which the nation (signified here by the metropole of Boston) moved but also a horizontal medium of national culture. All clocks, however, are not the same. "Clocks of every description put up with accuracy and despatch for exportation," the label's copy reads. Indeed, the engraving, while lacking great detail, clearly shows clocks in a number of different forms. By the 1840s, American companies were producing a bewildering variety of different clock designs, partly in response to a market that demanded novelty, and a shop such as the Bealses' would have traded in all sorts of different pieces. Many of these clocks incorporated multiple temporal signatures into their design and decoration. Clocks in the neoclassical or Gothic styles, or featuring painted images of historic buildings such as Independence Hall or Mount Vernon, or mythological tales, or pastoral scenes, or celebrations of their own technical ingenuity, continuously revised ideas about the relationship between past, present, and future, tradition and innovation, nature and culture, history and modernity.[8] As these commodities spread across the nation and the globe through the networks of commerce, they lent themselves to the ferment of temporal cultures in perpetual transformation. A clock marking the hours of work in an office would not possess the same social meaning as a clock employed in a Shaker community to coordinate religious life or a clock in the hallway of a bourgeois home whose function was mainly aesthetic.[9] Hence, the horizontal plane of present time was variegated, not uniform. The circulation of clocks (and, later, watches) as commodities through any number of distinctive social environments contributed to a welter of heterogeneous temporalities authorizing different ways of imagining the nation's relationship to the world and different possible routes through the vertical time of history—that is, different possible national futures.

Finding Time

The varied mechanical timepieces circulating through the American market in the nineteenth century embodied ideas about time in their construction, design, and use. Just as the social experience of natural time is a consequence of the real conditions of nature (the rising and setting of the sun, the phases of the moon, and the changing seasons), the social experience of mechanical time can only be understood in the context of those real, material objects. The most common type of clock in America from the seventeenth century until the early twentieth century was the weight-driven pendulum clock. During the nineteenth century, household clocks employed the same basic elements with which Americans had long been familiar: wooden or brass gears, weights to supply power to the movement, and a pendulum to regulate the speed of the movement. Strictly speaking, only a timepiece with a striking mechanism should be described as a clock (the English word "clock" is one of a large family of cognate words, including the French *cloche* and the German *Glocke*, all meaning bell), but then, as now, most people employed the term with much less discrimination. During this period, there was no technical change so dramatically apparent to users lacking specialized training as the introduction of the pendulum as regulator had been to the people of the sixteenth century, or as the introduction of electric power, quartz crystals as regulators, and digital displays would be to the people of the twentieth century. However, technical innovations did make it possible to produce clocks more cheaply and in different shapes and sizes. From the standpoint of cultural history, then, the technical achievements of nineteenth-century clock makers were important primarily because they made clocks available as consumer goods to great numbers of people and because they allowed for a greater variety of clock designs.[10]

During the first half of the nineteenth century, while clocks were establishing themselves as affordable commodities in the American market, watches remained expensive luxury goods. To be sure, enough Americans owned watches that these objects were also culturally significant, but their effect on American ideas about time was inflected by a very different class dynamic. Possessing and employing a watch would certainly have signified mastery of the sort of precise timekeeping demanded by market capitalism. However, because watches were assembled by hand by skilled craftsmen, they also connoted a preindustrial artisanal ideal that sat somewhat uneasily alongside the first signification, mastery of modern capitalism. In addition, because most watches were imported from England, France, or Switzerland, they also continued to evoke a sense of American dependence upon Europe long after clocks had become symbols of national independence and equality. When American entrepreneurs developed mass production techniques for watches in the 1850s, the cultural meaning of the watch shifted radically. Many of the same nationalistic and egalitarian ideas previously associated with clocks could now be applied to watches as well. However, even after the 1850s watches continued to produce a set of quite distinct ideas about time, ideas pertaining not only to portability and privacy but also to the deeply embedded popular association of watches with railroad timekeeping.[11]

This dissemination of unlike timepieces among the populace over the course of the century had important consequences. While Americans had had access to mechanical time from public clocks since the seventeenth century, bringing a clock of a particular design into one's home, or carrying a watch on one's person, created a very different relationship to the cultural ideas signified by that particular object. The function of clock and watch mechanisms themselves had not changed much since the eighteenth century, but Americans nevertheless assigned new meanings to mechanical time in the nineteenth century. In contrast to the theory that the mass production of mechanical timepieces resulted in greater homogeneity of temporal experience, the great diversity of clocks (and, later, watches) available as consumer goods in fact produced a heterogeneous tapestry of quite different temporalities within individual American homes and other spaces.

This great variety of design, incorporating aesthetics from the neoclassical to the gothic, allowed for competing ways of imagining the relationships between past, present, and future, tradition and modernity, liberty and power. In addition, Americans associated clocks and watches with culturally important (and often incompatible) concepts such as artisanship, the patent system, and mass production. The key to making sense of this chaotic mass of temporal signifiers was narrative. Just as national history writers strove to create narratives that would make sense of a paradoxical republican empire, so too did the production, dissemination, and employment of clocks and watches form the material basis of narratives that attempted to organize and make sense of cultural conflicts over the nature and use of time.

Mechanical timepieces both embody and produce ideas about time in their design, operation, and use. However, only part of the historical specificity of these ideas resides within the mechanism of the object itself. That is to say, even a single clock or watch, remaining in use for several decades, might inhabit very different networks of ideas about time. The mechanism itself makes possible certain ways of conceptualizing temporality that would not otherwise be available, but different individuals and groups produce their own ways of thinking about and making use of such objects. The social experience of time exists *between* human agent and nonhuman object.[12] The narratives resulting from these interactions provide a tangible record of how the Americans who set out to colonize time mapped the abstract territory through which they moved. The diverse array of clocks and watches produced within and imported to the United States in the first half of the century themselves constitute a series of narratives about time, narratives suggesting a temporal terrain as convoluted and difficult to navigate as anything found in the land of the West.

The field of material culture studies offers a variety of different ways of interpreting the stories told by such objects, ranging from the more empirical to the more intuitive and imaginative. For example, Jules Prown offers the following "reading" of a tall case clock:

> The tall clock stands slim and erect, slightly larger than human scale. It has human characteristics, and yet it is both more and less than human. It has a face behind which a surrogate brain ticks relentlessly. It is not capable of independent life, yet once wound its mechanism ticks on and its hands move without rest. The human occupants of the house are mortal with an allotted span of time to use or waste while the clock measures its irretrievable passage. Could the clock have played a metaphorical role as the unblinking toller of time who watches the inhabitants of the house, the agent of some extrahuman, divine power? . . . How does one explore the mental landscape, the beliefs, to validate or deny such speculations? Sermons, private diaries, poetry, and fiction are among the sources for the investigator seeking not only facts but also the hints or suggestions of belief. Even if such hypotheses or speculations remain unproved, they are not necessarily invalid.[13]

An academic historian would no doubt find this account idiosyncratic and "presentist," in that Prown projects his own ideas about time, design, and technology onto the clock. However, as Prown suggests, some of the materials more traditionally used in social history, such as sermons and diaries, might also be subject to the same critique. Given that Prown's work in art history is usually richly contextualized, we can assume that he is being intentionally tendentious in this passage. He employs the clock to provoke us to question how we can know anything about the past, and whether there are things worth knowing that we cannot know with certainty or even great probability. The fact that a particular interpretation cannot be proven empirically does not mean that it is wrong. In fact, many correct interpretations of historical evidence probably cannot be proven empirically, and so a steadfast commitment to empiricism may blind us to certain important aspects of history.

In my own analysis of mechanical timepieces, I hew to a more empirical methodology than the one demonstrated by Prown in the passage above, but I also try to remain sensitive to how difficult it is to know how people experienced something as abstract as time, what they thought about it, and what they tried to do with it. We can only learn about such things indirectly. In the pages that follow, I treat objects as tangible objectifications of abstract ideas about time.[14] However, I also insist that material objects such as clocks and watches are themselves producers of new ideas that circulate through the culture, rather than simply representations of previously existing beliefs. A clock might embody a variety of ideas about time held by the clock maker, cabinetmaker, and painter who worked on the object. When brought into someone's home, the clock puts these ideas into circulation with the pre-existing versions of temporality already present in the household. Thus, the clock is both a representation of existing beliefs and a source of new ideas about time.

The Persistence of Temporal Artifacts

One characteristic of material objects is their persistence. Especially in an age in which furniture was not considered disposable, households provided venues for the accumulation and juxtaposition of objects from different periods, producing a layering of the cultural ideas embodied in changing styles. Eighteenth-century clocks and watches were a common part of nineteenth-century temporal experience, and such timepieces ordinarily kept time with admirable precision. Handmade watches imported from Europe may have been more common than clocks among eighteenth-century Americans, and many of these objects were passed down as precious family heirlooms.[15] Tall case clocks (or "grandfather clocks," as they are now commonly known) were the most prestigious form of timepiece in the eighteenth century and retained a special place in the temporal imagination of the nineteenth century.[16] The provenance of such objects is complex. Some were simply imported complete from Europe. Often, however, American merchants would import just the movement of a clock and have a local cabinetmaker create a case for this mechanism. Sometimes these American merchants would engrave their own names and places of business upon the dials (a form of advertising). Sometimes American clock makers would import parts and assemble them into complete movements, while others made their own parts. Some clock makers had their own retail stores, while others sold their goods through middlemen.

In all of these situations, the construction of the movement and the case were separate processes. Clock makers made movements, while cases were made by cabinetmakers. Indeed, customers would often buy a movement from a clock maker and then hire a cabinetmaker to create a case for the mechanism. Painting of the case and engraving of the dial were distinct crafts sometimes, though not always, handled by other tradespeople. In addition, a clock might be modified after sale, as an owner could have the works repaired or installed into a new case, decorative painting redone, new finials or hands added, or a variety of other modifications made.[17] Similarly, watches imported from Europe could be set in cases engraved with the names of American resellers (usually jewelers) and then further embellished with papers, chains, and other accessories chosen by the owner.[18]

A timepiece constructed in the eighteenth century could well continue shaping temporal experience for decades to come. Many eighteenth-century clocks still keep good time today. Their durability suggests that such clocks must have been relatively common in middle- and upper-class homes of the nineteenth century.[19] This hypothesis is supported by the numerous nineteenth-century written and visual references to tall case clocks. "Through every swift vicissitude / Of changeful time, unchanged it has stood," Henry Wadsworth Longfellow wrote of the old tall clock at his in-laws' house in 1845.[20] A painting by John Lewis Krimmel, *Quilting Frolic* (1813), suggests that tall case clocks, though quite expensive items in the eighteenth century, had been disseminated more widely through the population by early in the nineteenth century (Illustration 2.1). Although both black and white servants, or perhaps individuals who have been hired to aid in the quilting, appear in the painting, social distinctions have evidently diminished in the chaos resulting from the arrival of guests to celebrate the completion of the quilt.[21] The family appears to enjoy middling economic circumstances, prosperous enough to hire help and to throw a party but not especially affluent.[22] The clock depicted in Krimmel's painting features heavy foliate scrollwork typically found in mid-eighteenth-century clocks. Such a style might have appeared on a clock made in 1813 but would, in any case, have appeared old-fashioned.[23] This clock's style might also allude to the local culture of Pennsylvania, where Krimmel (a German immigrant) lived and worked. Pennsylvania German clock cabinetmakers employed an ornate, heavy style long after it had gone out of fashion in New York and New England.[24]

Most tall case clocks depicted in nineteenth-century genre painting feature this type of rococo pediment characteristic of mid-eighteenth-century furniture design. William Sidney Mount's well-known *Rustic Dance after a*

ILLUSTRATION 2.1. *John Lewis Krimmel,* Quilting Frolic, *1813.*
Oil on canvas, 16¾ × 22³⁄₁₆ inches (Winterthur Museum)

Sleigh Ride (1830) depicts such a clock in its most common position in genre
paintings, anchoring one corner of the composition (Illustration 2.2).[25] The
clock's heavy foliate scrollwork is unlike the lighter broken scroll pediments
or simple lines typical of Federal period clocks. The household depicted
in the painting is, as the title indicates, rural, appearing to be neither poor
nor very affluent. The clock could be an eighteenth-century piece handed
down through generations, or it could be a modern piece with an antiquated
design.[26] In other words, the display of the rococo style on the clock in the
painting indicates not only that this clock may be several decades old but
also that this family's "rustic" taste connects them to tradition, whatever a
viewer of the painting might imagine the clock's actual age to be. Thus, in a
variety of ways, both of these paintings suggest that clock time is characterized by tradition, local culture, and, through their rustic settings, a connection to nature. The culturally significant hoods of both of these clocks are
brought clearly into the viewer's perception by the exaggerated height of the

ILLUSTRATION 2.2. *William Sidney Mount,* Rustic Dance after a Sleigh Ride, *1830. Oil on canvas, 22⅛ × 27⅛ inches (Museum of Fine Arts, Boston; bequest of Martha C. Karolik for the M. and M. Karolik Collection of American Paintings, 1815–65. 48.458. Photograph © 2008, Museum of Fine Arts, Boston)*

cases. They each appear to tower several feet above the heads of the people around them. Actual tall case clocks are rarely over eight feet tall, including the finials. The faces of the clocks in the Mount and Krimmel paintings appear to be at least nine feet above the ground. Clearly, the painters intend these clocks to be seen.

In contrast to the prominent role given clocks in early to mid-nineteenth-century genre paintings, watches were not commonly depicted in such paintings, though they were featured in a good number of portraits. This difference suggests that while portrait painters employed watches to suggest distinction, genre painters did not view watches as aspects of the ostensibly typical American scenes they portrayed. This prejudice against the watch and in favor of the clock on the part of genre painters makes sense when we consider that, even before the age of mass production, many clocks were domestically produced, albeit with the aid of imported parts, while almost all watches were imported in their entirety until the emergence of the American watch industry in the 1850s. The fact that these watches could be placed in American cases or decorated with American accessories does not seem to have Americanized them, in the eyes of genre painters, in the same way that an American-made cabinet could domesticate a set of clockworks of transnational provenance. For whatever reason, it was not until the 1850s that watches began to appear in genre paintings, such as Lilly Martin Spencer's *Listening to Father's Watch* (1857) (Illustration 2.3). Even in this painting, the watch itself is obscured by the hand of the little girl who holds it to her ear. While the idea of the watch is central to the meaning of the painting's narrative, the details of the watch itself are hidden. The treatment of the watch in this painting thus contrasts dramatically with the emphasis placed upon the faces and hoods of the tall clocks depicted in the paintings by Krimmel and Mount. Indeed, it is not even possible to determine if this watch is one of the new, mass-produced American models or an older, imported watch. Given the overall tenor of the painting, we might surmise that the watch is one that the father has owned for many years, and that his daughter's listening to the watch represents the continuity of time across the generations. While the painting would, then, attribute a certain kind of social significance to the time told by the watch, it would also make watch time much more private than clock time. While in Spencer's painting watch time contributes to an intimate domestic moment between father and daughter, in the Krimmel and Mount paintings clocks preside over scenes of celebration in which the home is thrown open to visitors.

A tall case clock whose works were completed by Newport clock maker James Wady between 1745 and 1755 exemplifies the complexity of the time told by the sort of eighteenth-century clocks depicted by Krimmel and Mount (Illustration 2.4).[27] This clock's dial includes two time tracks. The outer track divides the dial as a whole into sixty segments, each representing one minute of time as measured by the clock's minute hand. The inner track divides each hour into four sections. These sections are for use in measuring time using the hour hand alone. Seventeenth and early eighteenth-century clocks often came equipped with an hour hand only. As the markings of the inner time track on the Wady clock dial reveal, it is quite possible to tell time with a reasonable degree of accuracy using only an hour hand and quarter hour divisions. In the eighteenth century, the minute hand served less a prac-

ILLUSTRATION 2.3. *Lilly Martin Spencer,* Listening to Father's Watch, *1857. Oil on academy board, 16 × 12 inches (Currier Museum of Art, Manchester, New Hampshire; gift of Henry Melville Fuller, 1974.34)*

ILLUSTRATION 2.4. *James Wady, Newport, Rhode Island, dial plate of tall clock, 1745–55 (Winterthur Museum)*

tical purpose than it did simply to demonstrate the technical skill of the clock maker and, one must assume, something about the character of the clock's owner (for clock makers would not have made clocks with minute hands if people did not want to buy them). The Wady clock, like many finely made tall case clocks, also includes a separate dial to mark the seconds (directly beneath the chapter number XII). The seconds hand emits an audible *tick* as it moves, calling constant attention to the passage of time.[28] Thus, Wady's clock combines an allusion to old-fashioned practices of telling time in its inner time track with a more precise and modern time track for the minute hand and a seconds dial; this latter device serves no practical timekeeping purpose but celebrates technical achievement and makes the mechanical operation of the clock audible and visible in every moment.[29] The clock also provides the option, regulated by the "strike/silent" dial in the upper right corner of the face, of hearing each hour tolled off by a bell. Longfellow's poem records how the ticking of the old clock at his in-laws' house seemed to become a "voice" speaking to the inhabitants during quiet times.[30] For many nineteenth-century Americans, the ongoing operation of such objects in their houses may well have signified, both visually and aurally, the origin of clock time in cultural traditions of ongoing importance. The design of the Wady clock certainly evokes connections to previously established ways of thinking about time to a much greater degree than it evokes a break from such traditions.

Directly above the dial of the Wady clock is a separate mechanism, also common in tall case clocks, for tracking the phases of the moon. The anthropomorphized lunar face, progressing across the lunette in a circular pattern that mirrors the movement of the hands around the clock dial, draws a connection between clock time and natural time. This connection is made even more emphatically by the small dial in the upper left corner of the face. This dial is regulated by the same pendulum that regulates the main clock dial, but through ingenious gearing it makes a complete revolution once every fifteen days. In the process it tracks the changes of the tides.[31] Such a device would be important in a place like Newport; although the original owner of this clock is unknown, it seems likely that it belonged to a merchant who would have had good reason to want such information. The clock thus not only combines nature and mechanics in its production of time, it also does so in a way that reflects local needs and interests.[32]

Together, images and objects such as these suggest a pattern of association between clock time and cultural traditions rooted in economic modes predating free-market capitalism. The scene in *Quilting Frolic* represents economic activity as local and communal. The labor of creating the quilt segues fluidly into the party to celebrate the quilt's completion. All of this activity has the effect of bringing people together by blurring the distinctions between master and servant, members of the household and outsiders. The Wady clock, while conveying a more formal sense of bourgeois respectability, also connects the mercantile activity antedating the market revolution with the natural environment of a particular locality that makes that specific form of economic activity possible. As a group, these clocks (both real and painted) seem to form the temporal basis of an "imagined community" founded in the local and knit together through the synthesis of differentiated economic and social roles. The prominent place of these old-fashioned clocks in nineteenth-century paintings points toward the perpetuation of their temporal signatures into the period of American nation formation. While there must have been significant differences in the ways in which diverse people responded to such objects and images, these objects and images nonetheless make clear that nature and religion continued to play important roles in nineteenth-century thinking about time for many Americans even as clocks became pervasive. Clocks could express, in their design and operation, natural or religious ideas about time. Some of the most important consequences of this fact become apparent in the models of national affiliation proposed by writers like Catharine Beecher and Henry Thoreau, explored in the following chapter.

Federal Time

While ornate eighteenth-century styles continued in use on some tall clocks through the mid-nineteenth century, the majority of clocks constructed after the Revolution adopted the Federal style. This aesthetic movement carried great ideological significance. The Federal style's neoclassical designs linked the United States to the Roman republic and Greek democracy. As Wendell Garret explains, the neoclassical ideal "affected and influenced the everyday world of the decorative arts with a new aesthetic — cool precision of line, delicacy of detail, attractive contrasts of textures, and opulent simplicity and easy elegance."[33] Material culture connected the modern republic to classical republicanism through forms such as urns, lyre shapes, shields, and eagles.[34] The eagle was, of course, both an American and a Roman symbol of national power. Sometimes these neoclassical forms were incorporated into the shape of the object itself, as in the case of urn or eagle finials, or the shield backs of many Federal period chairs. Neoclassical motifs such as cornucopias, ram's heads, wreaths, acanthus, and guilloche and Greek key borders could also be painted onto furniture.[35] Mythological subjects were common in such decorative painting. When these forms appear on clocks or watches, the temporality of the neoclassical aesthetic is thus doubled—the time of the present marked as antiquity. Clocks and watches were more susceptible to illustration than most furnishings, since many clock cabinets featured painted panels of either wood or glass, while watch cases were usually engraved and watch papers painted. Illustrators frequently employed neoclassical and mythological motifs for such commissions.[36]

The model for the neoclassical style in America was the Englishman George Hepplewhite's *Cabinet-Maker and Upholsterer's Guide* (1788). Copies of this design book were available in North America, and its ideas were spread by English artisans such as Richard Lawson, who came to Baltimore in 1785 and went into business with cabinetmaker John Bankson. Their shop produced a variety of neoclassical tall clock cases, including one featuring an inlaid image of George Washington.[37] In truth, much of the patriotic imagery of the Federal period was indebted to foreign sources. The use of Hepplewhite's design standards after the Revolution meant that American neoclassicism was mediated through the standards of taste of a culturally influential segment of English society. In temporal terms, then, American neoclassicism connoted both a direct connection between the modern republic and the ancient and a more convoluted historical debt to England and its traditions of liberty. If neoclassicism sought to reproduce ancient civic virtues in the modern nation, then the transmission of these virtues through forms claiming to represent English culture suggested that the American project was not original but rather the fulfillment of England's promise. Depicting Washington on a finely made tall clock in the Hepplewhite style made him a Whiggish hero representative of what many understood to be the best of English politics and, crucially, taste.

Washington was also a popular figure in French clocks made for the American market in the early years of the nineteenth century. A mantle clock created around 1805 by Jean-Baptiste Dubuc exemplifies the neoclassical iconography of such pieces. Washington's pose is that of an ancient warrior-statesman, evoking the legend of the virtuous Cincinnatus (Illustration 2.5). A formally similar clock by Louis Mallet (Illustration 2.6) dates from slightly after the Dubuc Washington clock but illustrates the iconography with which Dubuc worked.[38] In the Mallet clock, the military figure gazes outward and slightly upward. His left hand is open toward the viewer. The figure conveys

ILLUSTRATION 2.5. *Jean-Baptiste Dubuc, France, George Washington mantle clock, about 1805 (Winterthur Museum)*

ILLUSTRATION 2.6. *Louis Mallet, France, neoclassical mantle clock, about 1810–30 (Winterthur Museum)*

an impression of pride, independence, and nobility, all virtues in republican political theory. His right hand holds a link of chain. Is he a liberator or a conqueror? In the case of Washington, the answer is clear. The pages of the book open to his right read: "July 4th 1776 The Birthday of Liberty . . . America the Asylum of the Oppressed." The surveying instruments to Washington's right add the quality of scientific accomplishment to the military achievements signified by his uniform. Like the military figure in the Mallet clock, Dubuc's Washington gazes outward and slightly upward. His gaze mirrors that of the eagle. Since Washington had died a few years before this clock was made, it is appropriate that he gaze heavenward. But the linking of his gaze with that of the eagle also signifies that he remains with America. Washington and the eagle both gaze away from a specific point in time, the national origin of July Fourth, 1776, and toward the future, a national future. As the "asylum of the oppressed," America will not conquer territory but rather dominate world history, assimilating the peoples of the world into its political model. In this way, the clock incorporates the romantic historical conceit that the conquest of time makes possible the seeming paradox of the empire of liberty.

It thus seems that, in this object, the horizontal temporal plane of the present, signified by the clock dial itself, is subsumed within the vertical temporal plane of romantic history. Indeed, the clock dial is rather overwhelmed by the decorative features of the object. A bit more must be said about this relationship, however. In dim light, the outer ring of the dial, where the chapter numbers are engraved, glows softly as the rest of the object is obscured. In the nineteenth century the clock would often have been in a room with dim illumination.[39] Thus, the clock incorporates two slightly different relations between the mechanical time of the dial and the historical time of the Washington theme. In daylight, the historical decorative elements predominate. In the evening, however, by candle or lamplight, the dial catches the eye while history is suffused in shadow. Through this clever device, the clock may signify the mysterious relationship between time in the present and the long sweep of history, between the moments of time of the individuals employing the clock and the romance of nationalism.[40]

Federal period pieces by American immigrant clock makers working with different design traditions produced other connections between clock time and national time. A clock by the Pennsylvania German artisan John Paul is adorned with the date "1815," the word "liberty," and various patriotic emblems (Illustration 2.7).[41] The date 1815 probably alludes to the conclusion of the War of 1812. Although the conflict was, in military terms, at best a

ILLUSTRATION 2.7. *John Paul, Dauphin County, Pennsylvania, tall clock, detail of cabinet, about 1815 (Winterthur Museum)*

draw for the Americans, its conclusion was interpreted by many as a new beginning of American independence. This clock celebrates the continuation
of American time into the future. The clock is thought to have been constructed in 1815 or soon after, so at the time it was completed the date would
have seemed a part of the present. However, with each passing year the date
must have come to seem more and more distant. Hence, the relationship
between present moments of everyday time and historical time expressed by
this clock would have evolved over the years. It is also interesting to consider
this clock in the context of other dated pieces of furniture. It was not uncom-
mon for handmade furniture of the nineteenth century and earlier to bear, in
a highly visible spot, the date of its completion or the date of a special event
for which the furniture was made (such as a wedding). Like the Paul clock,
such objects would continue to remind members of a household of their
connection to the past. Putting such a date on a clock anchors clock time
in history, integrating it into the world of objects rich in particular temporal
associations among which many Americans lived.

Together, the pieces discussed thus far—the pre-Revolutionary clocks
of transatlantic origin that remained in use for decades, the Federal period
clocks designed according to English standards, the watches imported from
Europe but placed in cases engraved with the names of American merchants
or with icons of American nationalism, the imported French clocks celebrating Washington, the Pennsylvania German clock commemorating the War of
1812—and the many others like them carried temporal signatures into the
nineteenth century that situated American national time within the context
of the transatlantic culture of the eighteenth century. The prevalence of such
objects in both private and public places meant that Americans were constantly reminded of the origins of their own nation in the histories of other
nations, including not only Britain but also France and ancient Rome. The
term "nation" here of course acquires a complex and ambiguous meaning.
The United States was the first modern democracy, the first "nation" to employ the model of the liberal-democratic state. France and Britain would, in
the decades after the American Revolution, move toward this model, sometimes through gradual reform and sometimes by convulsion. Nevertheless,
the United States adopted many of its legal and political principles from
those countries, to say nothing of more abstract national ideals. Hence, no
one nation could claim ownership or invention of the model. Similarly, the
civilizations of classical Greece and Rome were not organized in national
terms at all in the modern sense, yet they possessed many practices and in-

stitutions from which the Americans borrowed. American national time in the nineteenth century was filled with the complex political and cultural histories conveyed by eighteenth- and early nineteenth-century timepieces of transnational provenance.

Simon Willard and the Artisanal Ideal

The transformations and layering of ideas about time from the 1790s to the 1820s can be seen in three quite different pieces completed in that span by the most famous of the Federal period clock makers, Simon Willard. The Willard family dominated clock making in Massachusetts in the late eighteenth and early nineteenth centuries. Benjamin Willard was the first of four brothers to take up the trade, producing pieces as early as the 1760s. His brothers Simon, Ephraim, and Aaron all followed him into the clock business. The Willards made tall case and shelf clocks during the eighteenth century. Simon Willard's calendar shelf clock, completed sometime in the 1790s, epitomizes Enlightenment ideas about time (Illustration 2.8).[42] The case is composed of two distinct cabinets, connected, the smaller cabinet on top measuring eleven and a half inches in height while the larger lower cabinet measures sixteen and a half inches. Because the upper cabinet is so much smaller, it appears to sit on top of the lower cabinet, but the two sections are connected and the works extend through both. The upper cabinet houses the main parts of the movement along with a brass dial engraved with both Roman and Arabic numerals. The lower cabinet features a door that can be opened easily without disturbing the workings of the mechanism. Opening the door reveals a circular time track that mirrors the time track on the dial above but that counts from one to twelve twice in Roman numerals. There was, originally, a disc in the circular space in the center of this second time track that registered the phases of the moon. This disc revolved once every fifty-nine days, thus running through the twenty-nine-and-a-half-day lunar cycle twice, driven by the same weight and pendulum system connected to the hands marking hours and minutes on the dial above. In front of the space where the moon disc used to sit is a wooden cutout in the shape of a lunette. A printed sheet of paper pasted onto this cutout provides a chart for finding the day of the week of any calendar day between 1780 and 1860, using a system of dominical letters. Below the lunette is another chart showing the difference between solar mean time and apparent solar time for every day of the year. In the corners of the space around the double time track

ILLUSTRATION 2.8. *Simon Willard, Roxbury, Massachusetts, calendar shelf clock, detail of interior of lower cabinet, 1790s (Winterthur Museum)*

are drawings of the planets, along with their names and astronomical symbols. Through all of these design elements, this object connects clock time to astronomical time and hence technology to nature. Such connections are made especially emphatic by the way that the lunar disc in the lower cabinet turns along with the hands on the dial in the upper cabinet—clock time and astronomical time share the same movement. The chart at the bottom of the page, similar to those commonly found in almanacs, points out both the artificiality of clock time (in that the clock diverges from the time of the sun) and clock time's relation to nature (in that the divergence is regular; clock time ventures only a certain number of minutes away from apparent solar time and then, always, returns to match the sun perfectly twice each year). As a whole, this calendar clock invites users to open it up and explore its secrets, to consider the relationships between different forms of time and to think of the clock as, at once, both artificial and natural.[43]

In 1802 Willard began producing a very different object—the "patent timepiece" that brought him his greatest fame (Illustration 2.9).[44] Willard's patent timepieces were expensive, costing roughly $45–$50 in the early years of the century, but popular nonetheless. Now called the "banjo clock" by collectors for its distinctive shape, the "Willard's Patent" design was both licensed and illicitly copied by clock makers throughout New England. Indeed, the phrase "Willard's Patent" became an indicator of quality that was usually painted onto these timepieces (even those that were unlicensed).[45] As Paul Foley explains, "The ability to legally enforce a patent was questionable, but obtaining a patent for a product offered more than protection against competition. . . . Patent products in the public's mind were equated with quality and innovation."[46] Following Willard's introduction of the concept, the idea of the clock as a patented invention became increasingly widespread and culturally powerful; patent time represented the American artisan as a creative genius bringing prosperity to the nation. Willard eventually found it necessary to defend the integrity of his patent in the newspapers, placing advertisements such as the following:

> CAUTION. I believe the public are not *generally* aware, that my former Patent Right expired 6 years ago; which induces me again to *caution* them against the frequent impositions practiced, in vending *spurious Timepieces*. It is true, they have "Patent" printed on them, and some with my name, and their outward appearance resembles those *formerly* made by me: *thus they are palmed upon the public.* Several of them have lately been brought to me for repairs, that would certainly put the greatest bungler

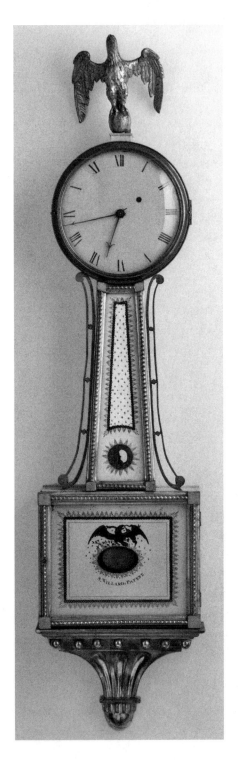

ILLUSTRATION 2.9.
Simon Willard, Roxbury,
Massachusetts, patent timepiece
("banjo clock"), about 1802–10
(Winterthur Museum)

to the blush. Such is the country inundated with, and such, I consider prejudicial to my reputation; I therefore *disclaim* being the same manufacturer of such vile performances.[47]

In making reference to his "reputation," Willard indicates how closely this product was associated with an artisanal ideal. The concept of authenticity applied equally to both the product and the maker, and thus "spurious" products constituted a threat to Willard's self-identity as an inventor and craftsman.

Historian of technology Carolyn Cooper has argued that the process of invention in this period "was to a significant degree socially constructed through patent management. . . . Since originality is the defining characteristic of any invention, the gradual social formation of decision rules for originality was tantamount to defining invention itself."[48] Obtaining a patent required convincing federal officials that one's invention was both original and useful. Since an object that did not meet those criteria could hardly be considered an "invention," obtaining a patent was a way of certifying the status of invention. The application process involved submitting detailed plans, along with a written explanation of the function of the invention and the way in which it differed from similar technologies already in use. In his patent application, Willard emphasized the technical superiority of his timepiece: "The weight falls only fifteen inches in eight days, during which time the regulator goes without winding up, whereas, the weight of the eight day clock falls not less than six feet in the same time." This innovation allowed Willard to put an accurate timepiece in a much smaller cabinet. In addition, the application notes that "the pendulum is brought forward in front of the weights, by which means it may be made longer and will consequently vibrate more accurately than the common method in which the pendulum was placed behind the weights."[49] This change would not be visible when the clock was operating while mounted on a wall, as it was intended to do. Indeed, it is unlikely that a user lacking technical knowledge of clock making would have any way of checking whether the slightly longer pendulum would be more accurate, since the difference would amount to only seconds per day.[50]

Hence, the patent timepiece produces ideas about time quite different from those of Willard's earlier calendar clock. The calendar clock foregrounds connections between mechanical time and nature that render the individual maker of the clock more an amanuensis than a creator in his own right. In contrast, the patent timepiece calls attention to the clock maker himself, emphasizing his role as inventor in producing mechanical time. The calendar clock makes the mechanics of time — both the equations governing the relationship between clock and sun and the movement of the time train — relatively transparent to any literate person who might have owned or used the clock. The patent timepiece contains no charts showing the equation of time, and its gears are hidden during ordinary use. The object must be taken down from the wall in order to be adjusted or cleaned. Through the agency of the inventor, the time of the clock is detached from nature and becomes a completed, self-contained product of processes to be marveled at but not observed in detail or understood by those not in possession of the inventor's special knowledge.

From a decorative standpoint, one of the most important features of the banjo clock is the painted glass (or *églomisé*) panel in the base of the cabinet. When Willard originally introduced this feature, he contracted with skilled painters such as Spencer Nolen to paint tasteful designs or pastoral scenes. As the nineteenth century progressed, other makers of banjo-style clocks and other forms of clocks as well began to introduce lower-quality painted images with a much wider variety of themes. Typically these paintings would leave an oval-shaped space of clear glass in the center, through which the bob of the pendulum could be seen as it swung back and forth. This clever effect provided a quick indication that the clock was, in fact, operating, but it also had an aesthetic purpose. As Willard states in his patent application, "The door of the regulator is set with glass painted and gilded with an oval space left, through which the motion of the pendulum is seen which has a pleasing effect." The swinging pendulum bob was the only part of the movement that could be seen during normal operation of the clock. Hence, unlike the calendar clock — which rendered virtually transparent the entire process by which a scientific principle, the regular motion of the pendulum, translated time from nature through a gear train into the hours and minutes of clock time — the banjo clock renders the process of translation opaque, simply alluding to time's source through the pendulum motion but not revealing the intervening sequence by which this motion is converted into clock time.

Willard's "lighthouse alarm clock," first produced around 1820, provides yet another interpretation of the nature of clock time (Illustration 2.10).[51] Each example of this clock style is designed as a three-dimensional model of a lighthouse. Although there are variations in individual pieces, the general design was inspired by the famous Eddystone Lighthouse in the English Channel. Like the calendar clock of the 1790s, this piece makes the moving

ILLUSTRATION 2.10. *Simon Willard, Roxbury, Massachusetts, lighthouse alarm clock, about 1820 (Old Sturbridge Village; photograph by Thomas Neill)*

works readily visible. Indeed, this visibility is even more pronounced in the lighthouse clock because the glass dome covering the works need not be removed to reveal the time train. While the clock face hides the gears from someone standing directly in front of the piece, anyone looking at the object from one side or the other would have a clear view of the movement in operation (Illustration 2.11). Since this clock was meant to be displayed on a shelf rather than mounted on a wall, it would often be seen from the side. Having this working mechanism visible in a room would convey a very different sense of clock time than would the closed case of the banjo wall clock. Time's movement is visible as a mechanical operation. The lighthouse clock makes its mechanism apparent both as an object of wonder (the glass cover makes it seem like a museum object) and as an object of inspection (one must remove the cover to wind the clock and set the alarm).

It is worth asking why Willard might have chosen to design a clock in the image of a lighthouse, and why he might have chosen the Eddystone Lighthouse in particular. As John Stilgoe explains, in the early years of the nineteenth century lighthouses represented the presence of the federal government in the American landscape. Indeed, in this period lighthouses were just about the only structure built by the federal government that many rural Americans were likely to see in their lifetimes. Moreover, they connoted the benevolent work of the government in protecting the people, as well as the skill required to do so: "Everyone understood that a lighthouse must function every night, through the severest storms, and that careful design and meticulous regulation alone assured such constancy."[52] Such reliability was, of course, also a quality one would want in a clock. The Eddystone Lighthouse, situated on a rocky reef several miles off the coast of southern England, was a famous marvel of engineering. It was also an aesthetic touchstone, a well-known subject of popular prints in both England and America. The structure's remote location was part of its interest. In his *Autobiography* of 1821, Thomas Jefferson recounts a conversation in which Benjamin Franklin described the Eddystone Lighthouse as "being built on a rock in the mid-channel, totally inaccessible in winter, from the boisterous character of the sea, in that season." Because of its remoteness and the difficulties involved in its construction, the lighthouse signified both human achievement and human insignificance in the face of nature, contradictory themes captured nicely in Herman Melville's allusion to the structure in *Moby-Dick*: "Nantucket! Take out your map and look at it. See what a real corner of the world it occupies; how it stands there, away off shore, more lonely than the Eddystone lighthouse."[53]

ILLUSTRATION 2.11. *Simon Willard lighthouse alarm clock, detail view from side, about 1820 (Old Sturbridge Village; photograph by Henry E. Peach)*

The Eddystone Lighthouse clock therefore provides a romantic interpretation of the mechanics of time, in which the ability of human beings to master nature, rendered so democratically accessible in the calendar clock of the 1790s, is now reserved to a few isolated master craftsmen. The clock's design invites individuals outside the clock-making trade to look on in wonder as the gears turn (though servants or slaves might have felt a sense of oppression or anxiety in addition). Indeed, because the Eddystone Lighthouse was a particularly well-known subject of prints that many Americans displayed in their homes, the lighthouse clock makes the mechanics of time into an aesthetic experience—time as object of picturesque contemplation. Writers and artists who represented the American West did so through formal conventions that brought that territory within the national imaginary.[54] Willard's lighthouse clock enacts a similar aestheticization of time. The object brings together the ability of the federal government to transform and nationalize the landscape with the aesthetics of the picturesque that facilitated the imaginative colonization of the West by federal explorers. But in articulating these themes in the form of a clock, Willard makes time itself into the territory of the colonial project—clock time dominated by a romantic conception of national power.

That three such different representations of time could have come from the same maker testifies to the richness of temporal experience in the period. In all of these objects, Willard represents American ingenuity as something solid, reliable, and productive of prosperity. As one newspaper memorialist wrote after Willard's death in 1848:

> In business Mr. Willard's desire seemed to be, that whatever work passed from his hands should be *well* done. The end for which most other people labor was with him a secondary consideration. Had he thought less of integrity and honor, and more of the "main chance" through his long life, he might have left more gold in bank, while he would necessarily have reduced the number and richness of those golden memories which now survive in the hearts of his revering successors.[55]

By the 1820s Willard's clocks no longer sold very well, most likely because of price and design competition from a welter of rapidly changing, highly commercial clock designs that could be produced much more cheaply. Yet Willard's image as an American artisan remained powerful enough to secure him the commission for the University of Virginia clock discussed in the previous chapter, and to evoke praise such as that expressed in the 1848 eulogy.

As market capitalism transformed the nature of production in the United States, Americans increasingly romanticized artisanal producers who had flourished in the era before the market revolution. Willard's most important legacy was contained in the idea of patent time; throughout the nineteenth century, clock manufacturers would boast of their "patent timepieces," paying homage to Willard even while flooding the market with pieces whose quality did not approach the artisanal ideal.

Patent Time and Mass Production

The first major blow to the dominance of artisanal clock production came in 1807, just five years after Willard had filed his famous patent, when an entrepreneur named Eli Terry began mass-producing wooden-movement clocks in a Connecticut factory. Terry, already an established clock maker in the more traditional mode of production, received a contract in 1806 to produce 4,000 wooden-movement clocks for the Porter brothers of Waterbury. This would have been an astounding number of clocks to make by hand. In order to fill the order, Terry converted a mill into a water-powered clock factory and began machine production the following year. By 1809 he had, to the surprise of many, fulfilled the contract.[56] In the ensuing years, Terry and two of his former employees, Seth Thomas and Silas Hoadley, became major figures in the Connecticut economy. Terry's "pillar-and-scroll" shelf clock, introduced in 1814, was the first wildly popular mass-produced clock. The example shown in Illustration 2.12 displays some of the most common features of these pieces.[57] The broken scroll pediment, urn finials, and columns on the sides are all neoclassical design elements. The connection between these elements and ancient republican traditions is made emphatically by the depiction in the *églomisé* tablet of Washington's neoclassical home at Mount Vernon. Over the course of the nineteenth century, Mount Vernon would become among the most common subjects of these paintings in mass-produced shelf clocks by many different makers.[58] Typically, these paintings would include an open space through which the pendulum could be seen swinging back and forth, similar to the description in Willard's patent. Very often, part of the time train (most notably, the "crown wheel," still made of metal even in this wooden-movement clock) would be left visible in front of the clock face. This may have been done to save space inside the cabinet, but not all pillar-and-scroll shelf clocks display this feature, so it should be interpreted as a design choice. Below the crown wheel was very commonly an

ILLUSTRATION 2.12. *Eli Terry, pillar-and-scroll shelf clock, 1817–18*
(Collections of the Henry Ford Museum)

American eagle emblem. Taken as a whole, then, the pillar-and-scroll clock situates modern clock technology within the national historical time of the Republic.

When the front door of the cabinet is opened up, Terry's clocks usually reveal a label reading "PATENT. INVENTED, Made and Sold by ELI TERRY, Plymouth." As Cooper's analysis suggests, the link between the patent and the idea of invention is a strong one. Despite the fact that these clocks were made by machine, they announce their own provenance in human ingenuity.[59] In stressing the role of the human inventor in creating the idea (which is, after all, what is patented) for a new kind of product that could be made at least partly by water-powered machinery, Terry's patent label plays an important role in situating the new technologies of the market revolution within traditional modes of production, however revolutionary the new processes might actually have been. Terry's employee Chauncey Jerome would later make this same point more directly, writing in the introduction to a trade catalog, "Clocks are not, as many persons appear to imagine, 'ground out' in a Mill; neither are they wholly manufactured by Machinery, but each one passes through two hundred processes in the hands of workmen before it is complete."[60] Both the patent label and Jerome's trade-catalog introduction promote the view that products created by the new processes are still "made" by an artisan-like individual, or, at least, skilled workers under the supervision of such an individual. However, when those products are "sold," in the language of Terry's patent label, they enter the modern market. Hence, the insistence on the artisanal quality of these machine-made products is not antimodern. Rather, it defines market exchange in terms drawn from traditional modes of production. Most importantly, when considered in the context of the relationship between historical time and modernity represented in the other design features of the Terry pillar-and-scroll clock, the patent label with its motif of "invention" performs a parallel function of situating modern time telling within culturally important traditions. Just as Mount Vernon represents a repository of national historical time that is, in turn, connected to ancient republicanism, so too is the modern manufacturer linked to his artisanal predecessors, and the market in which he sells his products is defined by its connection to past time.

This idea becomes even clearer in another important and popular timepiece, Silas Hoadley's "Franklin" clock.[61] Some of these clocks borrowed the general pillar-and-scroll design from Terry, while others had somewhat different external designs. However, these clocks usually featured the slogan

"TIME IS MONEY" painted on the exterior toward the bottom front of the clock, while Hoadley's label on the inside of the clock depicted a benevolent Benjamin Franklin gazing down from the clouds toward earth, beneath the same "time is money" slogan (Illustration 2.13). Franklin's "time is money" (from his short essay "Advice to a Young Tradesman, Written by an Old One" of 1748) was a very popular maxim in the nineteenth century. For example, in *The Young Man's Guide* (1834), William Alcott reminds his readers that: "Economy in time is economy of money—for it needs not Franklin to tell us that time is equivalent to money. Besides, I never knew a person who was economical of the one, who was not equally so of the other."[62] However, Hoadley's Franklin clock suggests that we do, in fact, need Franklin to remind us that time is equivalent to money. The title of Franklin's essay indicates that such wisdom descends from previous generations to the present. Hoadley's clock conveys the same idea for a new generation: modern mass-produced clocks may make it easier for common folk to tell time with greater accuracy, but cultural traditions are required to tell the present generation what to do with time.

In contrast to the way in which clock makers sought to connect themselves to an artisanal ideal that seemed to connect industrial capitalism to the past, American watchmakers, who began mass production in the 1850s, more frequently sought to portray their products as revolutionary and modern. For example, many of the Elgin National Watch Company advertisements depicted images such as an Elgin watch running ahead of a group of other chronometers from previous eras, or a female figure representing "Columbia" sweeping away, like trash, a collection of obsolete watches to make room for the new Elgin watch, thus emphasizing the modernity of this new form of chronometer. An 1889 advertisement for the Waterbury Watch Company of Connecticut depicted Father Time carrying a Swiss watchmaker and his watches back to Europe.[63] Despite these efforts on the part of watch manufacturers to portray their products in the most modern light, many public comments upon the newly emerging American watch industry emphasized connections to previous examples of American entrepreneurship. For example, in his *Illustrated History of the Centennial Exhibition*, James McCabe praised the "experienced and skilful workers" at the Waltham workshop exhibit and gushed that "Waltham watches have long been regarded as the best of American manufacture, and the universal testimony of all who have used them is that they are unexcelled by any in the world."[64] In McCabe's account, the Waltham watches represented not a departure from tra-

"TIME IS MONEY."

FRANKLIN CLOCKS

With the improvement of bushing the pivots with Ivory.

ARRANGED AND MANUFACTURED BY

Silas Hoadley,

PLYMOUTH, (CONN.)

WARRANTED TO KEEP GOOD TIME IF WELL USED.

ILLUSTRATION 2.13. *Label of Silas Hoadley "Franklin" clock, about 1830 (Photo by Paul J. Foley; courtesy of Delaney Antique Clocks, West Townsend, Massachusetts)* ditional modes of production but the culmination of a tradition of American ingenuity. Similarly, an 1870 article in *Putnam's Magazine* described the American watch industry as the "latest important application of human ingenuity to the making of timepieces," a triumph made possible by "investing American brain against Swiss and British poverty." Far from representing a dehumanization of production, then, "these great factories afford the best instances of the splendor and strength, the beauty and usefulness, of human thought."[65]

Yet another example of this perspective on the mass production of watches is furnished by George William Curtis's 1863 article for *Atlantic Monthly*, "My Friend the Watch." In this piece, Curtis imagines that his watch administers a patriotic lecture on the necessity for domestic manufactures as Curtis journeys by rail toward a tour of the Waltham Watch Company's factory, where he encounters the apotheosis of "inquisitive Yankee ingenuity."[66] In each of these examples, the mass-produced watch is portrayed in terms similar to the patented, mass-produced clock: as a natural development of an American tradition of artisanal skill and creativity. In its reception of the watch, then, the public seems to have accepted the claims of the watchmakers that their products were brilliant new innovations but contextualized that claim within a much more traditional, and probably comforting, view of the importance of the human element in production.

Peddling Material Time

Cheap, mass-produced clocks of the sort manufactured by businessmen like Terry, Hoadley, and Jerome were purchased by individuals all over the country primarily for use in their homes. Businesses would typically use more expensive and reliable but less elaborately decorated "regulators," though these were also made by the same firms. A network of peddlers spread the clocks through every region of the country, including the South and West.[67] The Yankee clock peddler became a stock character in popular culture of the nineteenth century, providing the antihero of Canadian writer Thomas Chandler Halliburton's sketches about "Sam Slick" and also finding his way into images such as John Ehninger's 1853 painting *Yankee Peddler* (Illustration 2.14). Unfortunately, although these clocks became ubiquitous, they were not always reliable. A handmade eighteenth-century tall clock would be likely to keep time more accurately than a mass-produced shelf clock. A cheap wooden shelf clock of the type mass-produced in the nineteenth century, transported for scores or perhaps hundreds of miles in

ILLUSTRATION 2.14. *John Ehninger,* Yankee Peddler, *1858. Oil on canvas, 25¾ × 32¼ inches (Collection of the Newark Museum; gift of William F. Laporte, 1925)*

the back of a peddler's wagon and left to the inexpert maintenance of a rural family, was unlikely to keep time with great accuracy for long. "As to the Yankee clock pedlars," traveler George Featherstonehaugh wrote in 1844, "they are everywhere, and have contrived, by an assurance and perseverance that have been unrivaled from the Maccabees down, to stick up a clock in every cabin in the Western country." Unfortunately, Featherstonehaugh reported, within a few months "all the clocks have stopped, as a matter of course, either because they were good for nothing, or because they have wound them up too often."[68]

This skepticism about the true use value of the goods spread across the country by the market informs the imagery of Ehninger's painting. The peddler appears to be something of a huckster, foisting his wares upon a gullible rural crowd. The clock that can be clearly seen in his wagon is perched at a precarious angle atop a pile of miscellaneous goods. The impression is of haphazard abundance rather than quality. However, the American flag carried by the little boy in the foreground indicates that this is a national scene. Philip Fisher has argued that, due to the geographic and ethnic diversity of the United States, American national identity was "profoundly dependent upon the mass-production and broad distribution that capitalism created."[69] For the rural folk depicted in Ehninger's painting, consuming the goods brought to their small town by the peddler, regardless of the quality of those goods, evidently constitutes a form of national belonging. But what is most interesting about the painting is the centrality of the clock to this process of national consumption, a centrality that raises somewhat recursive questions about the relationship of clock time to the national market.

Given the uncertain reliability of mass-produced clocks, it seems that what made the clock an attractive commodity to Americans of diverse regions and socioeconomic classes was as much its symbolic value as its functional value. The role that clocks played in mediating national affiliation through the expansion of the market is developed more fully in two other genre paintings, both by Francis William Edmonds: *The Speculator* (1852) and *Taking the Census* (1854) (Illustrations 2.15 and 2.16). Formally, these two paintings are very similar. In each, a family group in the home is confronted by an outsider. In the case of *Taking the Census*, this outsider is a representative of the federal government, while in the case of *The Speculator*, the outsider represents the market. The plan that the speculator shows the young couple depicts a town laid out in a grid with a large street called "Railroad Avenue" running diagonally across it. Interestingly, Edmonds, who was a banker, sat on the boards of several railroads.[70] Of course, the railroads were associated with time, since railroad travel was one way in which Americans would become aware of the constructed nature of time. When traveling from one city to another, even within a region such as New England, travelers would move between one local time and another (standard time zones for the nation were instituted in 1883 by the railroads). Railroad timetables were often confusing because they differed from local time in most cities and from the time on other rail lines.[71] However, in this case the railroad stands most directly for the idea of speculating in the market. The young couple's house is rather disorderly, with objects spilled on the floor, cracked plaster, and a picture of a bull on the wall above the mantle signifying their rusticity. The household does not look especially prosperous, and there are no children present.

The household of *Taking the Census* is, in contrast, clearly flourishing. The family's fertility is signified by the children and by the ears of corn

ILLUSTRATION 2.15. *Francis William Edmonds,* The Speculator, *1852. Oil on canvas, 25⅛ × 30⅛ inches (Smithsonian American Art Museum; gift of Ruth C. and Kevin McCann in affectionate memory of Dwight David Eisenhower, 34th president of the United States)*

hanging above the mother's head. This family is also literate, as there are a few books pictured in the scene, another contrast to *The Speculator.* The household is neat and tidy, with only a few objects on the floor, including the father's hat and cane, symbolizing paternal authority. This theme is reinforced by the portrait of George Washington hanging over the mantle, the same place where the family in *The Speculator* misguidedly features livestock.

At the center of the prosperous image of *Taking the Census* is the clock on the mantle, an object missing from *The Speculator.* The clock encapsulates the orderliness of the household. When interpreted in the context of the overwhelming amount of patriotic and nationalistic iconography in clock

ILLUSTRATION 2.16. *Francis William Edmonds,* Taking the Census, *1854. Oil on canvas, 23 × 38 inches (Metropolitan Museum of Art; gift of Diane, Daniel, and Mathew Wolf in honor of John K. Howat and Lewis I. Sharp, 2006 [2006.457]).*

design, it is hard not to see this clock as representing the connection be-tween the family and the state, as much as the portrait of George Washington that is next to it. Indeed, given the painting's subject matter we might expect the portrait of Washington to stand at the center of the image. However, the clock might be more appropriate for a painting that depicts the government's effort to collect data about the people. Maybell Mann notes that "new factors were introduced into the taking of the census in 1850," making the process both lengthier and more intrusive.[72] Mann speculates that this may explain why the family is huddled to the left of the painting, with one boy holding his finger to his lips as if to call for secrecy. However, this theme is counter-balanced by the kindly features of the old man recording the information, and by the well-dressed and attentive boy who holds a pen helpfully toward him. The census taker and his young assistant mirror the family group. In each case, an adult male stands for benevolent paternal authority. The boy's finger to his lips might be a respectful call for silence as the father ponders an accurate response to a question. The boy is mirrored by the respectful assistant to the census taker. Just as the father presides over a well-ordered family, so too does the government. And the clock presides over all.

The clock in *Taking the Census* could be either a handmade shelf clock from the late eighteenth or early nineteenth centuries or, more likely, a shelf clock of the mass-produced Connecticut type. Indeed, this clock could be any of the wide variety of shelf clocks with which Edmonds might have expected a viewer of the painting to be familiar. While the clock is featured centrally in the painting, it does not evince any especially detailed decorative features. In its very plainness and simplicity, its blankness, it stands for clocks in general. Hence, understanding the painting depends upon a knowledge of precisely those details of real, historical clocks examined in this chapter. Placing the painting in its proper context, a historical context in which anyone looking at the image would have brought a complex store of meaningful iconography to the very notion of a clock, allows us to see that the connection suggested in the painting between clock time and national belonging is quite rich with cultural associations.

In *Taking the Census*, then, the clock plays exactly the kind of important role in the process of national affiliation that theorists of nationalism have suggested. However, the clock's role is not to homogenize experience in order to render the nation uniform. Quite the opposite, in its very blankness in the image, this clock retains the ability to represent any of the cultural values that clocks commonly conveyed in the period. Furthermore, this role is consonant with the theme of the painting, the collection of census data by the federal government. If the census taker is indeed asking the head of household to answer a series of detailed questions about his family, as the 1850 census would have required him to do, then it is the family's distinctiveness that has become the object of national attention. If all families were the same, there would be no need for the census taker to do anything more than count the number of people. The actual process of the census depicted in this painting facilitates national belonging for heterogeneous families, making their particularities the foundation of national belonging. Nineteenth-century genre paintings represent what are supposed to be universal aspects of national experience through depiction of particular scenes from everyday life. In *Taking the Census*, the clock plays a parallel role, standing for the way that the particularity of time as experienced in one place by distinct individuals becomes integrated into the universal time of the nation—without losing its particularity.

Timing the Market

Thus far we have seen that the experience of clock time (and, to some extent, the time of watches) in the nineteenth-century United States linked local temporalities and distinctive traditions to national belonging. Both because of the persistence of older timepieces and the distinctive, culturally significant decorative styles of newer clocks, clock time integrated the historical and the local into the time of the modern nation in the present. The three paintings just discussed point toward the increasing importance of the market in making this connection between time and national identity. *Taking the Census* represents the market as a benevolent force that has brought a rural family their clock and other possessions. *The Speculator*, on the other hand, represents the market as threat. The family does not know how to manage its financial affairs and will be taken advantage of by the unscrupulous speculator. *Yankee Peddler* takes a more ambiguous position, since the quality of the goods in the peddler's wagon is unclear. Together, these images convey the conflicted response of the American public to the way that the increasingly powerful forces of market exchange and capitalist production were transforming everyday life. In *Taking the Census* and *Yankee Peddler*, the clock becomes an icon of a welter of changes that were really too diffuse to make sense of. Conversely, it is the conspicuous absence of the clock and the portrait of George Washington that most obviously distinguishes the household of *The Speculator* from that of *Taking the Census*. The clock, as a highly visible, iconic commodity circulating through the market, possessed the ability to represent both positive and negative qualities associated with the market in the American national imagination.

This phenomenon is exemplified in popular representations of the tumultuous career of Chauncey Jerome, especially Jerome's own autobiography, *History of the American Clock Business for the Past Sixty Years, and Life of Chauncey Jerome* (1860). If clock makers such as Eli Terry became iconic figures in a triumphal narrative of American national productivity, Chauncey Jerome's public and sensational career exemplified how the rise of market capitalism was also associated, in the popular imagination, with themes such as speculation, insincerity, and chance. Jerome had been apprenticed as a carpenter but began working in Terry's clock factory in 1816 (one antiquarian scholar argues that Jerome may well have been responsible for Terry's adoption of the pillar-and-scroll design).[73] By 1822 Jerome had his own business, and he was the most successful clock maker in the United States for many years, until his spectacular bankruptcy in 1855. While earlier clock makers such as Willard and Terry had achieved success primarily through mechanical ingenuity, Jerome's genius lay in case design and marketing. In his autobiography, he put these talents to work in the service of self-invention, or, perhaps more accurately, self-reinvention. In the wake of his public failure, Jerome tried to redeem himself by situating his identity within the clock business, asserting that the industry that continued after him, though in other hands, contained the essence of his contributions to American national development and, indeed, the essence of his own personhood.

In this respect, Jerome's autobiography constitutes a revision of that of Benjamin Franklin, the most important model for American autobiography. Echoing Franklin, Jerome tells a tale of humble origins, hard work, and commercial success. Certain scenes in Jerome's *Life* seem to be taken wholesale from Franklin, as when Jerome describes his first visit to his future home of New Haven: "I wandered about the streets early one morning with a bundle of clothes and some bread and cheese in my hands little dreaming that I should live to see so great a change, or that it ever would be my home."[74] Unlike Franklin's mercantile world, however, the free-market capitalism in which Jerome operates does not always reward hard work and the rational pursuit of perfection. While Franklin creates a strong and coherent version of self-identity based upon success as a tradesman in the eighteenth-century mercantile world, Jerome somewhat lamely attempts to reconstruct his self-identity out of his very failure in the nineteenth-century world of market capitalism. Jerome tells a tale of the sudden acquisition of immense wealth and the equally sudden, stunning loss of that wealth through no fault of his own (according to Jerome). His autobiography challenges Franklin's attribution of agency to human life, proposing instead that individuals exert little control over their economic destinies. However, Jerome does agree with Franklin that each individual possesses unique abilities whose value can be registered in economic terms. That the market strips individuals of the products of these unique talents does not make them any less a part of the self. Personhood, in Jerome's conception, is thus decoupled from the individual and set circulating through the market.

An 1872 recounting of Jerome's story for a popular audience by James McCabe suggests the extent to which the entrepreneur had succeeded in promoting such a market-oriented version of public identity for himself. "He had watched the market closely," McCabe writes of Jerome's entry into the clock business, "and questioned the persons engaged in the business, and he found that, so far from the market being over-stocked, there was a ready sale for every clock made."[75] McCabe's account of Jerome's life emphasizes how the clock maker's intuitive understanding of the market allowed him to create a career for himself, and hence to acquire a public identity. McCabe offers Jerome as a model to his readers, yet unhelpfully implies that Jerome possessed his attunement to the market more by instinct than by dint of any training. Nevertheless, it is clear that McCabe views Jerome's market-oriented psyche as an exemplary one for the modern age.

Jerome makes similar claims for his status as a kind of ideal economic man in his own book, opening the narrative by suggesting that there is little difference between his personal story and that of the industry in which he established himself as an entrepreneur:

> Many years of my own life have been inseparably connected with and devoted to the American clock business, and the most important changes in it have taken place within my remembrance and actual experience. Its whole history is familiar to me, and I cannot write my life without having much to say about "Yankee Clocks." Neither can there be a history of that business written without alluding to myself. (3–4)

The fact that McCabe would echo this language more than twenty years later indicates both how successful Jerome was in cultivating this image for himself and how receptive the culture was to it. The formulation pushes Franklin's model a step further; while Franklin merely suggests that a young man can create himself by succeeding in a trade, Jerome understands himself, retrospectively, to have been wholly constituted by a field of business. The "Yankee Clocks," the products of Jerome's ingenuity, are also subsumed, as individual objects, within "that business" as a whole. Jerome's focus on the clock business, rather than clocks themselves, contrasts with Willard's evident sense that it was the clock itself that was of greatest importance, much more so than the production or marketing of those clocks. Even Terry, while less obviously a craftsman in the traditional sense embodied by Willard, became most famous for the application of industrial processes to clock production—the emphasis remaining on the production of particular objects. But in Jerome's case it is the "business," the marketing and distribution, along with the development of a profitable company, that is most important. Hence, Jerome's own narrative and popular accounts of his career such as McCabe's disassociate the clock, as a symbol, from the realm of production and resituate it in the area of exchange.

The identification of clocks with commerce takes on somewhat comical tones when Jerome describes how he and some of his associates began using them as a form of currency. After leaving Terry's employ, Jerome struck out on his own in Bristol as a small clock manufacturer. At this point, Jerome was still acquiring the inner workings of his clocks from Terry. He would then make cases and sell the finished product himself. As the narrative explains, these clockworks had a stable value that allowed Jerome to exchange them for real estate:

> I worked along in this small way until the year 1821, when I sold my house and lot, which I had almost worshipped, to Mr. Terry; it was worth six hundred dollars. He paid me one hundred wood clock movements, with the dials, tablets, glass and weights. I went over to Bristol to see a man by the name of George Mitchell, who owned a large two story house, with a barn and seventeen acres of good land in the southern part of the town, which he said he would sell and take his pay in clocks. I asked him how many of the Terry Patent Clocks he would sell it for; he said two hundred and fourteen. I told him I would give it, and closed the bargain at once. I finished up the hundred parts which I had got from Mr. Terry, exchanged cases with him for some more, obtained some credit, and in this way made out the quantity for Mitchell. (45–46)

These transactions are not a form of barter, because the clocks are the medium of exchange—not the objects of exchange themselves—for a series of real estate transactions. In addition, the reference to credit situates the clocks within the system of market exchange as it was then understood. In the first decades of the nineteenth century, credit was associated with currency, especially bank notes, as media of exchange that were new and different from more traditional barter. In using the name "Terry Patent Clocks," Jerome emphasizes the credibility of this unique form of currency. Unlike bank notes, whose value might depend upon the fortunes and even the proximity of the financial institution, these clocks depend upon the (ostensibly) more stable reputation of Terry's patent. When Jerome describes himself adding value to the clockwork currency by enclosing the gears in cases, he indicates the extent to which he is not simply a clock maker but a master of the new economics of market exchange.

If this use of clocks as currency signifies the promise of the market to create prosperity and opportunity, then the panic of 1837 and P. T. Barnum play prominent roles in Jerome's characterization of the perils residing in that same market. Following the panic of 1837, the clock business collapsed, and many observers predicted that the vogue of Connecticut clocks had reached an end. One reason that wooden clocks were hit so hard by the recession was that they could not be exported. Wooden parts would be ruined by exposure to too much moisture, and hence could not be transported by ship. If European markets had been available, the industry would have been better able to withstand the collapse of the domestic market. Jerome recounts traveling on business during this time with a sense of despair at his business prospects. Then, he explains, one night in a hotel room far from home, he experienced an epiphany that led to the development of the cheap brass clocks he would famously export to England:

> One night I took one of these clocks [the then-conventional wooden clocks] into my room and placing it on the table, left a light burning near it and went to bed. While thinking over my business troubles and disappointments, I could not help feeling very much depressed. I said to myself I will not give up yet, I know more about the clock business than anything else. That minute I was looking at the wood clock on the table and it came into my mind instantly that there could be a cheap one day brass clock that would take the place of the wood clock. I at once began to figure on it; the case would cost no more, the dials, glass, weights, and other fixtures would be the same, and the size could be reduced. I lay awake nearly all night thinking this new thing over. I knew there was a fortune in it. (56–57)

Clock historian Ken Roberts notes that this is "an incredible tale" and that the brass movement was really "a natural development of the advancing technology."[76] If Jerome's story is not very believable, it is still of great interest for the way it represents the process of development of a new product. In an age in which mass production threatened to render human individuality and creativity irrelevant, Jerome represents his role as an entrepreneurial businessman in terms that recall Hawthorne's description, ten years earlier, of the creative process for writers of romance: "late at night, I sat in the deserted parlour, lighted only by the glimmering coal-fire and the moon, striving to picture forth imaginary scenes, which, the next day, might flow out on the brightening page in many-hued description."[77] As numerous critics have pointed out, this line (and the lengthy passage from which it is drawn) reflects not only Hawthorne's frustration at his own inability to create imaginative literature and make a living at the same time but also his sense of the uselessness of the writer in a culture devoted to commerce and industry. How ironic, then, to find a successful businessman apparently attempting to compensate for the inhumanity of the industrial process by adopting the vocabulary of the imaginative writer. If Hawthorne despairs of ever making fiction writing into a socially useful or economically productive endeavor, Jerome seems to feel less hesitation about his ability to transform a business career into the stuff of romance.

Jerome's imagination focuses much more on the commercial aspects of the process than on the actual production of the objects. Terry and his former employees Hoadley and Thomas continued throughout the nineteenth century to employ the conceit of the patent as a way of humanizing mass-produced clocks through the mystique of the mechanical or inventive genius. While Jerome also used patent labels in his clocks, in his autobiography he focuses on the role of the marketing genius in overcoming the dehumanizing effects of an economic catastrophe such as the panic of 1837. It is Jerome's knowledge of the "clock business," rather than any special expertise in the technologies of timekeeping, that allows him to survive the panic and prosper again. Later in the autobiography, Jerome criticizes Seth Thomas directly for resisting innovation and continuing to do things the same way throughout his career (102). Jerome offers the brass clock, then, as an example of his own ability to innovate. Beyond simply noting that the use of brass parts would allow for transportation of clocks over the ocean, Jerome emphasizes the superior exchange value of brass clocks on the international market: "As I have said before, wood clocks could never have been exported to Europe from this country, for many reasons. They would have been laughed at, and looked upon as coming from the wooden nutmeg country, and classed as the same" (61). What is most important is not simply that the use value of these clocks is superior—it is that consumers would perceive them as being worth more. Thus, when value is determined by the market, the inventor must make way for an astute businessman.

This movement of the clock from a primary imaginative association with production to a different set of associations with exchange and consumption was crucial to the extension of clock time through the market. In this respect, Jerome's narrative most fully elucidates a key development in the material history of clock time that was implicit in the nineteenth-century clock trade: the clock became not merely an object of trade, but a *commodity* in the full sense that that term acquired with the onset of market capitalism. Bill Brown has noted that the commodity acquires a curious double identity in this stage of economic history. On the one hand, the "phantasmatic social life of things," the fetishism of commodities that arises as the market revolutionizes social life, "depends on their abstraction—more precisely, on their abstractability, their fungibility, their capacity to have a relation to each other that is mediated by the abstracting measure of value." This state is precisely the one that the clock achieves in Jerome's narrative, to the point of hypertrophy, when it becomes currency, the measure of value itself. At this point the clock not merely is exchanged but actually becomes the medium of exchange; in a sense, it becomes part of the market rather than simply an object of market exchange. On the other hand, as Brown notes, the fetishism of the commodity also requires consumers to invest the object with all sorts of particular qualities, a process that "by no means etherealizes the object" but in fact individualizes it, through tropes such as pathos and prosopopeia.[78] Jerome's clocks also retain this particularity, this resistance to complete abstraction. Jerome perpetually brags about New Haven's clock industry and celebrates new clock designs. The clocks that his firm actually produced certainly engaged in culturally specific design trends, such as the Gothic revival (Illustration 2.17).[79] The individuality of the clock is most evident, however, in the remarkable passage quoted above in which he ascribes a romantic, inspired origin to a mass-produced commodity. Hence, Jerome's clocks are at once fungible measures of value and particular objects having their own histories and remaining linked to particular places and cultural moments.

In this way, Jerome's narrative reveals the tension inherent in the conceit of the patent invention that was so important to the clock industry as a whole. Far from a homey marketing ploy, the apparently atavistic insistence upon the individuality of the mass-produced clock by Terry and his successors turns out to be a way of making the clock into a commodity, invested with the commodity's paradoxical combination of abstract value and particularity, exchange value and use value. Through this process of fetishization, the clock reflects the transformation of human qualities into a marketable form. Hence, when Jerome's business finally collapses in the 1850s, it should not be surprising to find that he is able to imagine his personhood continuing on in the clock business as a whole.

The end of Jerome's business career was precipitated by an unfortunate affiliation with P. T. Barnum (the descriptive phrase "Barnum's connection with the American clock business" appears on the book's title page). Barnum had gone into partnership with Theodore Terry (a nephew of Eli Terry) as part of his larger scheme to develop the East Bridgeport area of Connecticut. Barnum hoped that merging his and Terry's company with Jerome's much larger concern, and moving Jerome's operation to East Bridgeport, would spur the local economy (as well as making a profit on its own). According to his autobiography, Jerome had retired from active management of his own company by the time the Barnum and Jerome concerns were merged.

ILLUSTRATION 2.17. *Chauncey Jerome, Gothic revival shelf clock, about 1844–55 (National Watch and Clock Museum, Columbia, Pennsylvania)*

Nevertheless, Barnum still held Jerome personally responsible for the failure. The two great marketing geniuses and self-promoters would each later accuse the other of having misrepresented the financial situations of their respective firms in order to conceal untenable levels of debt. In *Struggles and Triumphs*, Barnum would describe the entire episode as a great "deception that had been practiced upon my too confiding nature" and himself as having been "cruelly swindled and deliberately defrauded."[80] Meanwhile, in his own autobiography Jerome describes how, during the crisis, Barnum's reputation was devalued:

> Thus the news went abroad that poor Barnum was hunted and troubled on every side with these clock notes. It was reported that he was quite sick in England and could not live, and, at another time, that being much depressed and discouraged on account of his many troubles, he had taken to drinking very hard, and in all probability would live but a short time; while at the same time, he was lecturing on temperance to the English people, and was in fact a total-abstinence man. These stories were extensively circulated; the value of his paper was depreciated in the market, and was, in several instances bought for a small sum. (113)

Here the "clock notes" that Barnum had issued to the merged company's creditors develop into an unstable version of the clockworks that had functioned so reliably as currency earlier in the narrative. At the same time that these notes become devalued in the market, Barnum himself physically sickens, signifying the close link (as Jerome sees it — this is his account, not Barnum's own) between Barnum's self and his career. Jerome also calls attention to Barnum's insincerity, the roles that he performs for economic gain, a gesture that again elicits the tension between different forms of value. Barnum is able to trade on perceptions of himself that differ from his substance, a distinction equivalent to that between exchange and use value. Barnum has, Jerome implies, become all exchange value, all surface, and hence lost his value in the market precisely because he no longer embodies the tension between use and exchange value that is integral to the commodity. Rather than an object one would want to buy, Barnum has become more akin to a bank note with no backing.

While scholars have not been able to determine what really happened in this affair (the secondary sources simply cite Jerome's and Barnum's own accounts), it is clear that Barnum eventually recovered, both financially and personally, while Jerome was ruined for good.[81] In contrast to the aftermath of the panic of 1837, this time Jerome was not struck with saving inspiration while gazing at a clock by lamplight. As he explains near the conclusion of his autobiography, this final catastrophe drained him of vitality: "The troubles that have grown out of the failure of this great business, have left me poor and broken down in spirit, constitution and health. I was never designed by Providence to eat the bread of dependence, for it is like poison to me, and will surely kill me in a short time. I have now lost more than forty pounds of flesh, though my ambition has not yet died within me" (116). Even while losing his flesh, physically disappearing from the material world, Jerome retains his ambition. With his body no longer able to carry that ambition forward into the future, Jerome imagines his life's work being fulfilled by the market itself. This idea depends upon the commodification of the clock. Jerome's own human qualities, his creativity, ability to innovate, and business acumen, become part of the objects his company produced and would continue to produce after he himself had been ruined. "The manufacture of clocks has become one of the most important branches of American industry," Jerome boasts on the first page of his autobiography. "Its productions are of immense value and form an important article of export to foreign countries" (3). Since the entire narrative was written after the collapse, these nationalistic lines can only be read as a way of redeeming Jerome's reputation—and, more importantly, his sense of personhood—from the ruins of his own business career. The lines accomplish this move by locating Jerome's enduring contribution to American national development within the clock business—not precisely within the clock itself, it should be noted, but the "industry" surrounding the clock, especially the process of export.

In the book's conclusion, Jerome returns to this nationalistic rhetoric, and especially the emphasis on the export trade, when he identifies New Haven as the metropole of a new empire and clock time as the distinguishing mark of the progress of civilization. Indeed, Jerome associates his worldwide trade in clocks with the power of American civilization to establish itself on the world stage and the primacy of New England in leading national progress:

> For many years I have extensively advertised throughout every part of the civilized world, and in the most conspicuous places, such a city as New Haven Connecticut, U.S.A., and its name is hourly brought to notice wherever American clocks are used, and I know of no more conspicuous or prominent place than the dial of a clock for this purpose. More of these clocks have been manufactured in this city for the past sixteen years than

any other one place in this country, and the company now manufacturing, turn out seven hundred daily. (134)

This passage echoes others that occur throughout the book. To Jerome, the mass production of clocks provided a model for industry in general, and the clock then in turn provided a vehicle for the imagined spread of an American ideology of industrial progress throughout the world. Just as Connecticut clocks colonized the pastoral South and West, so too would they aid in the Americanization of the world. Indeed, in Jerome's view, only those parts of the world where there is a market for clocks are civilized.

In the end, then, Jerome makes the history of the clock business into a story about several different sorts of time. Clocks themselves indicate civilization in the sense that it is civilized to keep track of time. They also present civilization to the rest of the world as objects carried by the market, springing from the metropole of New Haven to form connections with other parts of the world that are, perhaps, less far along (he recalls learning of a missionary using one of his clocks in the Sandwich Islands) or that have fallen behind the leading edge of modernity (his clocks are exported to "Europe, Asia, South America, Australia, Palestine, and in fact, to every part of the world; and millions of dollars brought into this country by this means" [61]). Still, clocks resist the homogenizing tendency of the market by proudly declaring their place of origin to the world. Jerome's imagined clockwork empire thus encapsulates the tensions within America's self-conception that are evident throughout the material history of time. First, the clock business crystallized, for the American public, the antithetical senses of promise and crisis implicit in the emergence of a market economy. Moreover, as generations of clock (and watch) designs layered upon each other in American life, the social meaning of time became increasingly complex. Objects such as eighteenth-century tall clocks, imported European watches, the artisanal clocks made by the Willards, mass-produced clocks alluding to the heroes of the Revolutionary generation, Jerome's gothic clocks, and finally, in the second half of the century, domestically produced watches all shared space in American homes and contributed to the rich network of temporal ideas circulating through the culture. Even while this dense particularity was accumulating, the increasing importance of the clock (and, later, the watch) as a product on the market exerted a contending impulse toward homogenization, a flattening out of particularity in favor of the universality of exchange value. This investigation of the material history of mechanical timepieces themselves has been crucial to understanding these developments within the context of the production and exchange of commodities. The next chapter of this study turns to literary narratives to explore how mechanical time functioned within the culturally central practice of consumption—that is, how Americans imagined themselves making use of mechanical time in everyday life in order to remake themselves into members of a heterogeneous national community.

CLOCKWORK NATION

Chauncey Jerome's tumultuous career illustrates how the clock became a representative commodity within the capitalist market that increasingly dominated economic life in the United States beginning in the 1820s. From Gillian Brown's classic analysis of "possessive individualism" to Jeffrey Sklansky's recent work on "the soul's economy," numerous scholars have shown that the advent of market capitalism facilitated the emergence of new forms of self-identity in nineteenth-century America.[1] As Jerome's autobiography suggests, clocks came to signify the triumph of American ingenuity, and hence purchasing a clock allowed one to share in this national achievement. However, clock time could also stand for the chaos of the market and the uncertainty of self-fashioning within a market-oriented social world. Jerome's move to structure a narrative of self-identity within the context of his career as a clock maker, and to situate his legacy as a human being within the commodities he had introduced to the market, represents a form of fetishism in which inanimate objects are invested with human qualities. This chapter will present an array of other narrative accounts illustrating the centrality of the reified experience of time to market-oriented forms of self-identity, and hence more broadly to social and national belonging in nineteenth-century America.

Clock time's utility for linking the market to the self in such powerful ways resided in its status as exemplary commodity. As Marx and a number of theorists writing in the Marxist tradition have shown, the commodity acquired new powers with the advent of market capitalism. Most important was the process of reification through which the commodity came to objectify human labor.[2] Because human beings are linked together socially through their labor, objectifying this activity in the form of the commodity alienates human beings from one another. Human beings come to understand their relationships indirectly, through objects circulating in the market. Georg Lukács argues that "as the capitalist system continuously produces and reproduces itself economically on higher and higher levels, the structure of reification progressively sinks more deeply, more fatefully and more definitively into the consciousness of man."[3] However, the process of reification does not merely threaten to dehumanize human beings; it also presents the possibility of humanizing the market. That is, as much as social and cultural activity can be reduced to commerce, commercial activity can also become social and cultural. Indeed, the theory of reification, present but not fully articulated in Marx, was developed by later theorists such as Lukács precisely to combat the "vulgar Marxism" that reduced culture to an aftereffect of the economic base of society. Once we recognize how the reification of commodities structures social reality within market capitalism, we can begin to assign historical importance not merely to the process of production but also to the exchange and consumption of commodities. It is especially in these realms that the commodity came to play a much larger role in the imaginative and affective lives of the people than it had in previous economic systems, including the mercantile capitalism of the eighteenth and early nineteenth centuries. Hence, while both clocks and wage labor have been bought and sold throughout human history, the social meaning of these transactions was not the same as that which would emerge following the market revolution.

The centrality of the process of consumption to middle-class identity formation in nineteenth-century America has been documented by a number of historians. As these scholars have shown, consumer goods did not simply serve material needs or occupy domestic space in nineteenth-century America; they enabled the imaginative creation of a new way of life structured around new kinds of social relations. The rise of consumerism in the 1830s formed, in Stuart Blumin's words, "a family strategy, a more or less deliberate attempt to shape the domestic environment in ways that signified social respectability, and that facilitated the acquisition of habits of personal deportment that could set a family apart from both the rough world of mechanics and the artificial world of fashion."[4] While "taste" was important to establishing membership in the middle class, there was also a more imaginative engagement with one's possessions that resulted in a domestic environment in which, as Lori Merish puts it, "material goods lift one beyond the body and are integrated with one's 'higher' faculties and sentiments."[5] In its capacity as a location of consumption, the home became a venue for very personal types of productive acts in which individuals reshaped themselves as social beings. By consuming time, regulating their domestic lives according to reified standards of temporal economy, middle-class Americans brought the market into their bodies while simultaneously abstracting themselves outward into the market and the modern nation.

Even more important to national belonging than the status of clocks as material commodities, then, was the way Americans began to treat the time that clocks told as an imaginative commodity whose abstract, quantifiable nature gave it a synecdochal relationship to the market as a whole. Just as the clock business was perceived as a representative modern business, the time that clocks told not only shared in but to a large extent exemplified the processes of reification and fetishism that give the commodity such central importance to the cultural life of an increasingly capitalistic society. Material commodities could represent the market in an inert way and through association, but time, in its living, reified form, embodied the market in its essence and made that market available for consumption. Like currency, that other newly important way of thinking about value, time as fungible unit of commerce provided the necessary abstraction to make sense of market exchange. Because it not only circulated within the market but also defined value in ways fundamental to the market's logic, time, like money, began to take on a life of its own, a reified existence that lent it a cultural significance far beyond its practical potential to mediate exchanges of goods and labor.

However, many of America's social and political thinkers in this protean period embraced market-oriented temporality only by imbricating it upon other forms of temporal experience, refusing to relegate those other forms to "premodern" oblivion, and in the process infusing the time of the market with values extrinsic to the demands of capitalist moneymaking. Time provided a way for writers to resolve some of the cultural conflicts between home and market precisely because it lacked money's frightening and distasteful associations with speculation and avarice, while still serving as a reified trope of the market itself. While the nineteenth century produced a copious advice literature enjoining readers to control their finances, mastery of finance was always uncertain, and too close an attention to pecuniary matters reflected badly upon one's character. Patrick Brantlinger has shown that the English-speaking world had associated entanglement in the complexities of finance with moral corruption since the eighteenth century at least. Moreover, as Brantlinger notes, in the decades before the Civil War the American economy even when booming "seemed paradoxically to be the thriving flotation of a welter of different currencies and monetary experiments," a situation engendering widespread distrust.[6] Money, while sharing time's special relationship with the abstract logic of the market, seemed to represent that market as chaos.

The conditions of American life in midcentury demanded a model of personhood that could at once rise above the seemingly impenetrable dilemmas of cash, credit, and interest while still promising mastery of the very market to whose functioning such dubious institutions were essential. By the 1830s, life for the emerging middle class was structured around a tense dichotomy between the private, personal sphere of the home and the public, dangerous, and amoral world of market competition. As Brown demonstrates, texts such as Harriet Beecher Stowe's *Uncle Tom's Cabin* (1851) and Herman Melville's "Bartleby, the Scrivener" (1854) portray domestic spaces under pressure from market forces threatening to turn the self into a commodity and set it on a round of endless circulation—a fate not unlike that which Chauncey Jerome depicts for himself in his autobiography. In light of this and subsequent work that has continued to uncover the complexity of the public-private relationship in this period, Lora Romero's description of the home as a "front" where competing cultural forces collide with one another seems most apt.[7] Hence, while clock time was central to the way Americans experienced the market revolution, it was also subject to trenchant contestation and creative appropriation by individuals who sought to play active roles in shaping the norms and values of the social world emerging along with the market. The significance of the discourse of temporal economy in this period is thus double. First, it provided the foundation for market-oriented personhood, enabling individuals to adapt to historical change in ways that promised mastery over current conditions. But second, it also opened up the possibility that imagining these new models of personhood might transform the market itself, making it a container for values other than the pecuniary.[8]

Consuming Time

Myriad texts from this period exemplify how the prevalent concern with the proper use of time could be employed to reshape social reality by narrativizing new forms of personhood. Early in Catharine Sedgwick's 1835 novel *Home*, for example, the male protagonist, William Barclay, explains to his new wife, Anne, how he has managed to furnish their house comfortably at moderate expense. "I was offered a remarkably pretty Geneva clock," he recounts, "which cost fifty dollars in Paris, for thirty dollars. A clock I thought essential to the punctual arrangement of house affairs; and to convince myself of the propriety of buying this particular clock, this *bargain*, I reasoned as people do when they would persuade themselves to that, which in their secret souls they know is not quite right." Tempted by this attractive commodity, a false bargain, William is on the verge of buying when the proprietor of the shop informs him that "if you really want the clock for a timepiece merely, here is an article of excellent mechanism, which costs only five dollars." Finally deciding on use value over frivolous ornamentation, William buys the cheaper clock and places it in the kitchen, that powerful locus of domestic ideology.[9] In choosing the five-dollar clock, which readers would probably associate with those mass-produced in New England factories, over the expensive Swiss clock, William illustrates one of this didactic novel's main points: that the market makes a well-furnished home available to any middle-class couple who manage their personal finances efficiently. The very democratic, and patriotic, suggestion of this episode is that the less expensive American-made clock will produce a better-regulated and happier kitchen and household than would the overly expensive, "pretty" import. Compensating for the clock's relative plainness will be Anne's own power to invest objects in the home with sentimental value. As Merish argues in her analysis of this novel, it is not the possessions themselves that make the home but the way that Anne's "approval and woman's touch" transform objects "rescued from the market" into accoutrements of a loving home.[10] Hence, it ultimately does not matter which clock William purchases, since it is not the material attributes of the commodity itself but Anne's "loving" character and skill as a homemaker that allow her to make the household and its furnishings into a tasteful and nurturing environment (11).

Anne acquires this powerful ability to manage the home through her employment of that other, more truly valuable commodity accompanying the clock: reified time. The material components of the clock itself are merely "pretty," but Anne shapes her character as housekeeper by internalizing the time the clock tells, and, as a result, clock time becomes the foundation of the social world of the household. Everyone in the Barclay family, including the children, comes to meals punctually, a practice that makes eating an occasion for sentimental bonding and moral instruction. "The right ministration of the table is an important item in home education," Sedgwick's narrator explains. "Mr. Barclay had a just horror of hurrying through meals" (27). William comes home from work every day to spend exactly one hour at dinner, then returns to his business right on time in the afternoon. The narrator makes clear that this is time well spent, for if "the working men and working women of our country" will give up a little potential earning for "*time*, and devote that time to such a ministration of their meals" as will benefit the health and good character of the family, then "they will find the amount of good resulting to the home circle incalculable" (28). If spending time wisely results in "incalculable" gains, then spending time is itself a productive act. That is, it is a form of consumption (the time is obtained in exchange for money, in the form of lost potential income) that results in the production of something of value—the healthy and moral personhood of the members of the family.

This use of time as a productive resource in the household was also promoted in nonfiction domestic advice manuals. In *Letters to Mothers* (1838), Lydia Sigourney echoes Sedgwick's theme when she explains to her female readers that the purpose of temporal economy is to enable mothers to spend time effectively in molding children into virtuous individuals:

> The same judgment which so admirably regulates food and clothing, it would be desirable to apply to another and higher department. It is to mothers, with the care of young children, that these remarks on economy are peculiarly addressed. They have the charge of immortal beings, whose physical, mental and moral temperament, are for a long period, exclusively in their hands. Nothing save the finger of God is written on the tablet, when it is committed to them. It is important that they secure *time* to form deep and lasting impressions.[11]

As Sigourney's emphasis of the word "time" suggests, in her view the crucial goal for middle-class mothers is to clear away time from other tasks to spend more time with their children. Sigourney even advises middle-class women to hire domestic servants in order to create this time. While industriousness in the world of commerce is only laudable if it actually produces financial gain, in the domestic sphere work acquires value if it leads to the production of "deep and lasting impressions" upon the characters of the family members. Work performed without such an end in view is fruitless, literally a waste of time, and the province of errant housekeepers who, in Sigourney's words, "are deceived by specious appearances, without knowing how their domestics spend their time; or they impose toil, at the proper seasons of rest."[12]

Just as it is possible to waste money on frivolous furnishings, it is also possible to waste time's potential returns by mismanaging it. This concept is illustrated in *Home* when one of William's business associates, Mr. Anthon, joins the family for dinner. Mr. Anthon is astonished to find that William spends so much time at the noon meal, exclaiming, "An hour! bless my heart!

We get through in our house in about ten minutes,—never exceed fifteen" (43). A subsequent chapter contrasts the chaos of Mr. Anthon's table with the order of the Barclays'. Mr. Anthon rushes in and out, unable to restore his "strength and spirits" as William does. In spending ten or fifteen minutes at dinner with his family, Mr. Anthon produces nothing. He is unable, in that time, to contribute anything to shaping the characters of his children. By investing more time in his family, William receives much greater returns. Mr. Anthon has wasted his ten to fifteen minutes a day, while William has spent his hour wisely and thus displayed more real economy. William credits Anne's management for his ability to profit from this time, for he is always able to enjoy a full hour with his family, "never abridged by want of punctuality on her part" (43). Anne's power to manage time so effectively ensures that time will be spent well—that is, productively—within the household.

As the various visits that William and his business associates pay to the home suggest, the way that Anne synchronizes the activities of her family with her husband's schedule as a businessman creates a connection between the private sphere of the home and the so-called public activities of commerce and paid employment. They are, effectively, parallel and adjacent cultural spaces sharing the same organizing logic. However, while clock time might have provided the mechanism by which the cultural logic of the market could move between commercial and domestic realms, this did not mean that the home was simply remade in the image of commercial exchange or industrial production. Rather, the home became a place in which the market encountered and absorbed values not intrinsic to capitalist moneymaking. The home provided a venue for forms of productivity that would, themselves, transform the nature of the market. Lukács's analysis of reification emphasizes the recursive relationship between such "cultural" activities and what traditional Marxists would call the economic "base" of society. If, as Lukács suggests, the economic activities of market capitalism transform "the consciousness of man," the cultural activities of the home also transform the market.

This process is apparent in the domestic manuals of the period that predicate success in the modern world upon management techniques derived from local tradition. For example, Mrs. E. A. Howland's popular domestic advice manual, published in 1845 as *The American Economical Housekeeper and Family Receipt Book* and in 1847 as *The New England Economical Housekeeper and Family Receipt Book*, includes an engraving in the frontispiece depicting an orderly kitchen over which a clock presides (Illustration 3.1), an image similar to Edmonds's *Taking the Census*. While the

ILLUSTRATION 3.1. *Frontispiece to* The American Economical Housekeeper, *by Mrs. E. A. Howland, 1845 (Old Sturbridge Village; photograph by Henry Peach)*

Howland image would seem to signify that the kitchen will run like clockwork, a reading of the book reveals that this is not literally the case. None of the procedures in Howland's recipes call for precision timekeeping. Since most food preparation in the 1840s involved techniques such as roasting and baking, the time intervals are quite long and imprecise. For "chicken pie," for example, Howland advises to "bake it in a moderate oven two hours, or two and a half."[13] The vast majority of the recipes call for these types of long, slow cooking, in which a half hour more or less makes no great difference. There are also many references to "quick" and "slow" ovens, a rough approximation of temperature. Even when time measurement is required, the clock is never mentioned. For example, in the instructions for "heating the oven," Howland directs, "For pies, cakes, and white bread, the heat of the oven should be such, that you can hold hand and arm in while you count forty: for brown bread, meats, beans, Indian puddings, and pumpkin pies, it should be hotter, so that you can only hold it in while you count twenty."[14] This painful-sounding method of timekeeping and temperature measurement must have been handed down through generations. It persists in the face of the widespread availability of cheap wooden shelf clocks. In fact, as the James Wady clock discussed in Chapter 2 of this book makes clear, it is quite possible to tell time as accurately as Howland's book requires without recourse to a minute hand at all.

Nevertheless, the presence of the clock in the frontispiece to the book indicates that the kitchen clock, with its hour and minute hands clearly visible, is in some way important. It is significant that the hands mark precisely nine o'clock on the dial. In the nineteenth century, as now, this setting was a conventional one for display clocks. Nine o'clock sharp seems to suggest precision, accuracy, and orderliness, but of course to be truly accurate the clock must move off of the hour. A clock standing directly at the hour represents the idea of precision without enacting precision. What does it mean for a kitchen to run like clockwork when the clock is not really used to measure precise intervals of time?

For the contemporary users of such a receipt book, that question could only be answered through recourse to the particular traditions that had been passed down from one generation of women to another. Unlike the cookbooks that emerged in the twentieth century, such as *The Joy of Cooking*, Howland's receipt book is written for someone who already knows what she is doing. While *The Joy of Cooking* explains techniques in sufficient detail that a complete novice can carry them out, it would not be possible to read Howland's book and then make the recipes with no prior experience. This experience would have to have been acquired from an older female in the household. Hence, it seems that in a receipt book in which the clock is represented as the arbiter of what takes place in the kitchen, time is actually employed according to traditional precepts. The clock has not displaced traditional ways of reckoning and employing time. Instead, this text imagines the home as a place where tradition and modernity intersect in moments of present time.

What is at stake in the way we read such a text is the degree of cultural agency we assign to activities taking place in the domestic sphere. Reading the home as a venue for the transformation of the market, and hence the production of new forms of market-oriented personhood, makes the domestic sphere and the women who inhabited it central to the production of modern social and economic worlds. In contrast, the traditional interpretation of the home as either a refuge from or a reflection of the world of the market, the world outside the home, relegates domestic labor (and hence, obviously, women's labor) to a peripheral status. For example, Philip Zea and Robert C. Cheney assume that the image of the clock in Howland's receipt book reflects the extent to which the standards of factory production had been adopted in the kitchen: "This meal would be ready on time. Workers and housewives had learned the importance of the designated times for working and taking breaks, and clock makers responded with timekeepers in many shapes and sizes."[15] The ease with which Zea and Cheney, usually very careful historians attentive to the complexities of such evidence, connect "workers and housewives" attests to the power of the notion that cultural activities such as homemaking are simply reflections of economic conditions outside of the home.[16] However, while domestic advice manuals did, indeed, emphasize economy of time, the techniques employed in cooking and other household duties did not, in fact, require close measurement by the clock in the same way that industrial labor was quantified by the clock. The mere presence of clocks in the home does not indicate, in itself, that these clocks were employed in the same manner and for the same purposes as they were in factories. What domestic writers meant by emphasizing the productivity of time and the necessity of economizing time was qualitatively different from what industrial managers meant.

Redeeming the Market

More specifically, in American domestic texts of the nineteenth century, moments of time function as conduits for the salvation of a morally imperiled, market-oriented consumer society through the redemptive power of cultural traditions. In these texts, tradition effectively saves the modern world of market capitalism from its own emptiness not by disavowing the market but by filling it with value. For example, Mrs. H. C. Gardner's short story "Labor; Or, Striking for Higher Wages," published in Cincinnati's *Ladies' Repository* in 1859, tells the story of Mary Currier, an admirable young woman from the country who, after marrying a city businessman named Paul, begins to run the household so efficiently that her husband prospers in business. Paul initially admonishes her to leave the domestic work to the servants, but Mary persists in managing the household actively. When Paul finally becomes fully aware of Mary's activities toward the end of the story, he exclaims:

> I begin to understand, what has been truly a mystery to me, the secret of our success in life. Your hidden knowledge has directed our domestic machinery and secured the clock-like regularity so essential to my success as a business man. I have often wondered how it should cost others with the same apparent needs so much more to live than it does us. There is

Charles Olmstead, with only his wife, vainly trying to live on twice the income that we expend. And in our home not a comfort is lacking.[17]

In this story, as in Sedgwick's *Home*, the market-derived equivalence between units of time and units of money creates the logical foundation for linking the domestic sphere with the business world. More than simply providing a pleasing domestic complement to the world of business, Mary makes the home environment "essential" to the proper functioning of the business environment outside the home, and thus, like Anne, proves her value according to the logic of the market.

Most importantly, Mary achieves this success not by adapting herself to city ways but by employing the traditional housekeeping skills she had learned as a girl in the country. Indeed, Sedgwick also makes her heroine, Anne, a country girl by origin. Gardner's Mary has been raised by her aunt in rural Massachusetts, but she must relocate to Boston when her father returns from a ten-year absence in "a foreign land" (7). Mr. Currier is a successful businessman, and Mary is suddenly thrust into a world of "the splendid house and its luxurious furniture, the elegant carriages and numerous servants, and the constant influx of gayly-dressed visitors" (8). Her father objects that the housekeeping skills and domestic economy that she has learned from her aunt in the rural village will be useless to "a young lady in her station" (7). He tells Mary that she will "soon have too many pleasures to find time for work" and remarks acerbically to the aunt that "if you had been training her for a servant all this knowledge of pickles and jellies would not come amiss" (7). When Mary finds a husband, he is at first equally indifferent to her domestic skills, for "Paul Franklin had never thought of woman as a helpmate" (9). Mr. Currier and Paul Franklin both represent the possibility that the excessive wealth created by commerce could undermine the very values of thrift and hard work that created that wealth. Many women writers such as Gardner were especially concerned that a life of leisure would turn women into the useless household ornaments of their businessman husbands. Mary's efficient management must contend not only against the immediate financial peril posed by wasteful spending but also against the moral peril posed by an urban, modern life of leisured affluence.

Gardner characterizes the urban setting in terms of pretense, insincerity, and excessive consumption. When Mary first comes to the city, the narrator describes her as "obliged to leave her quiet country home for her more pretending city one" (8). Gardner implies that theft and sloth are common among servants in bourgeois households: "I have changed the servants several times," Mary complains to her father, "but find none that are proof against the temptations to which we expose them" (9). Because Mary has learned to do housework herself, she is able to keep the servants from cheating her father and her husband. When the cook in the Franklin household succumbs to greedy impulses and goes on strike for higher wages just before an important dinner party, the heroine is able to prepare everything herself and still act the part of the gracious hostess due to her organization and industriousness. Efficient organization is essential, for "at first it seemed impossible to arrange the necessary work so as to give her husband no idea of her intention, and, what was of still greater moment, so as to secure leisure to entertain her guests" (11). But the one faithful servant, Jenny, reassures Mary that she will be able to complete everything and still find "plenty of time to dress" (11). Dressing here represents the larger preoccupation with composing oneself for society; dress, manners, and taste were all important elements of this process for nineteenth-century Americans. Gardner portrays efficient time management as the necessary precondition for achieving such a tasteful and socially acceptable self-presentation.

In keeping her machinations secret from her husband and the guests, Mary maintains the separation between front and back of the house that Karen Halttunen has shown was so important to the rising middle class. Halttunen notes that "the crucial test of the well-ordered household was the dinner party."[18] Mary's efficient time management allows her to play the role of the relaxed hostess in front of her husband and guests while giving no hint of the labor she has undertaken to prepare for their enjoyment. As Halttunen indicates, the goal of middle-class conduct was to create a perfect synthesis of social tact and sincerity. Because Mary is so self-disciplined in her use of time, she really is able to relax before her guests and sincerely enjoy the dinner. Her self-discipline has become natural to her; by internalizing time discipline, she achieves the ideal synthesis of sincere self-control. In the end, Paul praises Mary by noting that she has "an efficient hand" in managing the household. Indeed, because she keeps her machinations secret from her husband, Mary in effect becomes Adam Smith's "invisible hand," embodying in her character the logic of the market.

Thus, in Gardner's story, as in Sedgwick's novel, modern efficiency and the virtue it cultivates seem to be obtainable only by recourse to the country. It is interesting that in both cases, the entrée of the virtuous young housekeeper into the urban setting is brought about as a result of family connections. Both writers locate the future of the modern nation symbolically in the past and suggest that this virtue is accessible through recourse to genealogical continuity—the bloodlines linking the present and the past. These narratives thus situate modern time, signified by the employment of the clock to promote economic efficiency in the household, within historical time, signified by the intergenerational continuity of cultural traditions. National time resides not in one of these or the other, but in the intersection of the two—national time is a clock time grounded in tradition.

Sarah Josepha Hale was among the most important shapers of American social norms in the first half of the nineteenth century, and her 1845 novel *Keeping House and House Keeping: A Story of Domestic Life* exemplifies the process by which a narrative account of modern domesticity could make use of the management of time to transform the market-oriented social order by incorporating important local cultural traditions into a national vision of modernity. Hale's novel relates the story of an urban middle-class couple, the Harleys, who learn the value of systematic housekeeping after almost bankrupting themselves. The novel's plot revolves around the problems created by Mrs. Harley's love of fashion and distaste for domestic economy, and, most importantly, her penchant for misusing her time. Mrs. Harley believes that it would be beneath her station to supervise the household servants, whom she views with an aristocratic contempt. In the novel's first chapter, she persuades her husband that they must dismiss their efficient servant, Nancy, because she impertinently asks for time off to go to church, attend improving lectures, and visit her aged mother. This step proves to be an unfortunate one. The industrious, honest Nancy is quickly snapped up by another family, while the Harleys make their way through a series of drunken, lazy, flattering, dishonest, and thieving replacements. The dramatic climax of the novel occurs when Mrs. Harley throws a fashionable, expensive party that almost bankrupts the couple and that no one enjoys because she has invited too many insincere guests. Finally, Mr. Harley asks his Aunt Ruth to come from the country and set the house in order. The novel ends happily when Aunt Ruth is able to teach Mrs. Harley the value of domestic economy.

Throughout the novel, Mrs. Harley's crucial failing is misspending her time. Rather than investing her time in her family, she squanders it on an indolent social life. After the party, Mr. Harley recounts to Aunt Ruth that his wife had "spent her time and thoughts upon it for a number of weeks, and today she has been in the 'horrors,' lest they [the guests] saw something to be offended or to laugh at."[19] Spending her time vainly endeavoring to cultivate the approval of fashionable society has left her lacking moral authority in her own household and, hence, unable to shape the character of her family. In this way, she directly contradicts one of Beecher's most important injunctions: "No woman has a right to put a stitch of ornament on any article of dress or furniture, or to provide one superfluity in food, until she is sure she can secure time for all her social, intellectual, benevolent, and religious, duties" (167). Blumin provides a cogent gloss for what has happened to Mrs. Harley when he explains how a woman's "moral superiority, proclaimed so often by men as well as women, could be squandered . . . if she played the role of consumer too aggressively and in service of the wrong ambitions."[20] Mrs. Harley attempts to defend herself to Aunt Ruth by protesting, "You know I have not much time to give to domestic concerns, as John [the baby] requires so much care. Besides, ladies must go out a great deal, and be dressed to receive company: how can they do all this and work?" (109). Despite her protestation, Mrs. Harley spends almost no time with her baby, devoting her time instead to her social affairs. In neglecting the baby she squanders the productive power of her time. Mrs. Harley's failing lies not in having servants or money, but in failing to put those resources to use for the proper ends.

Mrs. Harley's poor management of her time affects not only her child's welfare but also her husband's ability to conduct business efficiently. Early in the novel, she wishes him to look at some flowers she has been arranging for her hair, but he refuses, saying, "I am in such haste, my dear, I cannot look at them now. Let's have dinner: I engaged to meet a man on business at three this afternoon" (26). Unfortunately, dinner is not ready, because, as the Harleys discover to their horror, the incompetent girl hired to replace Nancy does not know how to cook. Later in the novel, Mrs. Harley returns "late from making some fashionable calls" and finds Mr. Harley "waiting for her to dine" (58). On another occasion, when the cook threatens to quit, Mrs. Harley is so distraught that she goes to consult her husband at work, but "Mr. Harley was just negotiating some business of importance, and was not in a situation to be troubled with home affairs" (85). Far from creating the efficient domestic environment advocated by advice writers such as Beecher and Sigourney, and illustrated by the examples of Anne in Sedgwick's *Home* and Mary in Gardner's "Labor," Mrs. Harley produces domestic disorder that even intrudes unseasonably upon Mr. Harley's place of business. Her temporal misconduct thus links the domestic sphere to the market in precisely the wrong way: it threatens to undermine the family's moral integrity while also destroying its material prosperity.

In keeping with this theme of inversion of effective economy, Mrs. Harley reveals herself to be fully competent to manage her time effectively in the most inappropriate of circumstances: this is, when it comes to planning the all-important party. For example, at one point when she is dealing with the knotty problem of persuading her husband to spend more money on the party, the narrator tells us that "she looked at her watch, and finding there would be time to make a call before tea, slipped on her cloak and bonnet, and went to consult one of her fashionable confidantes as to what she could do" (62). Later, when the problems with the servants have become so bad that even Mrs. Harley grows concerned, she thinks that she must not ask her husband to make another change until after the party, for "that was the first and last thought about which time and money were alike expended" (66). She suggests to Mr. Harley that "we had better send out our invitations soon. Let us set a time, and shape our purposes accordingly" (67). Finally, when the dishonest housekeeper steals money from Mr. Harley's desk and he becomes set on dismissing her, Mrs. Harley again beseeches him to wait until after the party, for the "mere thought of being obliged to oversee the house, just as she wanted all her time to herself, was what she could not endure" (80). Mrs. Harley begs him, "Do, husband, let her stay till I get my dress. What time shall I have to go out if you leave me alone with Sally [the cook]?" (81). In all of these activities, Mrs. Harley endeavors to spend time productively, but the effort is hopeless from the outset because what she is trying to produce, a fashionable social life, is of no value in the moral universe of domestic fiction. Time has the power to produce personhood, but only when it is spent well and invested wisely. In striving to develop herself into a fashionable socialite, Mrs. Harley in effect invests her time in producing a kind of personhood that turns out to be ephemeral, a shoddy product of little value.

When Mrs. Harley finally reforms, she confesses to Aunt Ruth that the party left her dissatisfied with fashionable life because "it is provoking . . . after one has exhausted so much time, and spent so much money, to find we derive so little real enjoyment from it" (124). In describing how she has "exhausted" her time, Mrs. Harley perfectly captures the negative sense of futile consumption that produces nothing. After Mrs. Harley stops devoting so much of her time to a fashionable life and begins studying Aunt Ruth's lessons in domestic economy, she is able to put her domestic affairs in order: "The calls were ended, and Mrs. Harley's family experienced the comfortable, rational enjoyment which springs from a well-regulated home" (125). Aunt Ruth is able to effect this change in Mrs. Harley by offering "well-timed hints" for reform, encouraging her not only to learn domestic economy but also to read the Bible and attend church. By the time Aunt Ruth returns to her country home, Mrs. Harley has internalized the value of system and order to such an extent that she no longer cares for fashionable life. She tells her husband, "Since Aunt Ruth was here, I don't care much about such things, she impressed me so strongly with the folly of permitting them to engross my whole time" (129–30). Mrs. Harley even decides she does not wish to attend a fashionable party to which they have been invited. Significantly, the narrator describes this moral progress in terms of redemption of time lost: "By steady, but somewhat difficult steps in the commencement, Mrs. Harley proceeded in redeeming the past time; but never did a week go by that she did not find some relic of her former self, which she had not shaken off. So closely do our follies cleave to us when once they have gained the mastery" (130). Mrs. Harley's progress toward virtue must be measured against her former vices; the narrator creates a kind of temporal balance sheet in which time spent profitably must add up to redeem time lost. Because the relics of her former self reappear each week, Mrs. Harley is constantly reminded of the necessity to redeem the time. Her personhood is ultimately composed of an accumulated quantity of virtuously spent units of time. A virtuous person is defined by moments, hours, days, and weeks spent well. This modern method of redemption and character formation thus aligns the process of becoming an economic success in the market-oriented consumer culture of the mid-nineteenth century with a traditional New England rhetoric of salvation.

In conveying these traditional notions of redemption through Aunt Ruth, Hale, like Sedgwick and Gardner, locates the source of tradition in the country. In so doing, she maps the temporal relation between tradition and modernity spatially by suggesting that an agricultural or rural way of life must be the repository of traditional values and good housekeeping. Similarly, both Sedgwick and Gardner take pains to point out explicitly how their heroines' traditional values, instilled in a country upbringing, enable these characters to resist the temptations and superficialities of modern city life. In making the relationship between past and present equivalent to the relationship between country and city, these writers paradoxically insist that the past exists now and that tradition coexists with modernity—if only their readers knew where to look for it. The success of these characters in managing modern households symbolically perpetuates the traditional virtues of colonial and early national American character even while appropriating them for a more modern era.

In a neat piece of circular thought, this move to legitimize the present by connecting it to the past also implicitly turns the past into a "premodern" state. That is, if the modern social world retains many of the best attributes of traditional society, and in many ways arose out of that society, then logically the past must be a precursor to the present. "With all our ceiled houses," rhapsodizes the narrator of Harriet Beecher Stowe's *The Minister's Wooing*, "let us not forget our grandmothers' kitchens!"[21] Simultaneously idealizing their grandmothers' kitchens while also indicating how the present has improved upon the past, many domestic writers created a teleology in which modernity was understood not as a departure from the past but as a perpetuation and fulfillment of it. Some of the domestic writers who constructed this teleology emphasized the moral, Christian qualities of colonial American life at the same time as they described its efficiency and orderliness. In describing household management, these things are one and the same. Hence, colonial America provides the template for a moral version of modern life; that is, everyday life organized according to the logic of the market, which logic itself allows Americans to model themselves after a Christian God characterized by orderliness.

Propagating Domestic Time

Such texts exemplify the kinds of raw materials out of which Catharine Beecher and Henry Thoreau formulated systematic domestic theories based upon the mastery of time. Unlike Sedgwick, Gardner, and many other writers who dealt with this theme in parts, both Beecher and Thoreau fully theorized the importance of time and used it to create quite different templates for what each writer saw as a morally perfect America. Beecher's *A Treatise on Domestic Economy* (1841) was the most important manual of domestic instruction in the United States before the Civil War. It may seem odd to place Thoreau in the context of domestic writing, but *Walden* (1854) is about homemaking as much as it is about nature. Indeed, as Cecelia Tichi has recently shown, Thoreau's "longtime identity . . . as a nature writer" has led readers to ignore "how carefully" Thoreau must have "scrutinized the domestic furnishings and housekeeping practices of the moment" in order to produce a very detailed critique of normative middle-class domesticity.[22] There are so many correlations and antiphonies in the ways that Beecher and Thoreau analyze the use of time in the domestic sphere that the two writers are, in effect, engaged in a debate over issues of central importance to the culture.

"A wise economy is nowhere more conspicuous," declares Beecher in *A Treatise on Domestic Economy*, "than in the right *apportionment of time* to different pursuits."[23] In the modern middle-class household Beecher envisions, organizing units of time and spending them in useful activity demonstrate the economic efficiency perceived as essential to success in the new world of the market. Thoreau offers a competing but equally didactic model of the employment of time in an alternative domestic environment. Thoreau's small, rustic house strategically appropriates and reimagines elements of Beecher's ideal middle-class home. As Barksdale Maynard points out, Thoreau always refers to his dwelling as a "house," never a "cabin" as generations of readers have tended to call it. This smaller dwelling provides the venue within which Thoreau develops a critical personhood by transforming Beecher's temporal efficiency into a parodic diligence in not working during as many moments of time as possible: "There were times when I could not afford to sacrifice the bloom of the present moment to any work, whether of the head or hands."[24] Both Beecher's industry and Thoreau's idleness are framed in economic terms that link their advice to the logic of the market. Beecher writes, for example, of spending time wisely: "The economy of time, and our obligation to spend every hour for some useful end, are what few minds properly realize." Thoreau, in turn, protests that he cannot "afford" to waste time by working. Even though Thoreau's domestic economy purports to invert Beecher's, as a temporal economy it is precisely the same, in that it attaches equal value to moments of time. Saving time so thriftily provides, for Thoreau, a way not of rejecting but of engaging critically with the newly emerging middle-class norms by inhabiting and reconfiguring their economic logic. Together, these two texts illustrate how writers with diverse political and cultural agendas made clock time into a venue for debates over the ideal form of representative American personhood in a new age characterized by market activity.

What is of greatest importance for both writers in this debate over the employment of time is not how best to resist the capitalist market, but how best to mobilize the power of that market to remake the American social world. Beecher's use of the term "obligation," for example, points toward her sense that time is something given to us by God, and that its proper use is determined as much by spiritual concerns as by the secular needs of capitalist moneymaking. "Christianity teaches us," Beecher writes, "that, for all the time afforded us, we must give account to God." Indeed, Beecher defines God as a "Being of perfect system and order" and argues that "He has divided our time" in order to facilitate a more Christian lifestyle (159). Beginning with the division of the days of the week and the recurrence of the Sabbath every seventh day, Beecher proceeds to sketch out a system by which women might schedule their own recurring domestic duties through a "systematic apportionment of time" and so become beings of "perfect system and order" themselves (160). Ultimately, however, the spiritual "account" resulting from this strict program of time management must be reckoned by equating time with material wealth, so that in assigning the "right apportionment of time" to various daily tasks individuals should feel "bound by the same rules, as relate to the use of property" (181). Beecher thus carries the market through a cycle of ideologically important associations: first she locates the origin of systematic time management in God, then she shows how individuals might make themselves Godlike by emulating this logic, and finally she reconnects the notion of clockwork time to the market by equating time with property. Hence, Beecher's way of managing the market's integration into the household qualitatively transforms capitalism by locating its origin in the "system and order" she attributes to the Christian God.[25]

While value in the market might be defined in strictly monetary terms, Beecher's ideal domestic manager adds another form of value that transcends dollars and cents. In the marketplace, Beecher proposes, time has value because it can produce money or goods, while in the home, time has value because it can be used to produce Christian human beings. As she explains in *A Treatise on Domestic Economy*:

> But, besides economizing our own time, we are bound to use our influence and example to promote the discharge of the same duty by others. A woman is under obligations so to arrange the hours and pursuits of her family, as to promote systematic and habitual industry; and if, by late breakfasts, irregular hours for meals, and other hindrances of this kind, she interferes with, or refrains from promoting regular industry in, others, she is accountable to God for all the waste of time consequent on her negligence. (185)

In this passage Beecher fleshes out a model of familial behavior that is only suggested in Sedgwick and Gardner's fiction. For Beecher, the definition of virtue in the domestic sphere lies in doing the same things at the same times every day, and at the same time as the other members of the family. Meals must be eaten at regular hours. Everyone must arise early and at the same time. And in order for this punctuality to really constitute character formation, it must be habitual; that is, it must be internalized so as to become natural and effortless. This model of the family moves the language of spending, saving, and wasting from the public economic discourse of market capitalism into the private sphere of the home and makes it the basis of middle-class personhood. The language of clock time makes it possible for these economic metaphors to cross the threshold of domesticity—in both directions, as these newly minted persons then move outward from the domestic sphere into every other arena of American life.

Beecher's theory of modernization thus locates cultural production in the home. She resists the notion that industry, or the massive production of things that industry represents, are the defining features of market capitalism. Instead, she locates the spirit of capitalism in domestic consumer culture by showing how the market's ideal logic can be realized there and then disseminated outward. Indeed, five years after writing the first edition of *A Treatise on Domestic Economy*, Beecher would explicitly critique the use of time in precisely that industrial context upon which the historical accounts of E. P. Thompson and later writers such as Mark M. Smith focus. In 1846 Beecher visited the textile mills at Lowell and recorded her outrage at the way in which the operatives were made to hurry through their days. The operatives (and Beecher herself, when she visited) were "wakened at *five*, by the bells calling to labor," with "half an hour only allowed for dinner," followed by "work till seven o'clock, the last part of the time by lamplight." After supper, Beecher calculated, the operatives were left only ten hours for sleep and "shopping, mending, making, recreation, social intercourse, and *breathing the pure air*."[26] Interestingly, Beecher's critique here begins with the fact that factory operatives were awakened at five o'clock. Yet in *A Treatise on Domestic Economy* Beecher emphasizes the moral importance and health benefits of early rising, claiming that the practice "which may justly be called a domestic virtue, has a peculiar claim to be styled American and democratic" (123). The difference in the Lowell experience is that the operatives must rise early and then hurriedly complete their dress in order to get to the mills in time to work an excessive number of hours for the benefit of the owners. Here, time discipline is put to the service not of virtuous self-culture, but the opposite: the degradation of the operatives as moral beings. Beecher expresses particular concern at the lack of intellectual culture among the millworkers, writing that "in regard to intellectual advantages, such as night schools, lectures, reading, and composition, all time devoted to these must be taken from the hours required for recreation or needful repose."[27] In the mills, work steals time away from character formation. Like Sedgwick's William, who hates to hurry through any meal, Beecher deplores time wasted without production. The home, as she constructs it, is more productive than the factory, at least in those ways that she wants to make matter to her audience. That Beecher's protest against the rigid time-tables of factory labor is specifically made on behalf of women and children only adds emphasis to the fact that she sees these especially domestic beings as representative modern Americans; she relegates men and factory work alike to a secondary role when she asks "if it would not be better to put the thousands of men who are keeping school for young children into the mills, and employ the women to train the children" and emphasizes that factory labor degrades women's ability to be good mothers.[28] If the market extends between the factory and the home through the circulation of commodities, then Beecher demonstrates that both ends of this system are productive. The factory produces goods that are consumed in the home in ways that are themselves productive. Consumption within the organizing logic of temporal economy constitutes another, in fact a more powerful, form of production—the production not merely of things, but of personhood.

Reorienting our understanding of modernity toward domesticity, as Beecher's text invites us to do, toward private life and toward women, is itself a politically charged act. As Michel de Certeau points out, the systematic marginalization of processes of consumption is not incidental but endemic to the way that modern Western society has represented itself. Both academic theorists and the popular media depict production as vigorous (and, implicitly, masculine), while portraying consumption as a pleasant but somewhat embarrassing (and feminized) aftereffect of capitalism's massive productivity. "This is the logic of production," de Certeau writes. "Ever since the eighteenth century, it has engendered its own discursive and practical space, on the basis of points of concentration—the office, the factory, the city. It rejects the relevance of places it does not create."[29] If, however, the social networks arising from market activity were conveyed to individuals through the reified, imaginative power of clock time, then the spaces in which that time was consumed must be profoundly relevant to the creation of the modern social world. The home constitutes the location of that other form of production that de Certeau describes: "To a rationalized, expansionist and at the same time centralized, clamorous and spectacular production corresponds another production, called 'consumption.'"[30] Recovering the record of such spaces and unpacking the verbal artifacts of this protean period of historical change reveals the messy, complicated history of our modern social world. The rational grid of time and space that seems, in contemporary theory, always to have been an inevitable component of modernity was in fact a historical contingency created not by machines themselves but by individual human beings who employed those machines in a variety of ways during active moments of self-creation.

In the first chapter of *A Treatise on Domestic Economy*, Beecher asks, "Are we [Americans], then, a spectacle to the world? Has the Eternal Lawgiver appointed us to work out a problem, involving the destiny of the whole earth? Are such momentous interests to be advanced or retarded, just in proportion as we are faithful to our high trust?" The appropriateness of such questions for a practical treatise on domestic economy can only be understood in light of Beecher's commitment to the creation of a virtuous society through the culture of individual members of American families. As the daughter of a minister, Beecher had an acute sense of the spiritual traditions of New England.[31] Through their unmistakable echoing of John Winthrop's "A Model of Christian Charity," Beecher's questions draw the Puritan concern with a virtuous and well-ordered society out of the seventeenth and eighteenth centuries and reinvent it for the consumption of the nineteenth-century middle class. Crucially, Beecher's next question places the impetus of national success upon the self-culture of the individual American: "'What manner of persons, then, ought we to be,' in attempting to sustain so solemn, so glorious a responsibility?" (36). Beecher places her faith more in the perfectability of the temporal self than in God's power to save the nation, more in salvation through good works than salvation through grace, thus linking the Puritan tradition that was the Beecher family's religious heritage with the broader, ecumenical trend of Christian evangelism that played a central role in American national culture during the nineteenth century. The fact that this virtue is linked to the past lends it legitimacy, but it vigorously points the way toward mastery of the present and future.

Imagining the market in this way prepared the ground for Beecher's long-term social and political goals (many of which she shared with other domestic theorists) involving the creation of what Gillian Brown calls a "standard of harmony for America" that would "determine the characters" of the mass of Americans and result in a nation in which "socially and geographically, maternal power held sway over a limitless domain."[32] Beecher hoped to show how mastery of time's productive power could transform the moral peril emerging from the market revolution into a national opportunity for the production of virtuous selves. She warns of the danger facing the American family in the social chaos created by the market economy: "Every thing is moving and changing. Persons in poverty, are rising to opulence, and persons of wealth, are sinking to poverty. The children of common laborers, by their talents and enterprise, are becoming nobles in intellect, or wealth, or office; while the children of the wealthy, enervated by indulgence, are sinking to humbler stations" (40). In response to this peril, Beecher argues enthusiastically that, because American culture is modern and new, Americans have the potential to avoid the decadence of European society. As Nicole Tonkovich explains, in Beecher's theory "American women, unlike their European counterparts, do not partake of a heritable class. . . . Rather, they (and their children) acquire their social qualities and national identity through learning and overt instruction in behaviors that are uniquely American."[33] For Beecher the role of the wife and mother is to enact this pedagogical program, ensuring that the American family functions as the foundation of a society that neither perpetuates the evils of Old World monarchies nor allows the modern democratic nation to become chaotic and amoral, but instead draws on traditional New England values of thrift and industry to create a uniquely moral version of modern life.

In this way, while capitalism pushed a network of highways, canals, and railroads into more and more remote parts of the country, Beecher worked to extend a complementary array of Christian homes and schools into the West. This national pedagogical project provided templates for middle-class life that could be extended indefinitely, creating an "empire of the mother," in Mary Ryan's phrase, of limitless spatial and temporal demesne.[34] Articulating this standard through an economic logic modeled on the market provided Beecher with the ability to transmit her ideas through the spread of capitalism. Employing the rhetoric of temporal economy, Beecher made her version of domesticity market-like and thus employed capitalism's power to reproduce itself. Even as capitalism ineluctably transformed the pattern of everyday life in America, Beecher's domestic theory rode along and enacted a further transformation, extending across the space of America a national "market" in which moments of present time could be transformed, through economic consumption, into future salvation. Indeed, American space, in itself, was less important to Beecher's imaginative vision of a world made over than American time. "The mother forms the character of the future man," Beecher writes, "the sister bends the fibres that are hereafter to be the forest tree; the wife sways the heart, whose energies may turn for good or evil the destinies of a nation" (34). Beecher's domestic imagination, bent upon mastery of interior spaces, directs itself outward primarily in terms of time. Hence, for Beecher the "empire of the mother" exists not in the American land of the present but in the time of the future.

That Beecher was successful in promulgating this theory of cultural production is attested to by James Goodwyn Clonney's genre painting *Mother's Watch* (ca. 1852–56) (Illustration 3.2). In this image, two cherubic boys play with their sleeping mother's pocket watch. Meanwhile, another clock is visible on the wall above the boys' heads. The mother has fallen asleep while reading a heavy book with a lock, which can only be a Bible. The mother holds a pen in her hand. She may have been marking passages in scripture, or recording an important family event. In any case, she has been writing, a creative act that echoes her creative power as a mother. The painting correlates maternal love, Christian love, and the practice of child rearing with the passage of time. The clock time of the wall represents the time of the household, the mother's watch represents her synchronization with and mastery of that time, and the domestic environment as a whole is clearly conducive to the growth of the two boys into the next generation of American citizens. This woman has exhausted herself fulfilling the cultural work of motherhood, the production of two human beings who represent the national future. She has filled clock time with maternal love and made it a venue for Christian redemption. The fact that this image was painted by a male artist suggests the degree to which the domestic environment was seen as central to cultural production not only by women. To an important degree, the paradigm created by Beecher and other domestic writers had come, by the 1850s, to seem increasingly universal.

Disseminating a Natural Market

Like Beecher, Thoreau strives to fill time with value in order to create a template for representative American personhood compatible with the market but committed to moral perfection. Indeed, it is precisely this commitment to time, rather than space, that rescues Thoreau's *Walden* from the charge of ineffectual protest with which critics such as Philip Fisher, Robert Gross, and Michael Gilmore have labeled it. Gross claims that Thoreau's attack on the way that his contemporaries "rationalized their work and harnessed their lives to the clock" is "flawed by his idealization of the preindustrial order."[35] Fisher argues that an unlimited amount of space "could be carpeted from end to end with reduplications of Thoreau's experiment, but, in the abstemious pattern of asexuality, Thoreau's pattern could work for one generation only."[36] However, these critiques miss the tremendous productive power of time that Thoreau seeks to make available to his readers, and the way that he seeks to employ that productive power not in the service of exile to a premodern world but to refashion the modern world in

ILLUSTRATION 3.2. *James Goodwyn Clonney,* Mother's Watch, *about 1850.*
Oil on canvas, 27 × 22 inches (Westmoreland Museum of American Art)

which he and his readers lived. Despite his self-imposed solitude, Thoreau clearly intends to influence others, to persuade them to change their ways and adopt his vision. As Stanley Cavell observes, throughout *Walden* "the writer, basically alone, conducts himself as though he is founding and conducting the economy, at once the private and the public affairs, of his city, perhaps laying it up as a model in heaven."[37] Most fundamentally, Thoreau seeks to teach his compatriots what to make of the market. While Thoreau decries the excessive, thoughtless consumption of most of his neighbors — such as the deacon whose "trumpery" is auctioned off after his death to encumber the domestic "garrets and dust holes" of the rest of the community — he praises commerce itself as "very natural in its methods withal, far more so than many fantastic enterprises and sentimental experiments, and hence its singular success" (67, 119). As Ann Douglas has shown, members of the clergy were often thought of as feminine figures in this period, a fact that aligns the deacon with feminized middle-class domesticity as objects of Thoreau's scorn.[38] In contrast to the way Beecher depicts her ideal of a matriarchal Christian market, Thoreau admires the phallic and suggestively pagan sight of a "tall pine, hewn on far northern hills, which has winged its way over the Green Mountains and the Connecticut, shot like an arrow through the township within ten minutes." Given that "scarce another eye beholds" this avatar of a more masculine commerce, it is up to Thoreau to awaken his readers to its important signification (121).

By staging his life of material "simplicity" in a public way (both by making a spectacle of himself in the woods, crowing "as lustily as chanticleer" to wake his neighbors up, and by disseminating an account of this experience in print), Thoreau imitates Beecher's model of market-oriented personhood but substitutes a practice of saving time for Beecher's practice of productive spending, a repetition with a difference that competes with Beecher's own formulation. In a yoking of apparently antithetical concepts that recalls Beecher's conflation of Christianity and efficiency, when Thoreau writes of the "bloom" of present moments that he cannot "afford" to waste, he brings the modern world of the market into alignment with the natural world of Walden Pond. Throughout *Walden*, Thoreau preoccupies himself with the logic and practice of consumption to an even greater degree than Beecher or, perhaps, any other contemporary writer on middle-class culture or "economy." While Tichi argues that Thoreau joins Beecher and other domestic writers in seeking to create worlds apart from the capitalist market, Thoreau's use of the rhetoric of temporal economy indicates that he joins these other domestic writers in exactly the opposite way, in seeking to extend the logic of the market into a venue where it might be appropriated and put to the service of another social agenda. Thoreau's disagreement with Beecher does not concern the desirability of consuming goods purchased through the market, a practice that meets with both writers' qualified approval, as when Thoreau concludes that although "we might possibly live in a cave or a wigwam or wear skins today, it certainly is better to accept the advantages, though so dearly bought, which the invention and industry of mankind offer" (40). What Thoreau really objects to is the way that Beecher's version of domesticity, by appropriating clock time to women's sphere, makes the market as a whole a feminine province. Where Beecher imagines a domesticated, feminized, and Christianized market located in parlors and kitchens, Thoreau strives to produce a more masculine market in the woods, bragging that his days at Walden were not "minced into hours and fretted by the ticking of a clock" (112). The feminized diction of this line, "minced" and "fretted," signals a distaste for a variety of social norms that Beecher was helping to establish. In describing himself as a lustily crowing rooster, Thoreau clearly distinguishes himself from such a world; what is most significant is that in doing so he emulates Beecher's reformist method of infusing the time of the market with moral value. Hence, while as esteemed a critic as Robert D. Richardson reads *Walden* as expressing Thoreau's "major disagreement with Adam Smith," concluding that while "Smith wanted to see consumption maximized, Thoreau wants it minimized," it seems more accurate to say that Thoreau wants to rescue the process of consumption from Beecher's maternal project and restore it to its ostensibly "natural" masculine state.[39] The domestic world Thoreau imagines at *Walden* provides an alternative not to consumer culture as such but rather to the way that Beecher and her sister writers mince and fret away what Thoreau views as the robust time of a properly masculine capitalist market.

When Thoreau insists upon time, rather than money, as the fundamental measure of value, writing that "the cost of a thing is the amount of what I will call life which is required to be exchanged for it, immediately or in the long run," he finds agreement not only with the classical labor theory of value (as expressed, for example, by David Ricardo), but also with Beecher, who decries excessive consumption primarily because it steals time away from more productive pursuits (31).[40] Indeed, some of Beecher's pronouncements on this subject would not seem out of place in Walden: "It may be urged, that it is indispensable for most persons to give more time to earn a livelihood, and to prepare food, raiment, and dwellings, than to any other object. But it may be asked, how much of the time, devoted to these objects, is employed in preparing varieties of food, not necessary, but rather injurious, and how much is spent for those parts of dress and furniture not indispensable, and merely ornamental?" (161). Thoreau assesses the temporal cost of a fashionable middle-class lifestyle in very similar terms, as when he declares: "I did not wish to spend my time in earning rich carpets or other fine furniture, or delicate cookery, or a house in the Grecian or the Gothic style just yet" (70). Simplifying—that is, learning to live with fewer material possessions by economizing—yields a surplus of time that can itself be employed for better ends. "With a little more wit," he concludes in his discussion of consumer goods, "we might use these materials to become richer than the richest now are, and make our civilization a blessing" (40).

In pursuit of this blessing, Thoreau reproduces the kind of advice that one might find in domestic advice manuals, but he pushes the logic of this advice much further. Just as Beecher recommends, he tallies his household budget, bakes his own bread, and keeps his floor swept clean and white. "Housework was a pleasant pastime," he writes. "When my floor was dirty, I rose early, and, setting all my furniture out of doors on the grass, bed and bedstead making but one budget, dashed water on the floor, and sprinkled white sand from the pond on it, and then with a broom scrubbed it clean and white; and by the time the villagers had broken their fast the morning sun had dried my house sufficiently to allow me to move in again, and my meditations were almost uninterrupted" (112–13). Because the house becomes a symbolic representation of the total economic organization of his life, working on the house constitutes, in effect, the deliberate creation of a form of personhood founded on sound economy: "It would be worth the while to build still more deliberately than I did, considering, for instance, what foundation a door, a window, a cellar, a garret, have in the nature of man" (45). But where Beecher includes drawings and diagrams of modest but comfortably bourgeois Gothic cottages in her *Treatise*, Thoreau suggests that such middle-class norms are not, yet, economical enough: "An average house in this neighborhood costs perhaps eight hundred dollars, and to lay up this sum will take from ten to fifteen years of the laborer's life" (31). In constructing his own house for only $28.12½, a figure whose precision testifies to his economic mastery, Thoreau saves the years that others waste and shows how a solitary man can keep better house—and produce a sounder model of market-oriented personhood—than whole families operating on Beecher's scheme of synchronization.

If the riches Thoreau acquires through his wiser economy take the form of time, then the complement to his material simplicity must be the ostentatious complexity of his consumption of those luxurious moments. Echoing Beecher's praise for the democratic virtues of rising early to one's house-keeping, and the traditional New England wives' injunction to "get your work done up in the forenoon," Thoreau describes the salutary quality of his own domestic "morning work," for it makes a "fresh prospect" available "every hour" (112).[41] It is the economical organization of such labor within time, signified by the phrase "morning work," that brings it into accord with Thoreau's productive "meditations," his process of self-invention. "Sometimes," he writes, "in a summer morning, having taken my accustomed bath, I sat in my sunny doorway from sunrise till noon, rapt in a revery, amidst the pines and hickories and sumachs, in undisturbed solitude and stillness, while the birds sang around or flitted noiseless through the house, until by the sun falling in at my west window, or the noise of some traveller's wagon on the distant highway, I was reminded of the lapse of time" (111). The self-indulgence implicit in this scene of solitary bathing and rapture illustrates Thoreau's way of investing his time in himself. He goes on to write that he "grew in those seasons like corn in the night, and they were far better than any work of the hands would have been" (111). Where others might waste their time in physical labor exchanged for cash, Thoreau invests his temporal capital in self-development, cultivating his inner, imaginative life. By doing this, he unlocks time's productive power, describing these mornings as "not time subtracted from my life, but so much over and above my usual allowance" (111–12). The juxtaposition of an utterly simple outer life and a self-indulgent and richly imaginative inner life produces an irony that Thoreau nicely captures when he dreams, in the chapter "House Warming," of inhabiting "a larger and more populous house, standing in a golden age, of enduring materials" (243). This imagery once again makes the house into a metaphor for personhood, but this time representing the imaginative expansion of the self into a lavish interiority composed of an entire age of time.

Mirroring Beecher's household, Thoreau's woods also become the nexus of market logic, conducive to acts of self-making that link the personal to the commercial. "I have thought that Walden Pond would be a good place for business, not solely on account of the railroad and the ice trade," Thoreau remarks by way of explaining his choice to settle there (21). While there is certainly a joke in the semimetaphorical way that Thoreau uses the word "business," the joke derives much of its humor from the fact that it is possible to conduct real business at the pond, and that Thoreau himself does so, buying and selling, producing and consuming, in the course of which he effectively represents the market as indigenous to the woods around Walden. The most important symbol of Walden as a location of economic activity is the railroad; Richardson notes that the Fitchburg rail line had just been completed in 1844, and that an observer "could see the new railroad from almost any point on the pond."[42] As such, the railroad was an obvious, indeed unavoidable, sign of the incursion of commerce and industry upon the natural environment of Walden. Thoreau embraces the railroad, traveling to the village "along its causeway" and thus finding himself "related to society by this link." The railroad men acknowledge him "as an old acquaintance," he recounts, and even take him for an employee. "[A]nd so I am," he concedes: "I too would fain be a track repairer somewhere in the orbit of the earth" (115). In the metaphorical sense that Thoreau evokes through the imagery of a lofty "orbit," the work of track repairing must involve a kind of cultural rehabilitation. If the track leads between civilization and nature, through the intermediate world of the small farmers in the countryside around Walden, then Thoreau's task as "track repairer" must be to illustrate for his readers the compatibility of commerce and nature. Thoreau famously attends to the whistles of passing trains, but in his account, far from conflicting with nature, the railroad's whistle actually synchronizes with the songs of the birds: "Regularly at half past seven, in one part of the summer, after the evening train had gone by, the whippoorwills chanted their vespers for half an hour, sitting on a stump by my door, or upon the ridge pole of the house. They would begin to sing with as much precision as a clock, within five minutes of a particular time, referred to the setting of the sun, every evening" (123–24). Carefully avoiding any mention of cause and effect, Thoreau simply observes that the train and the birds both observe a similarly regular schedule, whose origin might be located as well in the clock as in the sun. This passage thus crystallizes Thoreau's vision of the commercial time of the railroad as natural, a way of thinking about the market that invests it with the spiritual value not of revealed religion but of nature. Indeed, the market appears immanent in the very waters of the pond itself when the gang of ice carvers appears to carve up the "skin itself" of the pond and disseminate it through the middle-class homes of America as a commodity akin to "so many barrels of flour" (295). Because the majority of the ice taken out melts before it can be sold, the pond "recover[s] the greater part" of its commodified waters, retaining undiminished its capacity to supply ice to the market (296). Like time, water signifies an ideal, perfectly fungible unit of value that takes on the commodity form as it circulates through the market, its transformation symbolized in its change of color from green to "frozen blue" as it turns to salable and consumable ice (297). The dissemination of these ideal commodities connects Thoreau's experiment in self-invention with "the sweltering inhabitants of Charleston and New Orleans, of Madras and Bombay and Calcutta," all of whom, Thoreau insists, "drink at my well" when they consume Walden's ice (297–98).

Thoreau thus conceives of Walden as the productive center of an inexhaustible natural market competing with the matriarchal Christian market theorized by Beecher. Just as Beecher employs the infrastructure of capitalist expansion to propagate her template for America, Thoreau imagines the railroad renaturalizing the market as it carries commodities, so that when the cattle train passes, the "air is filled with the bleating of calves and sheep, and the hustling of oxen, as though a pastoral valley were going by" (121–22). But more than material commodities, the railroad conveys time, the "startings and arrivals of the cars" becoming the "epochs in the village day," their whistle "heard so far, that the farmers set their clocks by them, and thus one well-conducted institution regulates a whole country" (117–18). Beecher's and Thoreau's two competing versions of the market meet at the point of the household clock, the moral quality of whose precisely measured moments both seek to define. In setting the clocks and attending to their time, the farmers actively link themselves to Thoreau's natural market, which enters their lives in the form of the railroad. "Here come your groceries, country," Thoreau exclaims while describing the train, "your rations, countrymen! Nor is there any man so independent on his farm that he can say them nay" (115). While there is, to be sure, something a bit ominous in the power of the trains to regulate the countryside, the notion of a well-regulated rural landscape peopled by small farmers each possessing a household clock evokes a kind of serene democracy reminiscent of Crèvecoeur or Jefferson. As Thoreau describes it, the market's compulsory power is mitigated both by the harmonious and prosperous quality of the social world it creates and by its anticipation in nature. The railroad becomes another sunrise, transforming America into a pastoral market as it travels; "I watch the passage of the morning cars," Thoreau reports, "with the same feeling that I do the rising of the sun, which is hardly more regular" (116). In the productive power of the "morning" time of this natural market Thoreau finds the possibility of a modern and morally perfect America inhabiting the territory of a utopian future.

In enjoining his readers to transform clock time into morning time, Thoreau does not wish to reject the clock, but rather to show how multilayered time can be. Additionally, he portrays time, in any form, as a tool created by human beings and used to imagine worlds: social, economic, natural, or, more aptly, some combination of all three. When he describes time as "but the stream I go a-fishing in," he does not deny the reality of time, any more than his subsequent statements that "I cannot count one" and "I know not the first letter of the alphabet" mean that he does not believe in the reality of mathematics or writing. He uses both math and writing in the course of creating his life in the woods, and so too does he make use of time. If, then, time in the end is "an illusion," as the "artist from the city of Kouroo" finds, it seems to be a necessary illusion, an "ingredient" of the imperfect personhood of human beings who live within history (326–27). The artist of Kouroo discovers Brahma when he transcends time. Most of us, Thoreau implies, must make the temporal world suffice instead, the world of the historical situation into which we have been born and which it is the labor of our lives to remake.

In thus appropriating both the logic of the capitalist market and the vocabulary of domesticity in the service of a "natural" way of life, an economy based on nature, Thoreau dramatizes the extent to which the modern social world that came into being along with the rise of a capitalist economy was shaped by cultural struggle. While Beecher fills the time of the modern nation with her version of traditional New England values, Thoreau revises Beecher's template and transforms the meaning of time once again. Together, these texts exemplify the heterogeneous quality of national time. They stage a debate over the meaning of clock time, thus employing clock time as the medium for an ongoing, inconclusive dialogue about American identity. In so doing, these texts make us aware that American history has always been structured by such irresolvable conflicts, and that the nature of the modern social world that emerged in the wake of the market revolution was far messier and more complex than the elegant mechanisms of the clock.

4

TIME IN THE LAND

Mark Twain's late satirical piece *Letters from the Earth* (composed around 1909 but unpublished during his lifetime) presents a series of bemused, touristic epistles ostensibly written by Satan to his fellow archangels Michael and Gabriel. While visiting the earth, Satan discovers all sorts of misconceptions, most of which lead human beings toward an undeserved sense of their own importance. The most egregious repository of such misinformation is the Christian Bible; in Twain's satire, although such biblical figures as God and Satan do exist, they are misrepresented in Christianity. The biblical story of Creation is an especially preposterous legend. "According to the Book and its servants," Twain has Satan write early in the satire, "the universe is only six thousand years old. It is only within the last hundred years that studious, inquiring minds have found out that it is nearer a hundred million."[1] In this line, Satan alludes to one of the most important intellectual and cultural developments of the nineteenth century: the expansion of the temporal scale from thousands to millions of years by the science of geology. It was, indeed, in the hundred years or so before Twain wrote *Letters from the Earth* that geologists had demonstrated to the satisfaction of other scientists and most lay people that the earth was far older than had previously been thought. Throughout *Letters from the Earth*, Twain makes the traditional biblical chronology an object of repeated satirical attacks; the belief that the world and humankind were both created only "six thousand years" before the nineteenth century comes to emblematize the benighted condition of the human beings Satan observes. God and the angels possess a true understanding of their place in time; this knowledge distinguishes divine beings from humankind.

Only a century before Twain wrote *Letters from the Earth*, the notion of a natural history stretching millions of years into the past would have seemed preposterous, rather than divinely enlightened, to most Americans. Although largely forgotten now, during the eighteenth and nineteenth centuries the 6,000-year timescale was well known throughout Europe and North America as an ecumenical Christian tradition. Beginning with St. Jerome, generations of theologians had tried to date the origin of the world and important biblical events such as the Deluge and the birth of Christ through analyses of biblical chronologies and genealogies correlated with astronomical and historical records from sources other than the Bible. At the turn of the nineteenth century, the most important such account in the English-speaking world was that of the Anglican archbishop James Ussher. In his *Annals of the History of the World* (1650), Ussher calculated that God had created the earth on the 23rd of October, 4004 BC.[2] Although the precision of this date may make Ussher's work sound silly to twenty-first-century readers, the archbishop was a learned man with a keen understanding of seventeenth-century natural philosophy. Such calculations were taken very seriously by educated people in Ussher's day and long after. The 6,000-year time frame was widely accepted in all strata of society through the early nineteenth century, and even in Twain's day it remained a commonplace allusion that any reader would immediately have understood. One example of the idea's persistence is provided by the drawing of the "Temple of Time" featured prominently in Emma Willard's history textbooks. On the back wall of the temple, at the metaphorical beginning of history, the words "Creation BC 4004" are clearly visible; this date remained in the drawing even in late nineteenth-century editions of Willard's text.[3]

Despite its continued legibility, the notion of the earth's origin in 4004 BC increasingly lost credibility as the nineteenth century wore on. The *Democratic Review* heaped scorn on the idea in an 1851 review of a book defending biblical chronology: "The author denies that the world is more than six thousand years old, or that the universe was made other than in six literal days, and thinks the deluge a 'far more credible and satisfactory' mode of accounting for the changes which the phenomena of the earth exhibit, than the theory of geology. . . . Really, when these bibliolaters, as Coleridge calls them, try their puny efforts to stop the car of science by interposing the verbal inspiration of Scripture, it is high time they should be told plainly and distinctly the absurdities in which they plunge themselves."[4] As this heated dismissal reveals, science and theology, which had been understood by most educated people as compatible, even friendly fields of inquiry at the dawn of the nineteenth century, had become somewhat hostile intellectual camps over the course of the century.[5] Most Americans continued to profess faith in God as the prime mover of natural processes, but belief in the literal veracity of the account of Creation reported in Genesis was increasingly perceived as an antiscientific and benighted attitude. The most successful and influential efforts to redeem the biblical account of Creation turned away from the literal and toward more metaphorical interpretations. Whereas in the eighteenth century science had had to steer carefully away from any claims that might conflict with religion, by the end of the nineteenth century it was biblical interpreters who risked censure if they contradicted scientific theory. By the time Twain wrote *Letters from the Earth*, the fact that the methods used by Ussher and other scholars for deriving the dates of Creation were rational and "scientific" had come to seem, in the minds of many, the height of absurdity, since these two worldviews had lost their compatibility.

Letters from the Earth ridicules the application of human reason to biblical exegesis by mixing, with intentional clumsiness, a scientific account of natural history with revisions of Old Testament narrative. Although Twain's satirical rendition of history employs biblical characters, it achieves its humor by placing these characters within a more scientific account of a vast cosmos filled with myriad stars and planets. Twain's God, unlike the God of the Bible, creates at once "a million stupendous suns," among which the earth is merely "a small globe" (3, 6). "You saw it, but did not notice it," God tells Satan, "amid the explosion of worlds and suns that sprayed from my hand" (6). Much nineteenth-century science writing for popular audiences emphasized the vastness of the cosmos and the ordinariness of the earth and its solar system. In the widely read (and anonymously published) *Vestiges of the Natural History of Creation* (1845), for example, the Edinburgh *litterateur* Robert Chambers wrote that it "has long been concluded amongst astronomers, that the stars, though they only appear to our eyes as brilliant points, are all to be considered as suns, representing so many solar systems, each bearing a general resemblance to our own."[6] Placing the Bible in the context of this scientific perspective, Twain's satire suggests that, if God does exist, he must have placed no great importance on human beings. Indeed, Twain's God describes humanity as merely one "experiment" among many he is conducting. "Time will show whether they were worth the trouble," God notes dismissively. In his first letter following his arrival on earth, Satan reports with astonishment that man "thinks he is the Creator's pet," and then asks rhetorically, "Isn't it a quaint idea?"

Beyond ridiculing the biblical account of Creation, Satan's letters make a mockery of various important events described in the Pentateuch by trying to reimagine biblical history in scientific terms. For example, one of the letters explains that the germs causing the notorious "sleeping sickness" in the nineteenth century had survived the Deluge centuries earlier because "Ham was full of these microbes, and when the voyage was over he discharged them in Africa and the havoc began, never to find amelioration until six thousand years should go by and science should pry into the mystery and hunt out the cause of the disease" (35). Satan's repeated references to "six thousand years" in the context of more scientific discussions of germ theory, speciation, and Malthusian population growth serve Twain's general dismissal of the logic of the Bible while also casting human efforts to comprehend the world through reason as inherently vexed. This absurdist mixture of biblical and scientific accounts of natural history reaches its peak when Satan describes a scene in which a multitude of immense prehistoric creatures seek unsuccessfully to escape the Deluge by securing places on Noah's Ark:

> Then at last, Noah sailed; and none too soon, for the Ark was only just sinking out of sight on the horizon when the monsters arrived, and added their lamentations to those of the multitude of weeping fathers and mothers and frightened little children who were clinging to the wave-washed rocks in the pouring rain and lifting imploring prayers to an All-Just and All-Forgiving and All-Pitying Being who had never answered a prayer since those crags were builded, grain by grain out of sands, and would still not have answered one when the ages should have crumbled them to sand again. (25)

Satan's description of the rocks on which the dinosaurs stand watching the ark sail away calls particular attention to geological theory. Although Satan repeatedly describes the Deluge as having occurred "six thousand years" before the present of the text, the description of the rocks "builded, grain by grain" and then "crumbled . . . to sand again" over the course of "ages" evokes the far longer spans of time required by the modern scientific account. In addition, the presence of the dinosaurs themselves is a jab at biblical chronologists. The discovery of the fossilized remains of extinct species in exposed rock strata had caused the majority of scientists to conclude that life had existed on earth long before human beings; this was another blow against the biblical account of six days of Creation. Twain spoofs those stalwart biblical literalists who insisted that, if the fossils discovered in the earth really were the bones of gigantic animals, then those animals must have lived at the same time as human beings. Twain's irony hinges on the fact that he reproduces this version of history, which he clearly views as preposterous, yet suggests that human beings and dinosaurs are equally misguided in believing that God is concerned with their welfare. Rather, like the ancient rocks, God is indifferent to the appeals of humans and dinosaurs alike. All of these living creatures fail to understand their relationship to the world around them, the insignificance of their brief lives in relation to nature's immense spans of time.

Geological Time and American Nationalism

I open this chapter with a discussion of Twain not because the great humorist was especially interested in geology, but for the opposite reason. While Twain had a lifelong enthusiasm for science and technology, and some of his works such as *Roughing It* and *Life on the Mississippi* display a working knowledge of the minerals and formations found in the western United States, geology was not a subject to which he devoted special attention.[7] Hence, his easy, casual invocation of geological ideas illustrates how familiar this field had become to the general public over the course of the nineteenth century. In particular, Twain's focus on the temporal aspects of geological theory is exemplary; for most nonspecialists, the most fascinating aspect of the scientific study of the earth was not what had been discovered about the nature of the rocks themselves but rather the immensity of time that was revealed in those rocks. The new chronology of millions of years of natural history captured the public imagination and seemed one of the great miracles of nineteenth-century science. In *Letters from the Earth*, Twain evokes the revolutionary quality of the new timescale by alluding not simply to the longer chronology itself, but also to the transformation in chronology, to the battles over the age of the earth that had raged among scientists and theologians over the course of the preceding decades. Hence, Twain's allusion suggests that cultural knowledge of that earlier way of thinking about time remained vital. The cultural prestige won by geology had not eradicated the memory of the biblical timescale. Rather, although the new chronology had gained broad acceptance, it was still perceived as revolutionary, a novel and strange way of understanding the world. It was precisely this quality that made geological time so important; its very newness made it a trope for revolutionary ways of conceptualizing the human relationship to history and nature.

Americans took an especially vigorous interest in this science of the land because it promised to provide something of a salve to feelings of cultural and political inferiority. Like all scientific revolutions, the discovery of deep time lent itself to many possible interpretations. Twain's sense that the geological timescale rendered human beings comically insignificant was not unique. Throughout the nineteenth century, American periodicals ran pieces musing on the implications of geological time for human history. For example, an 1850 article in *Harper's* (reprinted from an English magazine) suggested that geology "presents a variety of interest, and a revolution of events, before which the puny annals of modern history sink into insignificance."[8] Most Americans, however, preferred to try to integrate the new science into revised narratives of providential national destiny. As a self-consciously new nation, occupying the territory of a "new world," America sought historical roots for itself, to anchor itself in time. According to the romantic theories of nationhood that were current among the European intellectuals whom Americans most admired, a nation was defined by shared traditions, history, and roots in a particular land.[9] In his *Sketch-Book*, one of the first really successful books by an American author, Washington Irving noted ruefully that the picturesque English villages that he visited seemed to possess a far greater intrinsic connection to their landscape than did the towns of his own New York State. Irving's description of the power he felt emanating from Shakespeare's grave only confirmed for his readers that the glories of English culture were literally buried in the soil. American culture appeared, in comparison, more like a superficial transplant onto the surface of foreign soil; hence John O'Sullivan's self-consciously brash pronouncement, quoted in the first chapter of this book, that "American patriotism is not of soil."

Geology afforded Americans possibilities for imagining their relationship to the land as different from the unsuitable European models. Geology gave the American land a history and, through both scientific study and artistic representation, gave the people a felt connection to that history. In Chapter 1, I argued that statements such as O'Sullivan's exemplify how Americans imagined their nation developing primarily through time, and only secondarily across space. The land, I argued there, was important mostly because it provided a metaphor through which to imagine the real American territory, historical time. This chapter will build upon that way of rethinking the relationship between time and space by exploring how Americans perceived the land itself through the lens of time. Hence, while Chapter 1 focused upon time in an effort to ameliorate the neglect of time in favor of space in American studies scholarship, this chapter will strive to achieve a more balanced perspective on the way that those two terms were interconnected in the national imagination. The land ultimately acquired its great importance precisely because geological theory made it possible for Americans to imagine the land as a repository of time—ages of time stretching unfathomably far into the depths of the earth.[10]

A Revolutionary Chronology

The roots of the scientific revolution that made this way of thinking possible are complex, but historians of science concur in identifying the Scottish geologist James Hutton as a seminal figure in the English-speaking world at least. In 1795 Hutton published his *Theory of the Earth* (a book-length expansion of a paper originally presented ten years earlier), in which he made two important arguments: first, that we ought to assume that the same physical processes we observe in action in the present operated uniformly throughout past time; and second, that all existing geological phenomena could be explained by the operation of those observable processes if we would only concede that the earth was far older than 6,000 years.[11] In making these arguments, Hutton proposed what would come to be described as a "uniformitarian" theory of the earth's history that contested the established "catastrophist" theory. The catastrophists had sought to explain the origin of geological formations that clearly demonstrate the action of enormous forces by positing a series of epochal events. If such events had occurred, then the earth's crust could have achieved its broken and varied form in a relatively short time. Indeed, the more severe the catastrophes imagined, the less time required for the development of mountains, canyons, and other features. The uniformitarian theory posited, instead, the steady application of less intense forces over epochal periods of time. This perspective derived its name from its basic assumption: the uniformity of the laws and processes of nature. This view was, it need hardly be said, characteristic of the Enlightenment world in which Hutton and other early geologists were educated. In eighteenth-century Edinburgh, the orderliness and stability of the natural world were axiomatic. Many of these ideas remained powerful in the natural sciences even after the emergence of the romantic movement challenged many Enlightenment assumptions. In geology, uniformitarianism gradually won over the majority of both specialists and lay people, thanks not so much to Hutton himself, who had difficulty communicating beyond a very specialized audience, as to his compatriot John Playfair, a skillful writer whose *Illustrations of the Huttonian Theory of the Earth* (1802) made Hutton's ideas accessible to the educated reading public.[12] Later, Charles Lyell's uniformitarian *Principles of Geology* (1830–

33) became standard reading in Britain and North America, and Chambers's *Vestiges* provided a popular and sensational platform for a synthesis of theories from different branches of natural history, all positing the tremendous age of the earth.

As one might expect, the ascendancy of uniformitarianism was not uncompromised; the eventual consensus view among geologists synthesized viable ideas from both uniformitarian and catastrophist theory. A particularly important contribution to the resurgence of the catastrophist viewpoint was the glacial theory advanced by the Swiss-American naturalist Louis Agassiz.[13] In an 1868 review of the tenth edition of Lyell's *Principles* for the *North American Review*, Henry Adams politely noted that Agassiz's findings on climatic variation "seemed at first sight inconsistent with Sir Charles's argument," and by the time *The Education of Henry Adams* was published in 1905, Adams was asking acerbically, "If the glacial period were uniformity, what was catastrophe?"[14] Like Twain, Adams found that the development of geological theory provided occasion for skepticism not only about traditional understandings of revealed religion, but also about the potential of human reason to offer explanations of the world that were much more satisfactory. The Enlightenment faith in a world with rational laws had come to seem to Adams, by 1905, as a rather implausible form of mysticism. Nevertheless, in his 1867 review Adams, who had studied with Agassiz at Harvard, described Hutton's and Lyell's uniformitarianism as "certainly the most reasonable" of the two theoretical camps. As Adams reports, by the middle of the nineteenth century the views promulgated by Lyell in *Principles* had come to be understood by the majority of the educated reading public as mainstream geology. Ever since the first edition, Lyell's work had been "reprinted and widely read in America, where its views were commonly accepted."[15] It is the cultural privilege acquired by this particular body of theory, its wide dissemination and reception among the educated public, that is important for our understanding of how Americans thought about time. While many, including Agassiz and other important American scientists, continued to adhere to more of a catastrophist view well into the nineteenth century, by the late 1830s parties in both camps had come to accept the idea that the earth must be, at least, millions of years old, and that processes of geological change were continuing even in the present.

The importance of this shift in thinking about time quickly became apparent in scientific fields beyond geology itself. To cite only one important example, the discovery of geological time was a necessary precondition for Darwin's recognition of the evolutionary mechanism of natural selection, involving minute random changes over thousands or millions of years (readers of Darwin will recall his many geological observations). As Loren Eisley observes, "A change as vast as that existing between the Ptolemaic and the Copernican systems of the heavens had to be effected in Western thinking upon the subject of time before one could even contemplate the possibility of extensive organic change; the one idea is an absolute prerequisite to the other."[16] The discovery of geological time was, indeed, one of those great paradigm shifts whose importance to the history of science Thomas Kuhn has documented. Twain's intentionally absurd fusion of geological and biblical temporalities illustrates the sense of displacement engendered by this paradigm shift, as well as the extent to which the impact of this expansion of the temporal scale on Western thought went far beyond the natural sciences themselves. Adams credited his study of geology as a source of the "dynamic" theory of history he famously elaborated in the *Education*. Widespread acceptance of the notion that the earth was millions of years old prompted these and other social thinkers to reformulate their understanding of the human relationship to history and nature. If the naturalists of the Enlightenment era had fostered the notion that nature was a beautiful machine whose processes could be understood through the application of reason, the discovery of geological time prompted many thinkers in the nineteenth century to contemplate a nature whose immensity was beyond human comprehension.

An important painting by Frederic Edwin Church, *The Icebergs* (1861), encapsulates the feelings of awe and terror inspired by the sublimity of the natural forces revealed by geological theory. In the painting, a so-called erratic boulder and the mast of a wrecked ship serve as twin symbols of the power of nature and God (Illustration 4.1). Erratic boulders are found all over the world, often perched in seemingly impossible positions high upon mountains or balanced precariously one atop another. Before Agassiz published his work on glacier theory, most geologists had thought that such boulders were carried by water, whether ancient seas or massive floods. The erratic boulder thus had powerful religious connotations, since, according to this "diluvial" theory, one such flood would have been the biblical Deluge itself. In depicting the boulder carried across the ocean by the iceberg, a piece broken off from a glacier, Church's painting brings to life what were then the latest geological discoveries. The idea of massive sheets of ice carving stones from the sides of mountains seemed an awesome sign of the power of nature to shape the environment of human beings. The boulder, although much smaller than the iceberg, is positioned almost in the center

ILLUSTRATION 4.1. *Frederic Edwin Church,* The Icebergs, *1861.*
Oil on canvas, 64½ × 112½ inches (Dallas Museum of Art, anonymous gift)

of the painting. The iceberg is so large that it dominates the canvas even though only a portion of it is depicted. In a broadside written to accompany the painting, Church explains that all of the ice in the foreground and middle ground of the picture is intended to represent a single iceberg, most of which is, of course, submerged. Meanwhile, in the foreground lies the relatively tiny mast of a wrecked ship. Contemporary advertisements made note of the fact that Church's painting was based on scientific observation of real icebergs: "Painted from Studies made in the Northern Seas in the Summer of 1859" is how the work was advertised for its first exhibition in London.[17] Church had traveled in northern waters in order to observe icebergs firsthand and did several sketches and smaller paintings before undertaking his major composition on the subject. In the broadside, Church's naturalistic explanation of the characteristics of the ice depicted in the painting makes clear that the work is based on field observations and is intended to be as realistic as it is sublime. In addition to the scientific accuracy of the representation, however, the painting also conveys a religious theme. With its crow's nest, the fallen mast in the foreground forms the shape of a cross. This cross points directly toward the erratic boulder. The image is thus rich with possible meanings. The cross represents the possibility of salvation, yet, in pointing toward the boulder, it also alludes to God's wrath. Indeed, the ship to which this mast used to belong was not saved. The painting seems to depict humanity as lost or abandoned in the immensity of natural history. Hence, this image conveys one of the ironies of nineteenth-century science: the more human beings applied reason to understanding nature, the more inhuman the world threatened to become.

John McPhee has coined the evocative term "deep time" to express the abyssal character of the immense spans of time revealed by geological theory.[18] Adopting McPhee's term, Stephen Jay Gould observes that it is impossible for human beings to conceptualize time on such a scale with any degree of realism; as Gould puts it, "Deep time is so alien that we can really only comprehend it as metaphor." Hence, Gould notes, we seek to explain our relationship to natural history by analogizing time to other units of measurement: everyone has been taught that human history occupies but the last few inches of "the geological mile," for example.[19] It is this necessarily metaphorical quality of deep time that makes it so culturally important. In previous chapters of this book, we have seen that clock time was neither a property of machines themselves nor purely a cultural construct, but rather a fluid form of temporality arising continuously from the interactions between machines and human beings. Similarly, deep time was neither a property of the natural world itself nor a human invention. Rather, deep time arose out of persuasive interpretations of the natural world on the part of scientific thinkers who were capable of creating compelling narrative accounts of their discoveries.

Natural Theology in America

Both Church's *The Icebergs* and Twain's *Letters from the Earth* provide some indication of the difficulties that the emergence of deep time as a widely accepted scientific paradigm created for Christian theologians and the vast majority of lay people who continued to view the Bible as divine revelation. It had been easy for both scientifically minded theologians and devout scientists to reconcile biblical Creation with catastrophist theory, simply because catastrophism required so little time for its operation. However, as the nineteenth century progressed, most theologians eventually came to accept the mounting evidence in favor of the uniformitarian point of view, and, moreover, discovered that the new paradigm offered new forms of compatibility with Christian cosmology. If catastrophism had allowed some to continue to believe in the biblically derived 6,000-year chronology, then uniformitarianism at least held out the consolation of a cosmos organized by a benevolent controlling intelligence. As the *Southern Literary Messenger* put it in an 1839 review of William Buckland's *Geology and Mineralogy* (the fifth volume of the *Bridgewater Treatises*), "there is no reason to suppose it derogatory to the attributes of the Creator, that all the parts of this perfect machinery [of the earth], can keep on their destined motion, for a period of which we cannot form any conception."[20] The eight volumes of the *Bridgewater Treatises* and similar British works of Christian apology were favorably reviewed and commented upon in American periodicals and reprinted by American publishers. Because of its effort to reconcile natural history with Christian theology, this school of thought came to be called "natural theology" (this phrase had also provided the title for an enormously influential 1802 work by William Paley). Many important nineteenth-century scientists accepted the geological timescale of earth history while maintaining the older belief that the biblical account of the Creation of humankind had occurred only a few thousand years in the past. Georges Cuvier, for example, argued vigorously that while prehistoric animals might have existed millions of years in the past, there was no fossil evidence for the existence of human beings outside of the biblical time frame. Those who subscribed to such beliefs typically also emphasized the important role of the biblical Deluge in extinguishing previous species along with most of humankind (a position that Twain must have had in mind while writing *Letters from the Earth*). As John Lyon explains, Cuvier thought that the fossil record indicated that "the human race had existed for not much more than about 5,400 years since its rejuvenation by the great Flood described in the Pentateuch. According to the same Mosaic chronology, the period from Adam to Noah would be proportionately brief."[21] This was a point of view with which many Americans were sympathetic. An 1851 "Editor's Table" column in *Harper's*, probably written by Henry J. Raymond, made the claim that

> geology has created difficulties in the interpretation of certain parts of the Scriptures; but these are more than balanced by a most important aid, which in another respect, it is rendering to the cause of faith. The former are fast giving way before that sound interpretation of the primeval record which was maintained by some of the most learned and pious in the Church, centuries before the new science was ever dreamed of. The latter is gathering strength from every fresh discovery. We refer to the proof geology is furnishing of the late origin of the human race, and of the absolute necessity of ascribing it to a supernatural cause.[22]

Raymond, the founding editor of both *Harper's* and the *New York Times*, was an important Whig political figure and shaper of public opinion in the 1850s. Like many of his contemporaries, Raymond was taken with the idea that geological history was both progressive and guided by a divine hand. In addition, it was important to Raymond and most of his contemporaries that human beings continue to occupy a special place in the earth's history — precisely the view that Twain would later ridicule in *Letters from the Earth*. In the view of Raymond and many others like him, geological history could be integrated into a providential sense of America's national destiny. The North American continent had been formed by God for the special purpose of giving a home to the empire of liberty.

Adams's lengthy review essay and Raymond's column are only two examples of the assiduous attention the American press paid to the development of geological theory in Britain and continental Europe, both through book reviews and reprints of articles from British periodicals (a common practice for many American magazines at the time). "No science engages more attention at the present day than Geology," gushed a writer for *Scientific American* in 1847.[23] Lyell made two visits to America in the 1840s and published widely read travelogues describing both the rocks and the society and manners he encountered. Men of letters in the United States were delighted that an illustrious British intellectual not only had positive things to say about American society but also conducted field research in American territory. As a subject of international geological interest, the New World was not merely equal but perhaps even superior to the old. But Americans did not merely import their geology; the field was one of the most important branches of science in the United States, developed by influential native-born naturalists such as Benjamin Silliman, Amos Eaton, James Hall, Edward Hitchcock, and James D. Dana, as well as European immigrants such as Agassiz and Arnold Guyot. Although these men differed in their political affiliations, as a group they shared a progressive social vision that fused an Enlightenment-derived faith in the power of reason to solve human problems with Jacksonian optimism. The Scottish-born geologist William Maclure helped Robert Owen found the utopian community of New Harmony, Indiana, in 1826. Silliman founded the *American Journal of Science and the Arts*, or "Silliman's Journal" as it was popularly known, in 1818. The periodical frequently presented original fieldwork in geology by American researchers. By the time Hitchcock published his *Elementary Geology* in 1841, the *North American Review* was able to point with pride to the author's international scientific reputation and to his American originality: "Professor Hitchcock has been too long and favorably known to scientific men, both of the new world and of the old, to make it necessary for us to say, with what ample qualifications he undertakes the task before him. His work is no 'secondary formation,' based on the published works of European writers, but in every part bears the impress of acute and original observation."[24] As an American scientist conducting original research, Hitchcock was a source of national pride. But more than this, he was important because he was a geologist—a scientist who conducted original research of international importance on the very land on which the new nation was situated.

Hitchcock, professor of geology and president of Amherst College (and now remembered mostly for his influence on Emily Dickinson), was the foremost American proponent of natural theology. An active researcher—his *Geology of Massachusetts* (1833) was hailed as a model of fieldwork—Hitchcock was best known to the general public as the author of articles and books bearing titles such as "The Connection between Geology and Natural Religion" (1835) and *The Religion of Geology* (1851). His *Elementary Geology* (1840) provided a balanced account, from an overtly religious perspective, of contemporary geological theory for students in colleges and universities. In keeping with its intended use as a textbook, this work is composed mostly of technical descriptions and explanations of geological processes, but it also includes a substantial chapter titled "Connection between Geology and Natural and Revealed Religion." Here Hitchcock argues that "a minute examination of the works of creation as they now exist, discloses the infinite perfection of its Author, when they were brought into existence: and geology proves Him to have been unchangeably the same, through the vast periods of past duration, which that science shows to have elapsed since the original formation of the matter of our earth."[25] In this passage, in a manner typical of writings by many authors in this period, the ability to locate an orderly design in the uniformitarian theory seems to compensate Hitchcock for the potentially troubling expansion of the temporal scale. In *The Religion of Geology*, Hitchcock provided the most detailed American expression of natural theology, arguing that the "Mosaic account of creation" was not incompatible with discoveries in geology because the precise wording of the first chapter of Genesis left an unspecified amount of time between the initial creation of the earth and the later creation of human beings, and reiterating his core belief that the geological discovery of the vast ages of past time only made more visible the providential design of the Creator. This was the compromise at which Hitchcock arrived; over the course of his career, the different approaches he took to the problem provide a window onto the unsettled

ILLUSTRATION 4.2. A Bird's Eye View or Map of the Country from Lake Erie to Queenstown, exhibiting the Chasm formed by the retrograde movement of the Falls of Niagara. *Frontispiece to second American edition of* Introduction to Geology *(1833), by Robert Bakewell (Archives and Special Collections, Amherst College Library)*

state of geological theory in the period. His first writings, published before Lyell's *Principles*, unequivocally draw connections between catastrophist theory and such biblical events as the Great Flood. However, after 1830 this catastrophism is gradually mitigated by an increasing acceptance of uniformitarianism and a celebration of intelligent design in nature.[26]

The ability to locate signs of providence through geological study made the science an even more compelling way to assert the viability and providential destiny of American nationhood. The language of geological description that took shape in America merged scientific observation with religious teleology to create an iconography of cultural nationalism. American editions of British geological texts could be nationalized so as to emphasize the importance of the New World. For example, American editions of the British researcher Robert Bakewell's *Introduction to Geology* featured a "supplement" (actually a lengthy, original essay) by Silliman, offering his own interpretations of many of the topics discussed in the text. In addition, these editions featured as the frontispiece an illustration titled the "Chasm formed by the retrograde movement of the Falls of Niagara" (Illustration 4.2). Bakewell had toured North America in 1820 and famously calculated the rate at which Niagara was eroding its channel. When Lyell toured the United States in 1841, he visited the falls and reported in his travelogue that he thought the rate likely to be much slower than what Bakewell had suggested. Thus, one of America's best-known symbols of national identity became the object of an important dispute between two eminent British scientists. The *Democratic Review* explained how Lyell's slower rate of erosion implied a longer stretch of geological time for the falls to have arrived in their present form, writing that "our author has allowed thousands of years to the duration of the glacial period; other thousands rise before him as he considers the gradual emergence of the land from beneath the glacial sea, and then the falls begin within the present fossiliferous era, like a sublime clepsydra, to keep an account of those numerous centuries, that are but the moments of a geological day."[27]

A clepsydra, or water clock, is among the most ancient of human chronometers. Clepsydrae were notoriously unreliable due to the difficulty of maintaining the flow of water at a constant pace.[28] In calling Niagara a "sublime clepsydra," the *Democratic Review* renders the geological time marked by the water eroding the rocks superior to the human efforts to measure time in a mechanical device. In addition, the metaphor calls attention to Niagara's status as a national symbol because it was precisely the sublimity of the falls, their perfect expression of the ideals of a privileged aesthetic category, that made them important. Henry Rowe Schoolcraft writes:

> Sublime Niagara, glittering in the van;
> Pouring, as oft the traveler stops to hear,
> An Illiad of waters on the ear.[29]

As a natural epic poem, Niagara plays the same foundational role in American culture that the *Iliad* was understood to have played for the Greeks. As a "sublime clepsydra," then, the falls symbolize the sublimity of American national time, the awesome time imminent in the land of the nation. The fact that this phenomenon was noted by the two famous British scientists placed American time in the context of world history, situating American national identity in relation to the global progress of time through the "thousands of years" of the history of the earth.

American Territory and World Time

"While the republic has already acquired a history worldwide," Thoreau wrote in "Ktaadn" (1848), "America is still unsettled and unexplored." The lack Thoreau perceived was the connection of American territory to world history. Thus far, settlers had discovered "only the shores of America" —

this lament coming forty-five years after the Louisiana Purchase, in the year that Wisconsin became a state.[30] The universality of geological theory promised to reveal the deep connections between the American land and world history. Just as stadialist narratives made America part of universal history while also holding out the possibility that the United States might chart a new course through time due to its exceptional circumstances, the unique features of the American landscape could be taken to represent the exceptional role in the history of the earth that providence intended for the North American continent. In his *Manual of Geology* (1863), James D. Dana described for an audience of students and fellow professors how the particular physical situation of North America made it an ideal model of the progress of geological processes over time:

> On account of a peculiar simplicity and unity, American Geological History affords the best basis for a text-book of the science. North America stands alone in the ocean, a simple isolated specimen of a continent (even South America lying to the eastward of its meridians), and the laws of progress have been undisturbed by the conflicting movements of other lands. The author has, therefore, written out American Geology by itself, as a continuous history. Facts have, however, been added from other continents so far as was required to give completeness to the work and exhibit strongly the comprehensiveness of its principles.[31]

Dana's emphasis on the isolation of North America mimics nineteenth-century political rhetoric that described the position of the United States in relation to the rest of the world. Even American political thinkers such as Jefferson who favored strong cultural and intellectual connections between the United States and Europe felt that the geographical isolation of the United States would make it uniquely well suited to the development of democratic institutions, since its isolation would protect it from the effects of the wars and other catastrophes that regularly befell Europe. Dana develops this same idea out of the land itself, thus producing, through a shared vocabulary, consonance between natural and political history. In his review of Dana's *Manual*, Asa Gray, himself a noted American scientist, emphasized this quasipolitical isolation of the American continent even more strongly than Dana had done in his textbook:

> In studying the evolution of continents, Professor Dana turns with a natural preference to North America. This, he assures us, is a normal continent, a model specimen, standing by itself between the oceans, vast

enough fully to exemplify the system, and with no contiguous lands to disturb or complicate the action of the organizing forces. Its geology is correspondingly simple, normal, and the best fitted for the discovery and illustration of the grand principles of the science. Europe, on the contrary, is in close contact with Africa and Asia; indeed, a large part of it is only the western border of the Great Orient, answering to North America west of the Rocky Mountains; accordingly, its geological, like its civil history, is marked with complexity, conflict, and confusion; it is full of cross-purposes and incongruities, is broken up into many basins, and broken out into mountains of all ages, even down to the tertiary. It is better adapted for the study of special and subsidiary questions than for the clear exhibition of the general phenomena of the earth's structure, and of the general laws that govern them. These are best learned from the simpler geology of our own continent.[32]

Gray makes explicit what Dana had been content to leave implicit: the connection between natural and civil history. More than tracing cause and effect, Gray makes these two kinds of history equivalent. It is not simply that Europe's "mountains of all ages" and proximity to other continents (evidently populated by rather suspect people) have resulted in a confused political history. More importantly, Europe's geological and civil histories are "like"; that is, they display the same fundamental logic. By collapsing the distinction between natural and civil history, Gray implies that the United States, seated in the "model" continent of North America, provides the model for national development. The exceptional qualities of the American geographical situation will enable it to become universal, establishing a paradigm for other nations to follow in the future.

The structural parallels between civil and geological history theorized by scientists such as Dana and Gray made a new political vocabulary available to nongeologists who followed their work (as anyone who read the *North American Review* or just about any other American periodical in the nineteenth century could not help but do). Geological time was integrated into national history, thus reshaping the models of national development that Americans had inherited from eighteenth-century Europe. According to classic stadialism, a nation would progress through the various stages of history while expanding from and contracting back into the same geographical center. The language that scientists such as Dana and Gray made available offered another possibility, that stadialist development might progress further in the New World than it had in the Old World. In an 1851 essay loosely inspired by Guyot's *The Earth and Man* (1849), a writer for the *American Whig Review* traced the geological changes that had shaped the landscape of North America and then connected these natural processes seamlessly to the development and spread of democratic political institutions across the continent:

> On the skirts of civilization, unnoticed and in silence as the leaves grow at night, young States yearly germinate into life. Without strife, unconvulsed, almost without thought, quietly and naturally as the sap ascends the tree, these principalities, that yesterday were not, to-day take their seats in the world's councils. This is a link in the chain of events which began in Asia, and for which, through cycles of time, the earth's surface had been fitted. Distinct, yet homogeneous, wherever a handful of men of the nineteenth century meet, society instantly crystallizes into government.[33]

According to this author, the beginnings of civilization had emerged in Asia, but the "Asiatic steppes" were suited only for "the pastoral cohorts of the young world." Government in Asia had never progressed beyond a primitive despotism. Meanwhile, Europe lent itself to greater advancement because its mountainous terrain provided natural geographical divisions (note that this is a rather different interpretation of the same mountainous terrain described by Dana and Gray). These divisions encouraged the undifferentiated mass of humanity to disperse into smaller "localized and individualized" forms of political organization, a development that ultimately led to a greater emphasis on the individual. "Each tribe developed its type," our author explains, "and the individual man began to put forth powers and energies which hitherto had belonged alone to numbers."

While Europe prepared the way for democracy by encouraging this process of individuation, its limited amount of arable land ultimately meant that humanity could progress no further there. Only in North America could the individualism developed in the mazelike European landscape blossom into full-fledged democratic government, for the "superabundant natural wealth of the new world, too vast for the unassisted energies of infant humanity, is reserved as the field of the labors of its manhood." The author fuses natural history with stadialism, showing how the earth has providentially been formed through geological processes to take shapes appropriate to each stage of advancing civilization, moving always into the west in accordance with the *translatio imperii* that Berkeley had conveyed in his famous poem. In the end, the author speculates, the swelling population of North America will complete the circle by "bringing back the light of a new day to the ancient homes of the human family." This last development is described in rather apocalyptic terms; throughout the essay, providence plays an important role in both natural and human history, and the prophecy that a fully mature American civilization would one day begin migrating into Asia can only be described as millenarian. Science, theology, and history coalesce into one vision of national development through time.

Vertical Time

While writers such as Dana, Gray, and the anonymous *American Whig Review* author analyzed the surface features of geology for their relation to human history, others perceived that the truly novel and powerful aspect of geological theory lay in the verticality of deep time. That is to say, while progressive accounts of history often depicted time advancing horizontally across space, the geological revolution made it possible to imagine time extending perpendicularly into the territory beneath the nation. Jefferson and others had envisioned national time spreading like bands on a two-dimensional map across the continent from east to west. Jefferson's description of the progress of society, in his 1824 letter to William Ludlow, stopped at the Rocky Mountains, as though that geological disruption of the flat, fertile plains marked the proper boundary of a nation. Although Jefferson was fascinated by fossils (and even gave an address to the American Philosophical Society on the bones of the "megalonyx" found in Virginia), he died too early to assimilate deep time into his thinking. The arrival of modern geological theory in America made it possible for later writers to spin the Jeffersonian national temporality on its axis and plunge it directly down into the earth. In the graphical representations of American geological features that were quite popular in the nineteenth century, the built environment of human beings is typically depicted as the final layer atop the strata extending deeply below. Edward and Orra White Hitchcock's *Plates Illustrating the Geology and Scenery of Massachusetts* (1832) includes a long foldout cross-section of the topography of the state, with the names of towns worked into the folds of the crust of the earth (Illustration 4.3).[34] Engravings depicting typical scenes from around the state then contextualize human activity within the framework of this topography. The illustration *Sugar Loaf Mountain, Deerfield*, for example, shows houses and a boundary fence at the feet of a sharp elevation showing the lines of rock strata that have been pushed up from below (Illustration 4.4). Other pictures show human activities such as boats moving along a river or men fishing, situated within signifi-

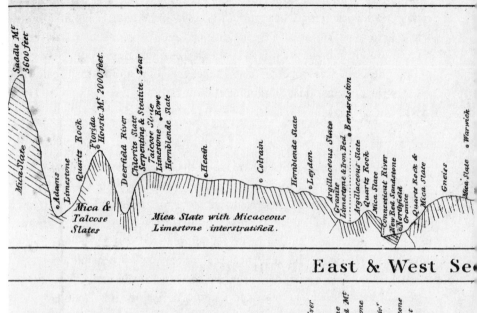

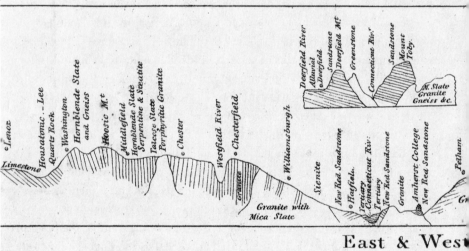

ILLUSTRATION 4.3. *Detail from "East and West Sections in Massachusetts," from* Plates Illustrating the Geology and Scenery of Massachusetts *(1833), by Edward Hitchcock and Orra White Hitchcock (Edward and Orra White Hitchcock Papers, Archives and Special Collections, Amherst College Library)*

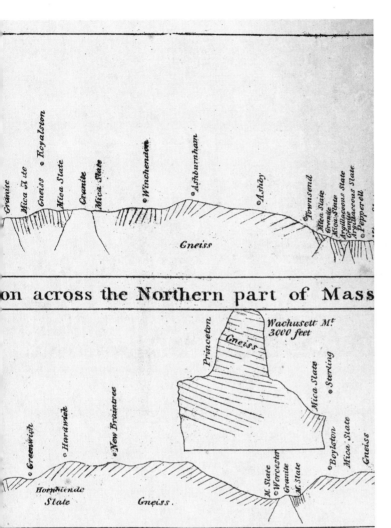

Granite
Mica Slate
Gneiss · Royalston
Mica Slate
Granite
Mica Slate
· Winchendon
· Ashburnham
· Ashby
· Townsend
Mica Slate
Granite
Mica Slate
Argillaceous Slate
Granite
Argillaceous Slate
· Pepperell

Gneiss

on across the Northern part of Mass

Wachusett M.t
3000 feet

Princeton
Gneiss
Mica Slate
· Sterling

· Greenwich
· Hardwick
· New Braintree
· Boylston
Mica Slate
Gneiss

Hornblende
Slate
Gneiss.
M. Slate
· Worcester
Granite
M. Slate

Section across the Central parts of N

SUGAR LOAF MOUNTAIN, DEERFIELD.

ILLUSTRATION 4.4. *Orra White Hitchcock,* Sugar Loaf Mountain, Deerfield, *from* Plates Illustrating the Geology and Scenery of Massachusetts *(1833), by Edward Hitchcock and Orra White Hitchcock (Edward and Orra White Hitchcock Papers, Archives and Special Collections, Amherst College Library)*

cant geological features. Finally, the book ends with several pages devoted to engravings of fossils that had been dug out of the earth of North America. Through artistic representations of geological formations, Americans aestheticized not merely the land but time itself, and thus became conscious of a new way of understanding their geographical and temporal position as a nation; rather than thinking about temporal change in terms of the progress of history from east to west, the old *translatio imperii,* deep time situated the nation atop a vast compendium of rock strata saturated with millions of years of natural history, progressing upwards from the remote past toward the present-day world of the surface. Hence, the American nation might be described as emerging through time from below rather than arriving on the eastern seaboard as the residue of European history.

   The popular religious writer John Harris invited his readers to imagine time in this vertical way in *The Pre-Adamite Earth* (1849). Harris's fanciful narrative guides readers on an imaginary journey through the different rock strata from the surface to the deepest recesses of the earth, "beyond the limits of recorded time."[35] As tour guide, Harris separates the strata into their proper periods according to then-current geological theory and takes note of the fossils that would be found in each layer. As Harris and his readers descend, he offers a series of different metaphors for deep time, each connoting different qualities. At first, descending into the earth evokes ancient mythology:

> As we descend through these, one of the most sublime fictions of mythology becomes sober truth, for at our every step an age flies past. We find ourselves on a road where the lapse of duration is marked — not by the succession of seasons and of years, — but by the slow excavation, by water, of deep valleys in rock marble; by the return of a continent to the bosom of an ocean in which ages before it had been slowly formed; or by the departure of one world and the formation of another. (67)

In reaching back to classical mythology, Harris suggests that the "pre-Adamite earth" is also pre-Christian, a pagan realm that precedes the more modern Christian world. The description of marble eroded by water over millennia also conjures up classical antiquity, for marble was best known as the building material of classical ruins in the Old World and neoclassical buildings in the New World. Invoking the aesthetic category of the sublime suggests a response of awe to this ancient substructure of the Christian world; it is a "world" whose "departure" was part of the deep history of "another," that is, the modern world of Harris and his readers. In other words, it is a world that is now forever beyond reach. Nevertheless, the overall effect of Harris's description is to render deep time more accessible. It is a myth, it is an ancient ruin — hence, it is subject to assimilation into culture.

Harris continues this work of assimilation as he imagines himself and his readers moving downward into another stratum of rock, one that offers "new proofs of the dateless antiquity of the earth." Explaining that the "oolitic" strata were deposited through the action of water over thousands of years, Harris observes that "so gradual and tranquil was the operation, that, in some places, the organic remains of the successive strata are arranged with a shelf-like regularity, reminding us of the well-ordered cabinet of the naturalist" (68). Having begun by looking to classical antiquity for a kind of prehistory of time, Harris now moves to the Enlightenment for a metaphor from science. Americans were quite familiar with the "well-ordered" cabinets, displayed in museums and pictured in magazines, that brought design to the apparent chaos of the natural world. Hence, Harris renders deep time wonderful—the giant shelves composed of rock strata—and comprehensible, just the response that cabinets in museums hoped to elicit. Finally, Harris concludes the strange journey by considering how the knowledge of deep time's existence might require a reevaluation of the significance of human history:

> Can we think of the thin soil of man's few thousand years, in contrast with the succession of worlds we have passed through . . . without acknowledging that the days and years of geology are ages and cycles of ages! Let us conceive, if we can, that the atoms of one of these strata have formed the sands of an hour-glass, and that each grain counted a moment, and we may then make some approximation to the past periods of geology; periods in the computation of which the longest human dynasty, and even the date of the pyramids, would form only an insignificant fraction. (70–71)

In comparing deep time to the time told by an hourglass, Harris suggests at once the enormous difference between the two, as well as the notion that this difference is one of degree, rather than kind. Deep time, Harris assures his readers, is the same phenomenon of time with which they are familiar; it is simply more expansive. Indeed, representing deep time does not even require the complicated technics of a clock. It is as familiar and comprehensible as the traditional hourglass that New England ministers employed to time their sermons during the seventeenth and eighteenth centuries. America lies on the uppermost layer of this vast repository of time, its history forming only an "insignificant fraction" of the whole, yet connected through its own marble structures, naturalists' cabinets, and hourglasses. As a progressive time akin to that which Jefferson had imagined striated across the land, deep time provides the grand foundation for America, culminating in the uppermost stratum, American history.

Thoreau's "Ktaadn" also contextualizes American history as the uppermost layer of a vertical continuum of deep time. The essay describes how a young Thoreau and a small group of friends ascended the eponymous mountain, located in Maine, in 1846. After the party has left the last vestiges of civilization behind, Thoreau marks the real beginning of the adventure by indicating the time at which the group sets out, six o'clock, for the mountain, "distant, as Uncle George said the boatmen called it, about four miles, but as I judged, and as it proved, nearer fourteen" (56). The uncertainty of the mountain's distance contrasts with the accurately known clock time of their departure; the journey to the mountain takes them away from the precision of modern life and toward a primeval land whose temporal location can only be described in mythic terms. As they approach, the naked rock of Ktaadn looms up in a bare ridge, "and we looked up at this blue barrier as if it were some fragment of a wall which anciently bounded the earth in that direction" (57). Thoreau knew well that mountains were rock thrust upward from deep inside the earth, and so Ktaadn represents the most ancient part of nature, rock once buried in the foundations of the world. It is appropriate, then, that Thoreau's party must travel there without "the slightest trace of man to guide us," for they are leaving the temporal realm in which humanity emerged and entering a different, more ancient world (56). As Thoreau describes the approach, he emphasizes the mountain's mythic quality by noting that it is only briefly perceptible at certain intervals of the journey: "At length we reached an elevation sufficiently bare to afford a view of the summit, still distant and blue, almost as if retreating from us" (59). As they get closer to Ktaadn's peak, they note that it is shrouded in clouds, symbolizing its mythic and unlocatable quality. Like the deep time from which it emerged, Ktaadn cannot really be seen. The route to the peak takes them up a ravine that is like "a giant's stairway" (60). With this image, Thoreau suggests the smallness and fragility of human existence in contrast to the vast scale of geological time. The world, Thoreau implies, was made for beings on a grand scale, and humanity only inhabits it awkwardly and transiently.

At first, Thoreau finds this natural grandeur compelling and is eager to experience more. On the second day of the narrative, when the party begins the final ascent of the peak, Thoreau leads the way and makes such speed, in his excitement, that he leaves his companions behind. "I climbed alone over huge rocks," he recounts, "loosely poised, a mile or more, still edging toward the clouds — for though the day was clear elsewhere, the summit was concealed by mist" (63). By emphasizing his aloneness and the contrast between the large size of the rocks and his own small body, Thoreau points to the ephemeral nature of the human being in relation to nature. The fact that the summit alone is covered in clouds suggests that it is a mythic place apart from the time of the present — "the day." After an arduous climb, Thoreau enters into this cloud realm and notes its seemingly eternal nature: "At length I entered into the skirts of the cloud which seemed forever drifting over the summit, and yet would never be gone, but was generated out of that pure air as fast as it flowed away" (63). This image of clouds that drift but never disappear suggests a possible form of transcendent being that Thoreau, by climbing the mountain, hopes to experience himself.

The mood of the essay changes when Thoreau reaches the cloudy region near the peak and realizes that this primal environment is alien to human beings. While Harris had had to imagine descending miles into the earth in order to discover the farthest reaches of time, Thoreau encounters what seems to be the beginning of the world at high altitude:

> The mountain seemed a vast aggregation of loose rocks, as if sometime it had rained rocks, and they lay as they fell on the mountain sides, nowhere fairly at rest, but leaning on each other, all rocking-stones, with cavities between, but scarcely any soil or smoother shelf. They were the raw materials of a planet dropped from an unseen quarry, which the vast chemistry of nature would anon work up, or work down, into the smiling and verdant plains and valleys of earth. This was an undone extremity of the globe; as in lignite we see coal in the process of formation. (63)

In this originary place, the beginning of time, Thoreau relies more and more upon metaphor—a quarry, chemistry, and finally mythology. "It reminded me of the creations of the old epic and dramatic poets, of Atlas, Vulcan, the Cyclops, and Prometheus," Thoreau explains. "It was vast, Titanic, and such as man never inhabits" (64). In contrast to Harris's humanizing myth, Thoreau employs the idea of a mythic prehistory to excavate nature's deep unfriendliness to human beings. "She seems to say sternly," Thoreau imagines, "why came ye here before your time?" (64). Later, reflecting upon his ascent, Thoreau admits that "it is difficult to conceive of a region uninhabited by man" (70). The habitual anthropomorphism of the human perception of nature both renders the reality of deep time invisible and leaves Thoreau helpless when he stumbles upon this primal scene, not yet given its "smiling" aspect and made palatable to human beings. It is an "undone" place, and Thoreau's language is undone by his attempt to represent it in what becomes increasingly futile figurative language.

Finally tearing himself out of the awestruck reverie with which he beholds the barren peak, Thoreau descends to a plateau where he finds his companions picking wild blueberries and cranberries. As they descend, they are able to see across the Maine wilderness for miles in every direction. Thoreau describes the forest below as "a firm grass sward" or "a farm for somebody, when cleared" (66). The party finally reaches the boat they had used as transport "by two o'clock" in the afternoon (71). They have returned to their own temporal frame.

Thoreau's description of his journey leaves his readers with a three-dimensional representation of national time. The horizontal plain of the present stretches to the horizons below the mountain, ready for domestication by families of settlers, while Ktaadn punctures the plain and pushes skyward, a perpendicular vector of time extending from deep within the earth and spiking through the national territory to disappear into the heavens. Ktaadn's towering presence represents the nation's movement through a history too long for human beings to conceive. Far above the plain of the present, the future remains veiled in clouds. "I am reminded by my journey," Thoreau remarks toward the end of the essay, "how exceedingly new this country still is" (81).

Deep Time and Stadialism

Thomas Cole employs this vertical understanding of deep time to provide a counterpoint to the stadialist historical narrative depicted in *The Course of Empire*. As Rebecca Bedell explains, *The Course of Empire* features the same erratic boulder occupying a prominent position in the background of each of the five paintings in the series. The boulder remains changeless as the empire depicted in the foreground undergoes its cycle of rise and decline. When Cole completed the series in the 1830s, before Agassiz had won widespread support for glacial theory, such boulders were thought by most influential geological theorists to have been deposited by water, including the biblical Deluge. By placing an erratic boulder in the background of his allegory of power and corruption, Cole provides a theological context for judging human history. A wrathful God had destroyed human civilization before and might do so again.[36] Cole conceptualized the paintings around the same time that Lyell's *Principles* was first published. When he completed these works, the artist had evidently read Lyell (I shall discuss the evidence for this below) but nevertheless still subscribed to the catastrophist view of geological change. This perspective was consonant with his use of the boulder to allude to the Deluge, since that most famous of biblical catastrophes was often cited as evidence of the compatibility of the Bible with geological theory. Cole's diluvian understanding of the provenance of erratic boulders seems to imply a God whose agency is more immediate in the world than the God suggested by Church's boulder in *The Icebergs*. Church, who was at one time a student of Cole, gestures toward religion with the forlorn image of the cross-shaped mast in the foreground of his painting. Cole, in contrast, places a sign of God's agency atop the mountain that looms over every image in the series.

What is interesting about the depiction of geological time in the paint-

ILLUSTRATION 4.5. *Thomas Cole,* The Subsiding of the Waters of the Deluge, *1829. Oil on canvas, 35¾ × 47¾ inches (Smithsonian American Art Museum; gift of Mrs. Katie Dean in memory of Minnibel S. and James Wallace Dean and museum purchase through the Smithsonian Institution Collections Acquisition Program)*

ings, then, is the absence of change. If Cole placed the erratic boulder in such a prominent position in each painting in the series in order to allude to geological catastrophes, as it seems clear he did, then *Destruction* might be expected to depict the earth shaking, a volcano erupting, flood waters rising, or, at least, the boulder tumbling from its perch. The final painting, *Desolation*, might similarly have shown not merely the ruins of human structures but an entire ruined landscape, scarred by earthquakes and defaced by floods. Cole had depicted just such a landscape in his earlier painting, *The Subsiding of the Waters of the Deluge* (1829) (Illustration 4.5). In this piece, Cole places the broken mast of a ship and a human skull in conjunction with jagged rocks that seem to have been tossed everywhere by the enormous forces of the flood. As Bedell observes, "Cole's inclusion of the jumbled masses of rocks in the foreground and boulders balanced on mountain peaks in the distance clearly indicate that he associated these geological features with the Biblical flood."[37] Since Cole had employed such imagery shortly before he began *The Course of Empire*, it is striking that he chose not to use it again in his epic series in order to illustrate how the processes of natural history provide the models for the cycles of human history. By choosing, instead, to leave the geological features in the painting unchanged throughout *The Course of Empire*, Cole distinguishes the violent events and rapid changes of human history from nature. As human history progresses, in natural history nothing appears to happen. The scale of geological time, even within Cole's understanding of the catastrophist paradigm, is so great that it frames and supercedes the events of human history. At some point in the distant past, the series invites viewers to imagine, some cataclysmic event deposited the erratic boulder upon the top of the cliff. While human history might replicate such cataclysms, the decades or, at most, centuries of imperial demesne play out in tiny irrelevance against the background of deep time.

Cole further complicates the tension between natural and human history through his use of shifting perspective in the series. In the first painting, *The Savage State*, the boulder atop the cliff is almost exactly in the center of the canvas (Illustration 4.6). The boulder dominates the entire image; even the other mountain peak is veiled in clouds and barely visible. Meanwhile, an American Indian village to the right of the canvas is oddly balanced against a hunter on the far left whose garb, hair, and pose connote models from European classical antiquity. Additional human figures of indeterminate cultural origin are scattered about the landscape. The amalgamation of different cultures beneath the dominating image of the erratic boulder implies the subordination of human history to what would seem to be a universal origin in a natural world characterized not so much by plants and animals as by the geological forces that shaped this landscape. That is, the time of different "empires," whose origin stadialists located in such primitive scenes as this, arises from a mythic, common prehistory in the earth itself. In the subsequent panels, Cole shifts the position of the cliff and erratic boulder in order to suggest different relationships between geological time and the events of human history represented in the foreground of each panel. In the second panel, *The Pastoral State*, the boulder has moved to the left of the canvas and a round stone structure reminiscent of Stonehenge has taken its place in the center. Nature's stone has shifted into the background in favor of stones shaped by human art. However, the tall peak in the far background of the painting has emerged from its veil of clouds, providing a more distant

ILLUSTRATION 4.6. *Thomas Cole,* The Course of Empire: The Savage State, *1834. Oil on canvas, 39¼ × 63¼ inches (Collection of the New-York Historical Society)*

signal of the power of geological time to reshape stone in ways human beings cannot. The artificial stone structure catches the viewer's attention first, but it quickly comes to seem small and less significant in relation to the immense mountain towering vertically above and behind it. In *The Consummation of Empire*, the boulder has moved across the canvas to the right side, where it forms a line parallel to that of the statue of Minerva that is the most striking image in the center of the canvas. The mountain on which the boulder is perched has been covered with white marble buildings, while the larger, more distant mountain is now entirely absent from the scene.

In the final two paintings of Cole's series, nature once again asserts its dominance of the scene. In *Destruction*, the erratic boulder has moved back into the center of the canvas and is now given further prominence by a circle of light shining from a distant point in the sky. This formal structure draws the viewer's eye upwards along the line of the cliff face and into the sky. In contrast, the buildings sitting horizontally on the mountain's more gradually sloping side are obscured by the dark smoke that dominates the foreground of the painting. In the last image, *Desolation*, the boulder shifts to the right, blending in with the ruins of the once-great empire, formally bal-

ILLUSTRATION 4.7. *Thomas Cole,* The Course of Empire: Desolation, *1836.*
Oil on canvas, 39¼ × 63 inches (Collection of the New-York Historical Society)

anced against a large column in the left foreground (Illustration 4.7). The
human artifacts in all of the paintings, such as the round stone temple or
the statue of Minerva, seem to echo the formal structures found in nature,
but because the built environment tends to obscure nature, the impression
left by the series is that the builders of those artifacts are unaware of these
echoes. Nature has shaped human activity powerfully but subtly. In addition, the built environment's mimicry of nature is attenuated. The flatness of
the round stone temple against the ground contrasts with the soaring height
of the mountain behind it. Throughout all five paintings, human activity is
confined primarily to a horizontal plain in the bottom half of the canvas,
while the vertical line of the mountain's cliff face extends through the erratic
boulder and toward the top of the canvas. The presence of this geological
signifier standing in the background of the history of the imaginary empire
depicted in the foregrounds of the paintings produces a tension between
two different temporalities. Like Thoreau's "Ktaadn," Cole's *The Course of
Empire* attempts to capture the mystery of deep time by representing it as
perpendicular to the horizontal plain in which human activity takes place.
Through this spatial metaphor, the artist conveys the heterogeneity of na-

tional time. Two different processes of change operate simultaneously — one observable, the other mysterious and ultimately, Cole suggests, of far greater significance.

The Geology of Ruin

In *Desolation*, Cole leaves the viewer with a juxtaposition of ruined classical buildings and geological features that would have seemed quite familiar to his contemporaries. The formal relationship between the deteriorating column and the vertical line of the cliff face and boulder is crucial to the mysterious relationship between the different temporal frames. Lyell had inaugurated a vogue of such comparisons when he used an engraving of the ruins of the Temple of Jupiter Serapis, at Pozzuoli near Naples, as the frontispiece to the first edition of *Principles*. Hitchcock's *Elementary Geology* and Dana's *Manual of Geology* would later make the same association of ruined structures with geological processes. Dana rewrote, in his own words, Lyell's analysis of how the marks and remains of shellfish on the columns revealed that the temple had been covered with water at some point, and the manual included a different illustration of the temple (Illustration 4.8). In addition to the evidence of immersion provided by the shellfish, Dana noted that the temple was still moving up and down in a way that was noticeable to the local population: "The pavement of the temple is now submerged. Five feet below it there is a second pavement, proving that these oscillations had gone on before the temple was deserted by the Romans. It has been recently stated that for some time previous to 1845 a slow sinking had been going on, and since then there has been as gradual a rising."[38] This finding was important because it provided proof that the land on which the temple stood had shifted vertically, relative to the level of the sea, during the time in which the temple had existed. This movement proved that geological changes in the earth were still going on in the present, an important component of uniformitarian theory.

The particular ruin that Lyell, Hitchcock, and Dana all used as an example was well known to Americans as a popular stop on European tours. Nathaniel Parker Willis described the Temple of Jupiter Serapis for American readers in an 1853 European travelogue:

> This was one of the largest and richest of the temples of antiquity. It was a quadrangular building, near the edge of the sea, lined with marble, and sustained by columns of solid cipolino, three of which are still standing.

ILLUSTRATION 4.8. *The Temple of Jupiter Serapis, illustration from* Manual of Geology, *by James D. Dana (first edition 1863; reproduction from 1866 edition)*

It was buried by an earthquake and forgotten for a century or two, till in 1750 it was discovered by a peasant, who struck the top of one of the columns in digging. We stepped around over the prostrate fragments, building it up once more in fancy, and peopling the aisles with priests and worshippers. In the centre of the temple was the place of sacrifice, raised by flights of steps, and at the foot still remained two rings of Corinthian brass, to which the victims were fastened, and near them the receptacles for their blood and ashes. The whole scene has a stamp of grandeur.[39]

Willis's description of the temple reflects what David Levin calls the "attitude toward the Past that one can find in almost any literary young American's letters home from Europe" in this period. I cite Willis's very conventional response for its representative quality. The ruin was a *topos* of the past, and as such it contained a standard package of ideas about the mutability and impermanence of the works of human beings; these ideas are adequately captured in Levin's pithy phrase, "the inclination to wallow in sentiment at the sight of ruins."[40] The very conventionality of the ruin indicates how completely it has been processed into the symbolic vocabulary of the culture; it is fully encoded with well-understood meaning. In this respect, the ruin represents the antithesis of incomprehensible deep time, and hence, the conjunction of the two presents an interpretive problem. It was all too easy to imagine that the movement of the ruin in response to geological forces meant that the ruin was somehow coextensive with geological time. The ruin provides a representational medium through which deep time is also brought within the circle of the known. What geologists really wanted to show, however, was that the vastness of deep time rendered the ruin's few centuries parochial.

Silliman grappled with this problem in his "Supplement" to the third edition of Bakewell's *Introduction to Geology*, where he also employed the idea of the ruin to reiterate Lyell's position regarding the ongoing nature of geological change. While Lyell and Dana had been content merely to show how human ruins moved with geological time, Silliman sought for a more elaborate trope that would represent the accretive process of change over time. Silliman struck upon the device of comparing geological change to the progressive development of a city:

The earth is unlike Memphis, Thebes, Persopolis, Babylon, Balbec or Palmyra, which present merely confused and mutilated masses of colossal and beautiful architecture, answering no purpose except to gratify curiosity, and to awaken a sublime and pathetic moral feeling; it is rather like modern Rome, replete indeed with the ruins of the ancient city, in part rearranged for purposes of utility and ornament, but also covered by the regular and perfect constructions of subsequent centuries.[41]

In rejecting the long list of abandoned cities as unsuitable, Silliman makes clear that geological change is an ongoing process. The earth moves perpetually beneath the feet of human beings whose senses are not attuned to the proper scale to perceive the movement. Hence, the earth is like an ancient city that continues to add new layers of construction on top of the old. Silliman's choice of Rome for his simile is especially intriguing given that this is the same city Freud would employ several decades later to illustrate his theory of the subconscious mind. Silliman's reference to "regular and perfect constructions" seems to represent the effort to contain or manage the problem of deep time. Geological theory imposed system upon something that was really incomprehensible through the use of inevitably somewhat arbitrary tropes. Similarly, Freud cautions his readers that the mind is not truly like a city. The subconscious can only be perceived obliquely and with less than perfect accuracy through figurative language. Most importantly, the spatial metaphor falls short because "if we want to represent historical sequence in spatial terms we can only do it by juxtaposition in space: the same space cannot have two different contents."[42] In this respect, then, Silliman makes the human relationship to deep time rather similar to the relationship Freud posits between the conscious and the unconscious mind. While it would be absurd to put too much interpretive pressure on this apparently coincidental choice of similes, understanding how Freud uses the Roman example does help us to see what Silliman is reaching for. In Freud's theory, the behavior of the conscious mind is shaped by the unconscious mind, yet this influence is deeply buried and the conscious mind forgets, in a sense, its true situation and motivations. Freud sees in Rome, then, a way to represent a powerful force that perpetually acts in hidden ways upon the everyday experience of which people are consciously aware. This force is an unacknowledged but intrinsic and essential part of that which it influences. Silliman wants to say something very similar about the relationship between deep time and the time of everyday life. Deep time is the real environment of humanity, yet human beings forget their true provenance and imagine that they inhabit a world small enough for them to understand. Despite this forgetting, deep time continues to shape the time of everyday experience. The spatial metaphors that Silliman and other writers and artists employed to try to represent deep time could never convey the thing itself. Deep time is the true medium of change for the earth and all of the biological organisms on it, yet it is beyond perception or understanding.

In all of Cole's many depictions of ruins in his landscapes, deep time seems to have come to the surface only in *The Course of Empire*. Cole had done a pencil sketch entitled *Ruins, or the Effects of Time*, in 1832 or 1833 when he was conceptualizing *The Course of Empire*. This sketch depicts a row of columns very similar to those in the engraving in Lyell's *Principles*. Elwood C. Parry III points out that it is hard to believe, based on the formal similarity of the images, that Cole had not read and been influenced by *Principles* when he made this sketch. However, Cole's reaction to *Principles* was evidently at least partly restrained, for his notes to the sketch prescribe a catastrophist interpretation of how "the effects of time" have brought the temple to its ruined state: "Broken mountains with huge rocks which seem to have descended from there and overturned columns in their downward course to the sea where a fragment is yet seen above the waves."[43] These notes place natural and human history within a unified temporal frame; both share the same catastrophic process of change. Over a decade later, Cole would produce remarkably similar descriptions of the ruins he encountered as a tourist in Sicily, published as "Sicilian Scenery and Antiquities," in the *Knickerbocker* magazine in 1844. "On every side of this elevated field," Cole wrote of the Temple of Jupiter Olympius, "lie the walls, entablatures, and columns in enormous fragments: the capitals of the columns look like huge rocks that have been hurled there by some violent convulsion of nature."[44] This travel sketch dwells often on the ways that the buildings of the ancients must have been brought to ruin by volcanic activity and earthquakes, two staples of the catastrophist paradigm. It seems, then, that the detachment between natural and human history in *The Course of Empire* cannot be attributed to some progressive evolution in Cole's thought. Both before and after painting his most famous series, Cole could articulate the classic catastrophist narrative of natural disaster striking down a proud civilization. The idea must have been one he had garnered while on tour, just as Willis had. The very nature of nineteenth-century tourism inculcated a standard way of thinking about the places visited and things seen. In the 1832–33 sketch, the violence of nature's catastrophic mutability destroys civilization, just as it does in the Sicilian travel narrative of 1844. In this conception, nature is threatening but at least comprehensible. Like Silliman's "regular and perfect constructions," the conventions of the touristic eye — the regular application of aesthetic categories such as the sublime and the picturesque — constitute a system of managing the unknown. When Cole painted *The Course of Empire*, he dispensed with this system and removed nature into deep time. *Destruction* conveys this unbridgeable difference in time; nature provides the unmoved, indifferent context to human mutability within time. However, the many formal similarities between natural and constructed forms in the series suggest that Cole still intuited a profound connection between the two; it seems simply to have been impossible for Cole to represent the nature of that connection. Deep time meant that nature's processes could never be understood. By 1844 Cole had once again buried the truly alien qualities of deep time beneath the familiar aesthetic categories of the sublime and the picturesque.

The Aesthetics of Geological Time

Art historians have shown that the general function of landscape aesthetics is to bring nature within the purview of culture. Angela Miller argues that American landscapes in the nineteenth century "drew collective inspiration from nature while containing and controlling its meanings. . . . Any unstructured encounter with nature threatened a kind of antinomianism that was the moral or spiritual counterpart of democratic anarchy."[45] Aesthetic categories such as the picturesque and the sublime schooled perception; if one had the proper education, then, as the travel literature quoted above illustrates, one would already know what to see when encountering a new scene. Aesthetics thus serves the purpose of bringing unknown nature out of "anarchy" and into organized culture. In her study of the representation of landscape in American literature, Kris Fresonke writes that the purpose of comparisons between nature and art in the picturesque aesthetic "is to contain and control in the lexicon of images the somewhat sprawling and random encounters with nature."[46] Barbara Novak makes a very similar point regarding another major aesthetic category of the nineteenth century when she writes that by the 1840s "the sublime was being absorbed into a religious, moral, and frequently nationalist concept of culture, contributing to the rhetorical screen under which the aggressive conquest of the country could be accomplished."[47] By representing geological features using these aesthetic systems, American artists and writers worked to bring deep time within national culture. Cole's *The Course of Empire* and Thoreau's "Ktaadn" are unusual for their acknowledgment of the truly alien qualities of deep time. Usually, as in Harris's *The Pre-Adamite Earth* or Hitchcock's writings on natural theology, the objective was to domesticate this mysterious substratum of the national territory. However, in both cases, the effect of representing deep time is to bring it within the symbolic vocabulary of the nation.

But what was it that had, through these aesthetics, gained admission to the national imaginary? In a picturesque description of the Merrimack River, Thoreau captures the ambivalence about the meaning of human institutions and activities prompted by the conception of American civilization residing atop a world of geological change:

> Unfitted to some extent for the purposes of commerce by the sand-bar at its mouth, see how this river was devoted from the first to the service of manufactures. Issuing from the iron region of Franconia, and flowing through still uncut forests, by inexhaustible ledges of granite, with Squam, and Winnipiseogee, and Newfound, and Massabesic Lakes for its mill-ponds, it falls over a succession of natural dams, where it has been offering its *privileges* in vain for ages, until at last the Yankee race came to *improve* them. Standing at its base, look up its sparkling stream to its source,—a silver cascade which falls all the way from the White Mountains to the sea,—and behold a city on each successive plateau, a busy colony of human beaver around every fall.[48]

In Thoreau's revisioning of the landscape, human settlements are recent additions to the surface of a world whose truly important processes of change go on underground, literally below the ground upon which all of this human activity takes place, and figuratively beneath the notice of the human beings preoccupied with the effort to "improve" nature—which Thoreau suggests cannot be improved upon by ineffectual human beings with their poor powers. These Yankees imagine themselves the possessors of perfect freedom, but they locate their cities in deference to a geography shaped by millennia of powerful forces that will continue working long after these cities are gone. "Perchance," he writes of the Concord River, "after a few thousand years, if the fishes will be patient, and pass their summers elsewhere meanwhile, nature will have leveled the Billerica dam, and the Lowell factories, and the Grass-bound River run clear again, to be explored by new migratory shoals, even as far as the Hopkinton pond and Westborough Swamp."[49] Here, in contrast to "Ktaadn," Thoreau's representation is lovely but conventional, rendering deep time an object of tame reverence, a picturesque frame for national history. Yet, even within this convention, Thoreau admits a hint of the profound critique of human agency contained within the concept of deep time. The aesthetics of time thus provided the medium of admission to the national imaginary of a potentially powerful critique of the voluntaristic model of human agency that was fundamental to the normative American construction of liberal democracy.

In Chapter 1, I claimed that we ought to take ideological representations of time seriously, as reflections (inversions, mirror images) of historical and political reality. Thoreau's picturesque descriptions of the millennia-long history of erosion associated with the Concord and Merrimack Rivers constitute one such expression. In the next, and final, chapter of this book, I shall consider another writer deeply immersed in the ideology of his culture: Ralph Waldo Emerson. Emerson's work has recently been at the center of academic debates about the merits of liberal democracy. At the same time, Emerson shared with Thoreau and other transcendentalist writers a fascination with nature, science, and the nonhuman world. For this reason, Emerson's works provide an excellent opportunity to demonstrate the centrality to American culture of a theory of liberalism whose structure is shaped by the recognition and ideological representation of deep time.

EMERSON'S DEEP DEMOCRACY

"We no longer measure by miles but by orbits of Neptune," Ralph Waldo Emerson wrote in his journal in 1856. "The old six thousand years of chronology is a kitchen clock, no more a measure of time than an hour-glass or an egg-glass since the durations of geologic periods have come in use."[1] In this entry, written at the age of fifty-three, Emerson acknowledges the degree to which the radical expansion of the temporal scale by geological theory had reordered the world during his lifetime. In comparing the 6,000 years of biblical history to a "kitchen clock," Emerson relegates both clock time and the traditional chronology of his ministerial training to obsolescence, since old, cheap shelf clocks were usually reserved for kitchen use.[2] The "hour-glass" and "egg-glass" also connote domesticity; together, these metaphors set up a dichotomy between the familiar world of domestic and religious time on the one hand, and the unknowable and newly revealed deep time of nature on the other. In comparing the scale of deep time to the spatial extent of astronomical distances, Emerson reprises the oft-employed strategy of attempting to understand time through spatial figures; in this case, however, rather than familiarizing deep time by comparing its extent to a common unit of measurement such as a mile, Emerson reveals how incomprehensible he finds deep time by analogizing it to interplanetary distances. This journal entry thus reveals the degree to which Emerson perceived deep time as profoundly different from more familiar forms of temporal experience — different not simply in quantity but, more importantly, in quality.

The present chapter, the final full chapter in this book, focuses on Emerson's response to deep time in order to show how such a temporal mode, circulating through the American world of ideas, could be put to work as a tool by a reformist thinker with an ambitious agenda. For Emerson, it was crucial that America existed *in time*, in a variety of shifting senses whose fluid intersections and oppositions captured what he saw as the dynamic quality of the newly emerging American democratic social world. Understanding the role of temporality in Emerson's thought allows us to see how the liberal democratic politics that have been central to America's national self-conception as a radically modern nation arose out of the ferment of heterogeneous temporalities of the nineteenth century. Just as the diverse meanings of mechanical time emerged out of the interactions between human agents and nonhuman objects, so too did the meanings of geological deep time arise from the imaginative encounters between human thinkers and the nonhuman world. To be more specific, Emerson perceived in deep time an opportunity to create a revolutionary version of American politics no longer wedded to humanism. For most of the figures discussed in Chapter 4, deep time presented a challenge by threatening the humanism that was widely understood to be the foundation of democratic society. These figures went to great lengths to create representations and narratives that would limit or manage deep time's threat to humanism, and hence to the democratic character of the American nation as they understood it. While many of Emerson's contemporaries responded to deep time's threat to humanism by reaffirming their perception in nature of the design of a divine providence with special affection for humankind, Emerson worked gradually on a project of reformulating democratic politics from an antihumanist perspective more consonant with the new cosmology implied by deep time. Emerson was hardly sanguine about the vitality of the form taken by American democracy in the Jacksonian era, and he perceived in deep time the tool that would enable him to redeem this ghostly spectre of democracy. Deep time undermined the humanist worldview that the Enlightenment-era founders had bestowed upon the Republic, but it made it possible for Emerson to imagine a new, more radical, more vital democratic politics.

Natural History and the Social World

The exclamation "I will be a naturalist," which Emerson recorded in his journal after visiting the Muséum d'Histoire Naturelle in Paris in July 1833, has received considerable attention in recent scholarship.[3] The consensus view of Emerson has situated science at the center of his intellectual interests and has placed his understanding of geological time within a larger project of using scientific ideas in general to create order out of the apparent chaos of the world. As Laura Dassow Walls puts it in the most important recent monograph on Emerson and science, "Emerson's culture of truth sought to erect in the midst of a disordered world a palace of order, whose precincts enabled a gracious, rational, and civilized life otherwise impossible, and whose boundaries were to expand until the enlightened principles of self-discipline and self-education had embraced everyone capable of cultivation—a kind of global church estate or university campus, networked from nation to nation, by means of language."[4] As this quotation makes clear, there are important social implications to Emerson's thinking about natural science. If Emerson did, indeed, think of nature through tropes such as the orderly garden and the naturalist's cabinet, then the social ideas deriving from this scientific perspective might well, as Walls suggests, also take on rational and orderly forms.

However, Walls's description of Emerson's scientific project is rather at odds with recent revisions of our understanding of Emerson's social and political thought. While Walls reads Emerson primarily in terms of a neo-Platonic or even Cartesian rationality, employing the image of an Apollinian "solar eye" of science as a controlling figure in her interpretation of Emerson, Michael Lopez has emphasized Emerson's Dionysian embrace of power and distrust of metaphysics. Cornel West and Russell Goodman have seen Emerson as the founding father of American pragmatism, a philosophical school at odds not with scientific method but certainly with conventional scientific claims regarding the objective status of truth. Stanley Cavell has read Emerson through Nietzsche with an emphasis on ordinary language, while George Kateb has also employed the Nietzschean lens to make Emerson a source of his theory of "democratic individualism." Kateb finds in Emerson the notion that "human unpredictability must be insisted on."[5] In short, it seems that the two major recent trends in Emerson scholarship—Emerson as naturalist and Emerson as political or social philosopher—have left us with antithetical Emersons, one devoted to the neo-Platonic transcendence of the particularities of the phenomenal world and the other committed to the Dionysian turbulence and contingency of the social world.

While the impeccable scholarship of Walls and others has shown conclusively that an idealistic strain certainly does persist in Emerson's thinking about nature throughout his career, a closer look at the relationship between his ideas about nature and human society reveals the existence of an equally strong Nietzschean inclination that becomes centrally important by the 1840s. The neo-Platonic, rational strain of Emerson's thinking about natural history was fully consonant with his social views early in his career, but in the late 1830s and early 1840s Emerson developed less idealistic ways of thinking about nature. These new ideas were fundamental to his radically democratic social thought.

Emerson had become acquainted with geological theory during his years as a student at Harvard (1817–21), and he had certainly encountered the idea of deep time by the 1830s. He borrowed John Playfair's *Works* from the Boston Atheneum in 1834 and the first two volumes of Charles Lyell's *Principles of Geology* in 1836.[6] The mid- to late 1830s were crucial years in Emerson's intellectual development. His first book, *Nature*, was published in 1836; the so-called "Transcendentalist Club" began meeting that same year; in 1837 he delivered the famous address that would become known as "The American Scholar"; in 1838 he quit the pulpit and delivered another of his most famous addresses to the Harvard Divinity School. It was during these same years that Emerson first penned in his journals and tried out on lecture audiences many of the lines that would later form the heart of his seminal essay collections of the 1840s. This was a period in which Emerson searched for his vocation and, in a simultaneous and directly related project, began to formulate his unique ideas about the nature and importance of American democracy. In part, Emerson's avid reading in natural history simply reflected the increasing importance of lecturing as his livelihood; audiences wanted to hear lectures on current developments in the sciences, and Emerson obliged them. However, Emerson's passion for science ran much deeper than this; Harry Hayden Clark was the first of many scholars to observe that Emerson's "interest in science helped to motivate, during his formative years up to 1838, his turn against ecclesiasticism and an antiquarian devotion to the past."[7] The journals of the 1830s and the subsequent development of ideas from those journals into the published works of the 1840s reveal the extent to which Emerson did not merely follow scientific developments but made them his own and appropriated them into his philosophy.

Emerson's early works, his published writings and lectures of the early to mid-1830s, respond to his reading in natural history by arguing for a humanist, anthropocentric cosmology not unlike that advanced by natural theologians such as William Paley and Edward Hitchcock. Most of Emerson's early lectures were on topics drawn from natural history. In a talk first given either late in 1833 or early in 1834, "The Relation of Man to the Globe," Emerson told his audience:

By the study of the globe in very recent times we have become acquainted with a fact the most surprising—I may say the most sublime, to wit, that

Man who stands in the globe so proud and powerful is no upstart in the creation, but has been prophesied in nature for a thousand thousand ages before he appeared; that from times incalculably remote there has been a progressive preparation for him; an effort, (as physiologists say,) to produce him; the meaner creatures, the primeval sauri, containing the elements of his structure and pointing at it on every side, whilst the world was, at the same time, preparing to be habitable by him. He was not made sooner, because his house was not ready.[8]

Here Emerson seems to echo ideas that had been put forth much earlier by natural theologians and that continued to be espoused by many of his own countrymen such as Arnold Guyot and James D. Dana. The phrase "a thousand thousand ages" clearly alludes to the geological timescale, but Emerson interprets those vast stretches of time in a way that aggrandizes human beings. All of this prehistoric time exists as part of an "effort," a design, to "produce" human beings. By describing the earth as a "house" for human beings, Emerson evokes the same imagery of domesticity that he later, in the 1856 journal entry, came to denigrate as antithetical to the temporality revealed by geological theory. Whereas later he came to see domestic time as quaint and irrelevant when juxtaposed to deep time, in the 1830s he was still trying to imagine the geological timescale in domestic terms.

In an 1836 lecture entitled "The Humanity of Science," Emerson again integrated a domestic sensibility with natural theology, this time by comparing geological time to the movement of a clock: "In Geology . . . we have a book of Genesis, wherein we read when and how the worlds were made, and are introduced to periods as portentous as the distances of the sky. But here too, we are never strangers; it is the same functions, slower performed; the wheel of the clock which now revolves in the life of our species, once took the duration of many races of animals on the planet to complete its circle."[9] Like the passage from "The Relation of Man to the Globe" quoted above, this passage reveals an attitude toward time precisely opposite to that displayed in the 1856 journal entry. Here, the discovery of deep time has not changed but rather simply extended the experience of time with which we are familiar through the everyday clock—the "kitchen clock," as Emerson puts it in 1856—the clock that was already a common household object by 1836. Hence, geology reaffirms that the understanding of the world available to us through our senses is essentially correct, and that, far from being historically unique, the experience of the world familiar to Americans in everyday life in the 1830s is universal.

Although passages such as those quoted above represent the main tenor of Emerson's thinking about time in the 1830s, some alternative perspectives do become evident as early as the middle of the decade. Emerson's journal entries from this period reveal that, even as his public statements echoed conventional opinion, he had already begun to perceive the need for a reformulation of ideas about time. For example, in October 1835, months before delivering the lecture in which he would publicly compare geology with the book of Genesis, he privately dismissed the chronology of Genesis as incompatible with real intellectual perception: "It will not do for Sharon Turner or any man not of Ideas to make a System. Thus Mr Turner has got into his head the notion that the Mosaic history is a good natural history of the world, reconcilable with geology &c. Very well. You see at once the length & breadth of what you may expect, & the mind loses all appetite to read."[10] In criticizing a historian such as Turner for accepting the "Mosaic history," Emerson suggests that what is important about "good natural history" is how it shapes our understanding of the social world. To make a "System" applicable to human society required understanding the nonhuman environment of human beings, an environment whose temporal dimensions geological theory had revealed. Robert D. Richardson notes that Turner's *History of the Anglo-Saxons* was one of Emerson's most important sources for historical ideas in his early lectures.[11] Hence, Emerson's private criticism of Turner in his journal reveals the conflicted state of his ideas in these years, the way that concepts from natural history were shifting the ground of his own developing intellectual system.

The first, rather veiled public expression of these shifting ideas about time appears in Emerson's first book, the 1836 *Nature*, whose mostly conventional, humanist, and idealist approach to natural history is disturbed now and then by inklings of a fresh perspective. *Nature* presents a beautifully written but intellectually derivative lamentation of the fall of human beings from an original, romanticized state of unity with nature. For the most part, Emerson's attitude toward time in the book is one of dismissal; redemption must be achieved by transcending time. In a vision patched together from the ideas of Augustine and Kant, Emerson portrays time as an illusion of the phenomenal world: "Idealism sees the world in God. It beholds the whole circle of persons and things, of actions and events, of country and religion, not as painfully accumulated, atom after atom, act after act, in an aged creeping Past, but as one vast picture, which God paints on the instant eternity, for the contemplation of the soul."[12] This passage illustrates how important geological metaphors had already become to Emerson's thinking, in its depiction of an "aged creeping Past," but it employs the concept of sedimentation to argue for the need to transcend time. Here Emerson clearly has not embraced the notion of time as an important medium for human development and action.

However, earlier in the book, in the chapter titled "Beauty," we find Emerson offering quite a different treatment of natural time. The chapter assesses the relationship between the human observer and the nonhuman world that is observed. What interests Emerson about this relationship is the possibility that a proper perception of beauty might lead an individual back into a state of unity with nature. In discussing the way in which the "inhabitants of cities" have lost track of natural time, Emerson characterizes nature's higher temporality in terms of perpetual change:

> To the attentive eye, each moment of the year has its own beauty, and in the same field, it beholds, every hour, a picture which was never seen before, and which shall never be seen again. The heavens change every moment, and reflect their glory or gloom on the plains beneath. The state of the crop in the surrounding farms alters the expression of the earth from week to week. The succession of native plants in the pastures and roadsides, which makes the silent clock by which time tells the summer hours, will make even the divisions of the day sensible to a keen observer.[13]

In the analysis Emerson offers here, it is not an entrapment within time that shackles human beings to a fallen state. Instead, it is entrapment within the wrong kind of time, the time of cities. The process of redemption requires individuals to attune their perceptions to natural time, characterized by endless change and diversity. To be sure, this idea is not fully developed in *Nature*. For the most part, Emerson treats time as a phenomenal illusion, as in the first quotation above. However, the passage from the chapter on beauty reveals that, even as Emerson encouraged his readers to transcend time, he had already begun to ponder other possibilities. Most importantly, he had begun to think about time as a medium of change, and this way of thinking would eventually make time central to his larger project of individual and cultural transformation.

While the passage from *Nature* portrays temporal change as a gradual, harmonious process, an entry from Emerson's journal of the following year employs geological imagery to imagine change in much more violent terms. As James K. Guthrie points out, the effect of geological theory and natural history on Emerson's thought became much more powerful after 1836; Guthrie notes that it is somewhat ironic that Emerson's ideas about nature grew more concrete and sophisticated only after he had published the book *Nature*, "probably because Emerson had not yet digested the significance of Lyell's new worldview."[14] Continuing to mull over the problem of perception that was central to "Beauty," Emerson, in his May 1837 journal entry, draws upon geological theory in a very different way, now making unity with nature into a frightening, destructive prospect:

> What was, ever since my memory, solid continent, now yawns apart and discloses its composition and genesis. I learn geology the morning after an earthquake. I learn fast on the ghastly diagrams of the cloven mountain & upheaved plain and the dry bottom of the Sea. The roots of orchards and the cellars of palaces and the cornerstones of cities are dragged into melancholy sunshine. I see the natural fracture of the stone. I see the tearing of the tree & learn its fibre & its rooting. The Artificial is rent from the eternal.[15]

As Barbara Packer observes, this entry "combines the language of traditional apocalyptic with the language of the science whose authority was busily destroying the ontological foundations of Biblical revelation: geology." The implication of this juxtaposition, Packer goes on to say, is that Emerson "suddenly sees the social and economic not as a given, something solid and inescapable, but as the end product of forces extending back into the unimaginable past."[16] We may expand upon Packer's remarks by noting that the passage also connects this unimaginable geological past with personal memory. Thus, Emerson's own memory, the repository of his own sensory impressions, is rent apart by the force of time. The apocalypse is not only "social and economic," as Packer indicates, but also personal, striking at Emerson's interior sense of continuous being. In contrast to the harmonious solar light that Walls and others have described Emerson finding in the scientific perspective, the revelation here casts a more unsettling "melancholy sunshine" upon the world and upon Emerson's sense of self.

In December 1837, Emerson again employed the language of geology in his journal, this time to consider a related but distinct implication of deep time, that is, that time denied a providential understanding of history in favor of one characterized by contingency: "The city of Chompawut was erected on Gneiss at the northern side of Choura Pany & was totally destroyed by the decomposition of the rock on which it stood. This is supposed to have happened 500 years ago. A few vestiges remain (sculptured fragments of granite of great magnificence) owing to the accidental circumstance of their having been erected on the more durable beds of rock."[17] This entry proposes a radically different paradigm for the relationship between human beings and nature. While human history is still dependent upon nature, as Emerson had insisted in "The Relation of Man to the Globe" and other early public lectures, in this journal entry Emerson portrays the connection between humanity and nature as essentially random. Natural processes do not fulfill themselves in human civilization; rather, cities (*civitas*, emblematic of the highest stage of progress in stadialist theory) either flourish or are destroyed as a result of "accidental circumstance." Human beings sculpt their built environment (which Emerson had termed "Artificial" in the entry from May of the same year quoted above) out of granite. However, the rock undergoes processes far more powerful and long lasting than human artifice. Human beings do not understand these processes; while they might well be orderly, subject to some laws, those laws are obscure due to the immensity of the time involved. No human being can know why an earthquake would destroy one building but leave another standing. If the cities that represent human civilization sit insecurely on the surface of a world of immense forces beyond human comprehension, then human history is shaped by nature in ways that can only be perceived in terms of chance.

In August 1837, between the dates of these two journal entries, Emerson would more cautiously integrate some of his burgeoning ideas about natural history into his oration titled "The American Scholar." In keeping with the celebratory occasion of this address, "The American Scholar" provides a more comforting depiction of temporal change than that recorded in the journals of the same year, but the address does challenge the members of the audience to reimagine their place in natural history. Whereas in *Nature* Emerson had imagined the time of a single day or a single year as a medium of endless transformation, in "The American Scholar" Emerson suggested that his contemporaries could empower themselves to transform the world through a proper understanding of the nature of deep time. After enjoining his listeners to embrace "freedom" as an essential quality of the intellect, Emerson theorized that a lack of self-trust in one's own powers could stem from the illusion that the world had long ago stopped moving:

> It is a mischievous notion that we are come late into nature; that the world was finished a long time ago. As the world was plastic and fluid in the hands of God, so it is ever to so much of his attributes as we bring to it. . . . They are the kings of the world who give the color of their present thought to all nature and all art, and persuade men by the cheerful serenity of their carrying the matter, that this thing which they do, is the apple which the

ages have desired to pluck, now at last ripe, and inviting nations to the harvest.[18]

This passage might, at first glance, seem to blame the geological timescale for the timidity of modern human beings. Deep time did, after all, portray humankind as having come only lately into the world. However, the passage's emphasis on the "plastic and fluid" nature of the world in fact aligns it with deep time in a positive way. Geologists had made clear that the world was still changing; ongoing change was, in fact, one of the foundations of the uniformitarian theory of Hutton, Playfair, and Lyell. The notion that the world had ceased changing long ago, and that modern civilization inhabited a twilight near the end of the world's history, was more akin to the biblical account of Creation, more aligned with popular American belief in an impending millennium. Hence, this passage in "The American Scholar" actually characterizes time in geological terms in order to give human beings a renewed sense of agency. If the world was still in transformation, still "plastic and fluid," then individuals still possessed the power to shape the world within time. "The American Scholar" thus reverses *Nature*'s dominant injunction to transcend time in favor of a program of individual and cultural empowerment within time. "See how nations and races flit by on the sea of time, and leave no ripple to tell where they floated or sunk," Emerson would caution a very different Harvard audience at the Divinity School in 1838.[19] To flit on the surface of time, leaving no ripple, to live outside of time, had come to seem to Emerson the absence of life.

"History": The New Perspective of Essays

The rather contradictory and haphazard ideas about time that germinate in Emerson's writings and lectures of the 1830s come to a more mature fruition in his second book, *Essays*, which he sent to the printer in January 1841.[20] Here we see Emerson reshaping a variety of conceptually imprecise images and metaphors from his earlier lectures and journal entries into a unified and intellectually rigorous work. The lead essay in the collection is entitled "History," and in it, Emerson reflects uncertainly that "Time dissipates to shining ether the solid angularity of facts"—quite a contrast to the confident optimism of his earlier lecture series on history. Although most of "History" is woven together out of passages from Emerson's earlier lectures and journal entries, this line is a new one, inserted within a paragraph originally penned in 1838.[21] The addition of new material such as this, along with the revision and recontextualization of previously written material from lectures and journal entries, make the *Essays* of 1841 into a new work, a re-imagining of ideas that had swirled less coherently through Emerson's mind in the 1830s. The twelve essays in the volume speak to one another, and their continuities and antiphonies form the foundation of the book as a whole. *Essays* thus presents a far more systematic formulation of the human relationship to nature through the concept of time as a medium for perpetual transformation.

"History" introduces *Essays* by situating human beings in relation to time, and Emerson makes clear that, even as he encourages his readers to create a vital American culture in the present, he views both past and future time in expansive terms. History is a "primeval world," or "the Fore-World," whose vastness extends beyond "the civil and metaphysical history of man" and into nature.[22] This temporal extension is fundamental to the way in which Emerson defines the human being: "He is the compend of time; he is also the correlative of nature."[23] Emerson's use of the two words "compend" and "correlative" illuminates the particular way in which time is important to his thought. Two things that are "correlatives" are related to but distinct from one another. That is, human beings correlate with, but remain outside of, nature. In contrast, if human beings are the "compend" of time, this means that they contain time within themselves, redact time into a concise form.[24] The essay "History" as a whole is structured to show how time extends between human beings and nature, for the first portion of the essay deals with the "civil and metaphysical history of man," dating back to classical antiquity, while the concluding portion of the essay turns to natural history. Thus, this introductory piece lays the foundation for Emerson's book-length consideration of the human condition in America in the moments of present time by establishing the basic ontological importance of time as the medium connecting human beings to their correlative, nature.

Since human beings could not exist without nature, in Emerson's view, it is essential that they extend themselves temporally from the moments of present time that constitute everyday experience into the vastness of natural time that lies before and behind them. Emerson makes the importance of this activity of imaginative temporal extension clear at the outset of "History," where he writes: "There is a relation between the hours of our life and the centuries of time. As the air I breath is drawn from the great repositories of nature, as the light on my book is yielded by a star a hundred millions of miles distant, as the poise of my body depends on the equilibrium of centrifugal and centripetal forces, so the hours should be instructed by the ages, and the ages explained by the hours."[25] Here Emerson still, as he had in "The Humanity of Science," focuses attention upon the importance of the human being within the grand expanse of nature. The individual's perceptions, ability to read and think, and bodily poise and integrity depend upon a harmonious relationship with nature on a scale that, as Lee Rust Brown puts it, "overwhelms normal conceptual frameworks."[26] But we may also mark here the maturing awareness that there is something tenuous and contingent about this relationship—it is itself a product of Emerson's imaginative activity, something he must assert and argue for, and even produce through acts of thought and living. Emerson depicts himself as a thinker, a maker, reading by starlight against the backdrop of ages of time. Extension through time, and hence connection to nature, results from this creative labor.

The wording of this passage in "History" also marks a shift away from a celebration of human beings as a collective—a stance that typified Emerson's early lectures as well as much of the writing in natural theology from which he drew inspiration for those lectures—and toward a more inquisitive focus upon the individual. Once again it is instructive to compare this passage with its antecedent. The original version of the passage appeared in the introductory lecture of Emerson's 1836–37 Boston lecture series, "The Philosophy of History." The passages are quite similar, but between 1836 and 1841 Emerson changed what had been a "we" into an "I": "As the air we breathe is drawn from the great repositories of nature: as the light we see by, is yielded by a star 100 millions of miles distant: as the poise of our bodies and the planting of our foot depends on the equilibrium of centripetal and centrifugal forces: so the hours should be instructed by the ages and the ages explained by the hours."[27] In part, the change from "we" to "I" in the two versions of this passage might be explained by the difference between occasions: a lecture as opposed to a published essay. Emerson might have felt it more appropriate to say "we" to an audience directly before him. However, there are numerous places in *Essays* where Emerson employs the first person plural pronoun (e.g., "In every work of genius we recognize our own rejected thoughts").[28] Emerson's use of the plural "we" is an important part of his strategy for constructing a relationship of trust and common purpose with his readers. He wishes his readers to join him in pursuing the philosophical project described in *Essays*, and the use of "we" facilitates this goal. Hence, when Emerson employs the first person singular pronoun, he does so with the intention of distinguishing these moments in some way from those in which he employs the collective "we." In the case of the passage from "History," the change from "we" to "I" transforms what had been a sense of similarity in our collective position in relation to nature into a sense of particularity in the individual positions of discrete beings in relation to nature. That is, in his writings of the 1830s, Emerson described the common position of all human beings in relation to deep time. In these earlier writings, Emerson represented the ontological condition of humanity as something given by the world, given to all human beings in the same way. However, by changing the "we" of the 1836 lecture to an "I" in the 1841 essay, Emerson implies that each individual possesses a different relationship to nature. While the fact of natural history is something common to all human beings, the meaning of that fact differs as individual human beings differ.

Such emphasis on the individual might seem to lead toward a romantic version of humanism, a reproduction of some shopworn ideas from half a century earlier about the importance of the individual creativity of the autonomous self in the face of sublime, inconceivable nature. However, Emerson's movement away from the collective and toward the individual really provides the means for a movement away from humanism and toward an antihumanist reconceptualization of human action. This direction in Emerson's thought becomes more clear if we consider his ideas in relation not only to those thinkers and writers who came before him, but also to those who came after. That is, rather than looking at Emerson teleologically as the fulfillment of a movement we now call romanticism, we ought to look at Emerson's ideas as coming somewhere in the middle of an ongoing struggle to define humanity in relation to nature, a struggle that begins with the earliest developments of natural science and continues to the present day. In particular, we can look at Emerson's ideas through the lens provided by one of his most enthusiastic readers, Nietzsche. While numerous philosophers and political thinkers have explored Emerson's influence on and connections with Nietzsche, the importance of natural history for both of these thinkers' perspectivalism and relativism has not been much noted.[29] Although Nietzsche developed many of his ideas about nature in response to Darwin, whose *Origin of Species* (1859) was published after Emerson had written his major works, both Nietzsche and Emerson grappled with very similar problems posed by geological theory and deep time. Nietzsche's 1873 essay "On Truth and Lie in an Extra-Moral Sense" employs a scientific cosmology that would have been perfectly comprehensible to Emerson, even before *Origin of Species*, to critique a humanist understanding of the history of philosophy. "In some remote corner of the universe," Nietzsche invites us to imagine, "poured out and glittering in innumerable solar systems, there once was a star on which clever animals invented knowledge. That was the haughtiest and most mendacious minute of 'world history' — yet only a minute. After nature had drawn a few breaths the star grew cold, and the clever animals had to die."[30] How small and powerless human beings are, Nietzsche playfully suggests. How vast and uncaring is the universe around us. And human knowledge, including philosophy, is merely a clever invention of an insignificant species of animals whose entire history comprises only a few breaths of cosmic time.

Such moments of strange perspective abound in Nietzsche's writings, which require us to imagine what sorts of things we would think about if we were cows, or to consider the moral terms in which sheep perceive birds of prey. To shift perspective is a central part of Nietzsche's effort to question values and reveal the constructed nature of foundations of knowledge. His project of "historical philosophizing" is based upon shifting temporal perspective: "Now, everything *essential* in human development occurred during primeval times, long before those four thousand years with which we are more or less acquainted; during these years, humanity may well not have changed much more. But the philosopher sees 'instincts' in present-day humanity and assumes that these belong to the unchangeable facts of humanity." In contrast to such naïve humanism, Nietzsche developed out of natural history an antifoundationalist philosophy that critiqued the "teleology" that he saw "built upon speaking of the human being of the last four millennia as something *eternal*, toward which all the things of the world have from their beginning naturally been directed. Everything, however, has come to be; there are *no eternal facts*: just as there are no absolute truths. — From now on therefore, *historical philosophizing* will be necessary, and along with it the virtue of modesty."[31] A historical consciousness that conceives of millions, rather than thousands, of years would certainly be conducive to human modesty, as well as a relativistic sense of values and a skepticism about the so-called truths that the human intellect has discovered. In keeping with this modest assessment of humanity, Nietzsche also invited his contemporaries to think of themselves as biological organisms in a way that probably would not have been possible before the nineteenth century, writing in *Beyond Good and Evil*, for example, that "by far the greater part of conscious thinking must still be included among instinctive activities."[32] Taken collectively, Nietzsche's use of concepts, images, and metaphors from the natural world and natural sciences forces his readers to shift their perspective away from an insular and self-aggrandizing human world and toward a suprahuman or even nonhuman world as a frame of reference for questions about knowledge and value.

Comparing Nietzsche's philosophy with Emerson's has a heuristic value, helping to reveal the kinds of imaginative vehicles for working through these problems that Emerson's philosophy had made possible; Emerson's "Time dissipates to shining ether the solid angularity of facts" becomes Nietzsche's "Everything, however, has come to be; there are *no eternal facts*: just as there are no absolute truths." Emerson did not draw all of the same conclusions that would later come to his successor, but his use of cosmic perspective served a similar interrogation of conventional wisdom regarding the status of the human being in relation to nature. Hence, in "History," Emerson revises his earlier representation of natural history as simply a preparation for the arrival of humankind into an insistence that human history must be rewritten within an extrahuman context.

> Hear the rats in the wall, see the lizard on the fence, the fungus under foot, the lichen on the log. What do I know sympathetically, morally, of either of these worlds of life? As old as the Caucasian man, — perhaps older, — these creatures have kept their counsel beside him, and there is no record of any word or sign that has passed from one to the other. . . . I am ashamed to see what a shallow village tale our so-called History is. How many times we must say Rome, and Paris, and Constantinople! What does Rome know of rat and lizard? What are Olympiads and Consulates to these neighbouring systems of being? . . . Broader and deeper we must write our annals, — from an ethical reformation, from an influx of the ever new, ever sanative conscience, — if we would trulier express our central and wide-related nature, instead of this old chronology of selfishness and pride to which we have too long lent our eyes.[33]

Since these lines are almost the last of the essay, Emerson does not elaborate on the forms such broader and deeper annals might take. However, it is clear from the examples of narrow and shallow history which he does offer — Rome, Paris, and Constantinople — that the new history would depart from a conventional nineteenth-century emphasis on the progress of empires. By comparing the histories of such empires to village tales, Emerson diminishes their size in relation to the temporal expanse and complexity of natural history. Natural history provides a more real frame for understanding human action. Just as it would be for Nietzsche, perspective is of vital importance to Emerson. In his journal, Emerson had asked, "Yet what is Rome to the rat & lizard?"[34] In the published version of the passage, Emerson shifts the perspective from the rat and lizard to the human. That is, while the nonhuman world may care little about "Olympiads and Consulates," it is of great importance for human beings to learn about nature. In stark contrast to the position taken in the lectures that human beings constitute the culmination of nature, here we see Emerson rendering human beings as rather marginal dependents, less important than lizards and rats but cruelly beholden to nature.

In response to this dilemma, Emerson calls for an "ethical reformation" that would enable human beings to exchange their shallow provincial sense of time for the deep time of natural history. Emerson does not propose that this reformation would come about as a result of the writing of deep history. Instead, he suggests that such a reformation is an essential precondition to the writing of deep history; historians must write "*from* an ethical reformation," rather than toward one. Hence, Emerson's call for a deep history comes at the end of the essay "History," rather than at the beginning. "History" critiques what Emerson sees as the prevailing ways of thinking about time, but the work of creating a new paradigm can only be carried on in the volume's subsequent essays, which investigate how an ethical reformation could be achieved that would make deep history possible.

Temporal Power and Revolution in Essays

"Self-Reliance," the next essay in the volume, initiates this work of ethical reformation by encouraging readers to perform a somewhat paradoxical operation: at once creating their humanity within present moments of time while simultaneously enhancing their awareness of the inhuman scale of the deep time of which those present moments form a part. It is very clear that by 1841 Emerson was committed to the position that a philosophical life could only be led by embracing the world rather than by searching for an abstract or numinous realm outside the world. In "Self-Reliance," Emerson describes the most desirable "sense of being" as one that "is not diverse from things, from space, from light, from time, from man, but one with them, and proceeds obviously from the same source whence their life and being also proceed."[35] To be sure, this way of thinking about being lends itself to the possibility of transcendence of one's individual isolation, but this transcendence would be achieved precisely by embracing the particulars of one's situation, one's time and place. Elsewhere in the essay, Emerson muses, "let me record day by day my honest thought without prospect or retrospect, and, I cannot doubt, it will be found symmetrical, though I mean it not, and see it not."[36] However, despite this commitment to immersion in a daily life without prospect or retrospect, Emerson's "true man" would also constitute "a cause, a country, and an age" and would require "infinite spaces and numbers and time fully to accomplish his design."[37] Hence, a robust commitment to the present provides access to the totality of time. Indeed, even if the individual who lives in the present does not see the long-term symmetry of his thoughts, the purpose of living in this way is nevertheless to achieve such symmetry. The purpose of living within the present moment is not to limit oneself to a single moment but to create a more expansive form of being that extends symmetrically, harmoniously across time.

This connection redounds throughout "Self-Reliance," as Emerson balances passages describing the extension of the self through vast stretches of cosmic time with other passages extolling the benefits of living within present moments. The most famous of these is his description of the roses that "make no reference to former roses or to better ones"; consequently, "they exist with God today" and each one is "perfect in every moment of its existence." Emerson adds to this description of existence in the present two parallel statements that seem to disavow the importance of time altogether: "There is no time to them"; and, three sentences later, writing now of a single rose, "There is no time to it." Because of these phrases, this passage has sometimes been cited as an example of Emerson's idealism and desire to escape from time. However, we must read the passage in the context of the many other passages in "Self-Reliance," and in *Essays* as a whole, that press the importance of embracing the world and time. Indeed, since Emerson clearly admires the way that the roses live fully and without regret in each present moment, it seems contradictory when he asserts that the roses have "no time to them." The concluding sentences of this passage, in which Emerson contrasts the discontent of human beings toward their temporal predicament with the perfect state of being of the roses, resolves the apparent contradiction. "But man postpones or remembers," Emerson writes. "He does not live in the present, but with reverted eye laments the past, or, heedless of the riches that surround him, stands on tiptoe to foresee the future. He cannot be happy and strong until he too lives with nature in the present, above time." The phrase "above time" resonates with the earlier repeated phrase "no time to them." These phrases seem to suggest that what is laudable about the roses is their escape from a temporal existence. However, "above time" is positioned syntactically within the passage's final sentence to echo and develop the sense of the previous prepositional phrase in the sentence, "in the present." Hence, to live "with nature" is to live both "in the present" and "above time." The spatial metaphor "above time" must represent a state of being in relation to time that is "in the present." If this state is "in" present time, then the preposition "above" cannot describe a position outside of time. Rather, it seems evident that the state of being "above time" can only be arrived at by achieving a state of complete immersion in present time. Through such an immersion, Emerson suggests, human beings can achieve a position of prospect over time. In literary history, the trope of the prospect is almost always associated with power; this association certainly informs the "Prospects" chapter of *Nature* and other sections of Emerson's writings. In the case of "Self-Reliance," then, the state of being "above time" represents not an escape from time but rather a position of power in relation to time.

This interpretation of "above time" as an empowered temporal position accords with Emerson's critique in the passage's penultimate sentence of the way that human beings revert their eyes and lament the past or else pine for an unachieved future. As Guthrie observes in his analysis of this passage, Emerson seems to feel that the modern individual "lives all too often in a state of temporal dissociation, so that when he 'postpones or remembers' he becomes fixated upon the future or the past, alienating himself not only from nature, but from himself."[38] To long to remove oneself from the present to some other place in time, either a nostalgically recalled past or a fantasy of a better future, really constitutes a rejection of being within time. If one cannot embrace the present, Emerson suggests, then one is powerless in relation to time. This weak state of being stems from the attitude that Nietzsche would later describe as *ressentiment*: a loathing of the human condition of being within time, a resentment of the changes that time brings to the world and a concomitant desire to escape time altogether. "Powerless against that which has been done," Nietzsche describes this condition, "the will is an angry spectator of all things past. The will cannot will backwards; that it cannot break time and time's desire — that is the will's most lonely affliction"[39] Nietzsche's strong spirit would accept and embrace being within time, which means affirming the mutability of the world. Longing for the past reveals a dissatisfaction with change. It is this inability to affirm the goodness of the course life has taken that causes most human beings, in Nietzsche's view, to reject the present and brood upon the past or concoct elaborate fantasies concerning the future. Emerson anticipates this position in "Self-Reliance" when he urges his readers to emulate the roses by embracing the present as the venue for being, and thus acquire power over the past and future. Earlier, I described how Emerson enjoins his readers to gain access to all time by committing themselves to the present. The parable of the roses reveals how difficult and complex a process this must be.

In "Compensation," the essay that follows "Self-Reliance," Emerson attempts to encourage his readers in this difficult pursuit by describing the panoramic perspective on change that one might acquire if one were able to live "above time." Emerson paints a positive picture of the life of ceaseless change within present moments that the roses of "Self-Reliance" represent. "Compensation" opens with a poem describing "Time" in terms of change and balance, "black and white, / Pied with morning and with night."[40] The overall argument of "Compensation" represents the world as a theater of contending but perfectly matched forces, perpetually shifting yet always ultimately returning to a harmonious balance. In this essay, Emerson depicts human life in terms of a "natural history of calamity" in which the "changes which break up at short intervals the prosperity of men are advertisements of a nature whose law is growth." This process of ceaseless alteration results in every soul's perpetually "quitting its whole system of things, its friends, and home, and laws, and faith, as the shell-fish crawls out of its beautiful but stony case, because it no longer admits of its growth, and slowly forms a new house."[41] Hence, our position in nature is one of endless transformation of being and situation. Far from constituting real catastrophes, however, such seemingly jarring changes are really just part of a larger pattern of harmony; the totality of time offers compensation for the seeming disharmony of individual moments, for "the sure years reveal the deep remedial force that underlies all facts," and "the man or woman who would have remained a sunny garden-flower, with no room for its roots and too much sunshine for its head, by the falling of the walls and the neglect of the gardener, is made the banian of the forest, yielding shade and fruit to wide neighbourhoods of men."[42] Through its imagery, this concluding passage of "Compensation" comments upon the conceit of the roses offered in "Self-Reliance." The roses of "Self-Reliance" are in fact sunny garden flowers, for Emerson introduces them as the "roses under my window."[43] By portraying the roses in such explicitly domestic terms, Emerson makes clear that they symbolize the American people in the nineteenth century—or at least one segment of that population, the segment for whom Emerson primarily wrote. That is, these roses grow within the comfortable but limited domesticity of the American middle class. Only through "calamity," as Emerson describes temporal change in "Compensation," can such garden flowers become banyan trees.

In "Self-Reliance," Emerson also describes the ideal state of being through a series of images from the natural world that range from the small to the vast: "The genesis and maturation of a planet, its poise and orbit, the bended tree recovering itself from the strong wind, the vital resources of every animal and vegetable, are demonstrations of the self-sufficing, and therefore self-relying soul."[44] The meaning of Emerson's concept of "self-reliance" is notoriously difficult to define, but here Emerson indicates that "self-reliance" is something found in natural history. This position accords with Emerson's more general insistence that an authentic humanity can only be achieved through a recognition of one's relationship to nature, to the ancient kingdoms of "rat and lizard" alluded to in "History." The analysis of "calamity" in "Compensation" maps the route one must travel from a domesticated rose to a banyan tree or even a planet. By embracing life within present moments of time, however painful the transformations those moments require of us, we extend ourselves from the garden to the vast temporal demesne of the planet.

In contrast to this salutary embrace of deep time, Emerson critiques the time of clocks and watches that had already become ubiquitous for middle-class Americans. In "Self-Reliance" Emerson calls critical attention to the "contrast between the well-clad, reading, writing, thinking American, with a watch, a pencil, and a bill of exchange in his pocket, and the naked New Zealander, whose property is a club, a spear, a mat, and an undivided twentieth of a shed to sleep under." The point of the irony here is, of course, to suggest that a watch is no better way to conceive of modernity than currency or commodities. And if, as Emerson argues in the conclusion of "Self-Reliance," property leads individuals to "measure their esteem for each other by what each has, and not by what each is," then the "fine Geneva watch" by which the "civilized man" regulates his day has led to inauthentic, unequal, and exploitative social relations within modern society.[45] In short, by the time of "Self-Reliance," the clock and the watch had come to represent to Emerson the failure of modernity to fulfill its promise, the impoverishment of the future for the sake of present gain and hence the impoverishment of the polity whose sense of belonging to the modern nation was predicated upon a shared hope for a utopian future America. Unlike Henry Thoreau or Catharine Beecher, Emerson did not see a hope of redeeming capitalism by employing the logic of the market to incite moral or spiritual reform. For Emerson, mechanical time had become market time, akin to currency as an aspect of capitalism's relentless effort to impoverish the social world through false promises of riches.

This critique of mechanical time brings to light once again the difficulty of Emerson's philosophical program. To embrace the present and affirm life's seemingly calamitous changes cannot be confused with venal greed or selfishness. As Kateb explains, Emersonian "self-reliance" is not selfish or isolationist, not self-directed, but rather directed outward, toward an acknowledgment of our mutual obligations toward one another. Kateb writes that Emerson wants "to see the human world's historical mutability and diversity as either a projection of elements in every soul or an enactment, on a large scale, of private events in any person's life. History could not be understood if all people were not similarly manifold and equally experienced."[46] The manifold quality of selfhood that Kateb describes enables the process of temporal extension that Emerson depicts in "Compensation." Indeed, the end result of attaining the prospect available from the position of being "above time" is a reformation of the self away from narcissistic individualism and toward a sense of continuity with the world outside of the self. The self that is powerful in time incorporates ceaseless transformation into a coherent being, balancing the inner life (what Emerson calls the "soul") with the external world. Near the end of "Compensation," Emerson pictures temporal change as a kind of fluctuating contact zone between the self and the world:

> In proportion to the vigor of the individual, these revolutions are frequent, until in some happier mind they are incessant, and all worldly relations hang very loosely about him, becoming, as it were, a transparent fluid membrane through which the living form is seen, and not, as in most men, an indurated heterogeneous fabric of many dates, and of no settled character, in which the man is imprisoned. Then there can be enlargement, and the man of to-day scarcely recognizes the man of yesterday. And such should be the outward biography of man in time, a putting off of dead circumstances day by day, as he renews his raiment day by day.[47]

This image captures Emerson's view that it is temporality's ceaseless transformations that connect the individual to the world outside the self. The more "vigor" an individual possesses, the more frequently will that person's life transform itself within time. Those who obtain Emerson's desired position of being "above time" become perceptible to others, present in the world, in contrast to the majority who are obscured by their less settled, less vigorous relationship to time. Paradoxically, in this condition in which the individual becomes recognizable to others, "the man of to-day scarcely recognizes the man of yesterday." Thus, to fully realize our own being requires inhabiting time, wearing it about ourselves like a membrane or second skin. Our sense of continuous self then becomes objective—we abandon our attachment to the past, and so our reality must be affirmed by those who perceive us. We give ourselves to the social world.

The imagery of clothing in this passage is clearly indebted to Thomas Carlyle, whose *Sartor Resartus* Emerson had brought to publication in its first book form in 1836 (it had been serialized in Britain in 1833-34). *Sartor Resartus* treats the philosophical problem of being satirically by presenting an ostensible history of clothing written by a fictitious German scholar named Diogenes Teufelsdröckh. In Carlyle's satire, Teufelsdröckh treats clothing as an authentic representation of the self, a kind of natural language revealing the self to the world. However, Teufelsdröckh's theories are presented via the medium of a nameless British editor, whose rational commentary contrasts with Teufelsdröckh's mysticism. The resulting dialogue between the novel's two voices undermines the credibility of Teufelsdröckh's theory and makes clothing into a symbol for the endlessly vexing and perplexing problem of representing the relationship between the self and the world outside the self. The contrast between the editor's anonymous but present voice and Teufelsdröckh's romantic but distant persona further complicates the text's initial claims to present a coherent theory of being. In the end, *Sartor Resartus* treats the self as an elusive and unknowable object of speculation.

Time plays an important role in *Sartor Resartus*, as Carlyle adheres to Kant's treatment of temporal phenomena as structural elements of the human mind, or "thought forms," that mediate human perception of the objective world.[48] Carlyle develops Kant's treatment of time as phenomenal by suggesting that when we cloak ourselves in time's folds we become entrapped in falseness, kept forever separate from the objective world and from any authentic experience of other human beings. The metaphor of clothing comes to stand for the artifice of time itself, which exists within our minds but not out in the world where we seem to perceive it. Thus, in Carlyle's dark satire it is impossible to achieve an authentic existence within time. The fundamental nature of our being leaves us powerless in relation to time, or, effectively, powerless in relation to ourselves.

Emerson reverses Carlyle's treatment of time by substituting an organic "transparent fluid membrane" for the Carlylian "heterogeneous fabric." Unlike the fabric, the temporal membrane affirms being's presence in the world. Carlyle's satire renders the self obscure and even incoherent, since neither the editor nor Teufelsdröckh seems to possess a fully realized humanity. Emerson suggests that most of his contemporaries do suffer from such a condition of incomplete selfhood and hence remain entrapped within the tattered garments of an improper relationship to time. However, unlike Carlyle, Emerson presents the possibility of transcending this state by achieving a different relationship to time. Like a piece of fabric, the membrane seems to be something that is at least partially a human creation. A certain program of philosophical labor is required to achieve this relationship to time. However, the membrane is also an aspect of nature, since it is of course a tissue of the body. The membrane is thus *between* the self and nature. Emerson revises Carlyle's Kantian understanding of time to suggest that time is, indeed, part of the objective world, and not merely a structural aspect of perception. Since time exists out there, in the world, our mastery of time, our achievement of a position "above time," makes us powerful in the world. In this way, we become visible to those around us, one of Emerson's geniuses.

The crucial point that Emerson makes through this image, then, is that we must acknowledge the objective reality of the world outside ourselves to become powerful and present within that world. Only when we acknowledge the reality of the world will the world begin to perceive our reality. Following the shifting of temporal perspective that "History" provides, "Self-Reliance" and "Compensation" thus lay out the program of "ethical reform" that Emerson had called for in "History." This relationship between mastery of time and authentic, powerful being is reiterated throughout the subsequent pieces in *Essays*, especially "The Over-Soul." At the conclusion of "The Over-Soul," Emerson writes that if a person achieves an existence within "a moment of time," then that individual "will weave no longer a spotted life of shreds and patches, but he will live with a divine unity."[49] The "spotted life" echoes the image of the "heterogeneous fabric" from "Compensation." In "The Over-Soul," Emerson goes on to connect this mastery of present moments with a position of power in relation to the entirety of time: "He will calmly front the morrow in the negligency of that trust which carries God with it," Emerson writes of the ideal person, "and so hath already the whole future in the bottom of the heart." Here Emerson ties the form of being within time that he had developed in "Compensation" to a prospect of the future. Hence, by this point in *Essays* we see that a position of power within present time leads to a powerful sense of possession of future time. The mode of being "above time" leads likewise to a more authentic relationship to the past. "Why do men feel that the natural history of man has never been written?" Emerson asks in the beginning of "The Over-Soul." "The philosophy of six thousand years has not searched the chambers and magazines of the soul. In its experiments there has always remained, in the last analysis, a residuum it could not resolve. Man is a stream whose source is hidden."[50] In these lines, Emerson dismisses the 6,000-year time frame of human history in favor of natural history, the temporality of "rat and lizard" that was central to the perspectival revolution of "History." The "ethical reformation" Emerson stages throughout *Essays* culminates in our retrieval of this last "residuum" of ourselves. By transcending our narrow subjectivity and acknowledging the reality of the world outside of ourselves, we finally come into complete possession of our own beings.[51]

Toward a Politics of the Inhuman

In *Essays*, then, Emerson transforms the expanse of natural history from a troubling fact given by the world into a tool available for use in his philosophical program. Like any other temporal form, deep time emerges out of the interaction between human actors and the nonhuman world. Just as an advice writer might produce a tract promoting a particular way of employing the time told by clocks, Emerson in *Essays* advocates certain ways of making use of the temporality revealed in natural history. Rather than seeking to contain deep time by rendering it compatible with already familiar religious or even secular humanist cosmologies, he embraces deep time's most radical potential in order to further his goal of fostering a more authentic condition of being among the American people. Such authenticity would, in turn, enable Americans to create more truly democratic social and political worlds.

After the publication of *Essays*, Emerson's writings increasingly emphasize the entropic qualities of nature in order to demolish the rational humanism that underlay both organized religion, as he had experienced it, and the utilitarian political economy of the nineteenth century. In the autumn 1841 address "The Method of Nature," delivered eight months after he had completed *Essays*, Emerson told a Waterville, Maine, audience: "If anything could stand still, it would be crushed and dissipated by the torrent it resisted, and if it were a mind, would be crazed; as insane persons are those who hold fast to one thought, and do not flow with the course of nature."[52] Here, Emerson has clearly adapted geological theory to his own use. Lyell or Agassiz would never have described natural history in such a way; indeed, Lyell's uniformitarianism, with its emphasis on the rational analysis of nature's stable, universal laws, is not at all compatible with Emerson's description of nature as a chaotic force and intellectual consistency as a form of madness. In the 1830s Emerson had repeated ideas gleaned from his reading to the audiences of his lectures. By the early 1840s, Emerson was transforming and making use of ideas from natural history for his own ends.

Through such entropic imagery, Emerson pursued the social implications of the reformulation of human identity that he had codified in *Essays*. The purpose of Emerson's profuse geological and biological metaphors is to seek the new form human social organization might take in a world of natural power on an inhuman scale. In the 1844 essay "Nature," Emerson writes: "Nature is loved by what is best in us. It is loved as the city of God, although, or rather because there is no citizen. The sunset is unlike anything that is underneath it: it wants men. And the beauty of nature must always seem unreal and mocking, until the landscape has human figures, that are as good as itself. If there were good men, there would never be this rapture in nature."[53] What is at stake in this passage is the status of the individual in relation to nature. Augustine's city of God lacked citizens because of the ubiquity of sin. Emerson's nature lacks human citizens because none have yet achieved the requisite ethical reformation. "When we behold the landscape in a poetic spirit," Emerson told the audience of "The Method of Nature," "we do not reckon individuals."[54] This lecture was delivered only months after Emerson had published *Essays*; how could the author of "Self-Reliance" suggest that there was something unnatural and unpoetic about the individual?

It is in this evident contradiction that the relevance of Emerson's thinking about deep time to his social and political philosophy becomes most apparent, for deep time profoundly reshapes Emerson's conception of the individual. "There is common agreement," writes Kateb, one of the most trenchant defenders of liberalism, "that the individual is the moral center of American life."[55] Emerson would undoubtedly have agreed with this statement, but would then proceed to ask what would be necessary for individuals to become moral, to achieve the ethical power that would make them the centers of their social worlds. As Kateb and others have illustrated, Emerson's concept of the individual is exceptionally complex. Indeed, his individualism often seems paradoxically contemptuous of individuals. In "The Over-Soul," for example, Emerson provides an almost postmodern description of selfhood as simply a residuum of nonhuman natural phenomena: "From within or from behind, a light shines through us upon things, and makes us aware that we are nothing, but the light is all."[56] This line is only one of many similar statements to be found throughout Emerson's writings. Emerson elevates the individual to the highest level of importance, yet he also situates the individual within a world of mysterious, inhuman power.

Statements such as these lead Christopher Newfield to find in Emerson the origin of what he terms "the submissive center" of American politics. Liberalism has put forward two ideals, Newfield suggests: personal autonomy and group intersubjectivity. In American liberalism's dominant, Emersonian mode, the balance between these two ideals has taken the form of submission to a quasi-religious "higher authority" that is "beyond the group" and "demands a submissive subject."[57] Sharon Cameron has gone even further in critiquing Emerson's "disillusion with the conventional idea that persons are separate and integral entities" by arguing that his "impersonal" conception of humanity is "ethically illegitimate." This is so because the "missing sense of a person" Cameron sees in Emerson's work results in an evasion of "the responsibility a person should take for his words," an acknowledgment of the material differences, contingencies, and suffering that must be the basis of ethical relations between human beings.[58] Kateb, in contrast, sees in Emerson's concern with "the gaps between persons" an ethical and philosophical commitment to "discover that others are real, as real as oneself, and that what is outside of oneself consists not of phantasms, but of reality."[59] Although I think that Kateb is more nearly right in his interpretation, Newfield's and Cameron's analyses usefully bring to the fore the tremendous threat to liberal democratic social theory that would be posed by the diminution of the individual human being.

What these critiques leave out is the historical context of Emerson's antihumanism. Emerson was not opposed to the individual per se; rather, he wished to redeem the concept of the ethically responsible individual by replacing an untenable form of individual identity rooted in Enlightenment humanism. Emerson did not invent the threat to this older concept of the individual; rather, the old form was undermined by the new nineteenth-century cosmology. "Geology has initiated us into the secularity of nature," Emerson writes in the 1844 essay "Nature," "and taught us to disuse our dame-school measures, and exchange our Mosaic and Ptolemaic schemes for her large style. We knew nothing rightly, for want of perspective."[60] Such broodings recur throughout his writings after *Essays*. In *English Traits* (1856), Emerson appropriates Lyell's analysis of the rise and fall of the land relative to the sea in order to suggest the brevity of human history in relation to natural history:

To the geologist, the sea is the only firmament; the land is in perpetual flux and change, now blown up like a tumor, now sunk in a chasm, and the registered observations of a few hundred years find it in a perpetual tilt, rising and falling. The sea keeps its old level; and 'tis no wonder that the history of our race is so recent, if the roar of the ocean is silencing our traditions. A rising of the sea, such as has been observed, say an inch a century, from east to west on the land, will bury all the towns, monuments, bones, and knowledge of mankind, steadily and insensibly.[61]

Emerson's use of the term "firmament" evokes the language of Genesis as translated in the King James Bible. Emerson's tale of the sea and land thus revises the Bible into a new story not centered upon human beings. More importantly, Emerson describes the historical insignificance of a nation far more ancient than the United States. In making specific mention not only of the towns of England but also of the "monuments" and "bones," Emerson casts history and culture into the depths of time. The visit to Shakespeare's grave is one of the central events in the cultural pilgrimage recorded in Washington Irving's *The Sketch Book*. While Irving's alter ego Geoffrey Crayon is intrigued by Shakespeare's birthplace, he is filled with a much more powerful sense of the permanence and majesty of culture when he stands within the church containing Shakespeare's tomb.[62] In recording his own journey to England, in contrast, Emerson imagines those bones and all of the accumulated "knowledge of mankind" that they represent disappearing into an immensely long, inhumanly patient geological shift.

Emerson acknowledges and articulates this threat to traditional culture in order to attempt to work out a solution that would redeem America from the looming abyss of deep time. It is this problem that both necessitates and makes possible his radical transformation of the individual. "If we measure our individual forces against hers," Emerson goes on to say near the end of the 1844 "Nature," "we may easily feel as if we were the sport of an insuperable destiny. But if, instead of identifying ourselves with the work, we feel that the soul of the workman streams through us, we shall find the peace of the morning dwelling first in our hearts, and the fathomless powers of gravity and chemistry, and, over them, of life, preexisting within us in their highest form."[63] This statement is another of the sort to which Newfield and Cameron object, since it seems to render the individual either submissive to a vaguely defined higher authority or devoid of ethical responsibility for his or her own actions. However, when we read a line such as this in the context of Emerson's concern with the massive and potentially devastating force of deep time, we can see that Emerson's aspiration here is not to strip the individual of agency but rather to seek a way to reconceptualize human agency within the newly revealed inhumanity of nature. Unlike Thoreau, who turns back when he nears the summit of Ktaadn, Emerson presses on.

For Emerson, conceiving of himself as a poet, the way to achieve this reformation is to employ language to mediate between the human and natural worlds. The "transparent fluid membrane" represents time, but in themselves the words on the page are not time but a metaphor.[64] That is to say, Emerson understood that human beings could only reform their relationships to time if they possessed a language in which to do so. Even before he conceived of his project in these terms, Emerson had been deeply committed to figurative language; from the beginning, his lectures and essays abound in the metaphors through which he strove to make sense of the world. Indeed, Emerson perceived figures of speech as themselves aspects of nature. "Every word which is used to express a moral or intellectual fact," he had written in a discussion of natural language theory in the 1836 *Nature*, "if traced to its root, is found to be borrowed from some material appearance."[65] Hence, in forming metaphors from and for natural history, Emerson is not appropriating nature but making its native connotations visible to humankind.

Such metaphors are woven into his work like a pattern for making sense of the world. In "Experience," for example, Emerson writes that "a man is like a bit of Labrador spar, which has no lustre as you turn it in your hand, until you come to a particular angle; then it shows deep and beautiful colors."[66] This line exemplifies the way that Emerson appropriated the discoveries of natural science for his own purposes by revealing their implicit metaphors. "In Henry VIII," he muses in 1845, assessing Shakespeare's relation to his source materials, "I think I see plainly the cropping out of the original rock on which his own finer stratum was laid."[67] If language is the medium between the human and the inhuman worlds, then Shakespeare, as poet, works with language as time works with rock. Linguistic influence and creative appropriation are versions of sedimentation, and literature forms the resulting strata. In "The Poet," Emerson draws a similar connection, but in this case he imagines the poet working in reverse of time, complementing the activity of sedimentation by following it backwards: "Language is fossil poetry. As the limestone of the continent consists of infinite masses of the shells of animalcules, so language is made up of images or tropes, which now, in their secondary use, have long ceased to remind us of their poetic origin. But the poet names the thing because he sees it, or comes one step nearer to it than any other."[68] Here the poet is a kind of linguistic geologist or archaeologist, while in the discussion of Shakespeare the poet is more like the process of geological change itself, laying down new strata atop earlier formations. In both cases, Emerson's belief in natural language theory makes it possible for him to integrate natural history and linguistic expression seamlessly.[69] For Emerson, language is a part of nature, and natural history is also the history of language.

The temporal dimension of Emerson's sustained intellectual project was to excavate America from sedimented language, instilling the idea of democracy with fresh life by recovering the vitality of its fossilized metaphors from the strata of history. Emerson sought the future promise of American democracy in forms recovered from the depths of time, a horizon of possibility both enticing and terrifying. The role of the thinker, artist, creator, then, is to provide us with an ability to face the inhuman enormity of the world without perishing. Emerson's search for "practical power" finds its complement in Nietzsche's "plastic power": the power of a being to "grow out of itself, transforming and assimilating everything past and alien, to heal wounds, replace what is lost and reshape broken forms out of itself."[70] Plastic power, or "practical power" as Emerson calls it, is bound up in this recursive problem of temporality, a medium that we both inhabit and create. In this way, an organism may become something other than itself, just as time and space are both of the self and alien from the self.

Making Camp in America

"Let a man learn to look for the permanent in the mutable and fleeting," Emerson writes in *Representative Men* (1850). "Let him learn to bear the disappearance of things he was wont to reverence, without losing his reverence; let him learn that he is here, not to work, but to be worked upon; and that, though abyss open under abyss, and opinion displace opinion, all are at last contained in the Eternal Cause."[71] These lines conclude his essay on Montaigne and skepticism. For Emerson, Montaigne was "the frankest and honestest of all writers" because of his commitment to truth and reality, his "impatience and fastidiousness at color or pretence of any kind."[72] Montaigne's skepticism is linked, as Emerson sees it, to a more realistic perception of the tenuous claim to coherence of the individual human being within nature. Reality, as Emerson understood it, compels us to admit that individuals exist subject to the whim of nature. And nature may produce individuals who are not always to our liking. In "The Method of Nature," Emerson says: "That no single end may be selected, and nature judged thereby, appears from this, that if man himself be considered as the end, and it be assumed that the final cause of the world is to make holy or wise or beautiful men, we see that it has not succeeded."[73] Evolution proceeds toward imperfection, elusive ends that deny our utopian aspirations. In his 1844 essay "Nature," Emerson concludes that "there is throughout nature something mocking, something that leads us on and on, but arrives nowhere, keeps no faith with us. All promise outruns the performance. We live in a system of approximations. Every end is prospective of some other end, which is also temporary; a round and final success nowhere. We are encamped in nature, not domesticated."[74] The domesticity of Emerson's earliest writings about nature has been displaced by a new metaphor, *encampment*, a trope that resists an objective, rational account of our position in relation to nature. Through such language, Emerson sought to contest the terms on which the modern world was constituting itself.

Stephen Toulmin has explored the work that modernity must do in order to represent itself in terms of Cartesian rationality. According to Toulmin, the "standard account" of the "modern age," understood to begin in the seventeenth century, rests upon the assumption that "the transition from medieval to modern modes of thought and practice rested on the adoption of rational methods in all serious fields of intellectual inquiry—by Galileo Galilei in physics, by René Descartes in epistemology—with their example soon being followed in political theory by Thomas Hobbes."[75] If Toulmin is right to say that modernity's self-representation has taken the form of Cartesian rationality—and I think that he is—then it is Emerson's great insight to see that time itself can change the Cartesian matrix. Deep time made it possible for Emerson to embrace change as the central fact of existence, and out of change, to make transition and power, rather than reason and order, the foundations of modernity. Emerson's celebration of Montaigne's philosophical skepticism even anticipates Toulmin's own call for a reformulation of modernity in which Montaigne, rather than Descartes and Bacon, would take on the central role; through Montaigne, Toulmin hopes to redeem Western culture from the "solipsism" of Descartes, in which "every individual, as a psychological subject, is (so to say) trapped inside his own head."[76] It is this kind of antidemocratic, pernicious individualism that Kateb seeks to locate a cure for in Emerson as part of his own effort to redeem liberal democracy.

Emerson discovers this more responsible version of selfhood in the position "above time" described in "Self-Reliance." When we wear time as a "transparent fluid membrane," we become visible to others. When we lose our weak desire to substitute the past or the future for the present, when we make ourselves able to affirm the present, then we abandon ourselves to the social world. We become dependent upon those others who perceive us to affirm our condition of continuous being, our ontological wholeness. Therefore, only when we become able to live "above time," able to forget our own yesterdays and tomorrows in the faith that others will affirm our continued existence, do we make an ethical commitment to emerge from our solipsism and trust in others for the care of our selves. We learn how to do this through the linguistic artistry of the poet, through the metaphors that the poet provides to enable us to perceive our relationship to the inhuman world.

The metaphor of encampment extends the earlier concept of being "above time" as a way of thinking about the relation of the individual self to this inhuman world. In opposition to domesticity, encampment provides a skeptical outlook upon the situation of the moment and its relation to other moments. Our encampment within temporality is, perforce, temporary. The question is whether this temporary (or temporal) condition will prevent us from committing fully to being within time. Encampment does not imply a lack of concern for the present moment. On the contrary, only when we recognize that every present moment will disappear, only when we acknowledge the mutability of life within time, can we make a fully responsible, philosophically meaningful commitment to the present. We must commit ourselves to that which we know will cease to exist in a moment. This is difficult, far more difficult than allowing ourselves to drown in nostalgia, or to be swept up in the teleology of romantic historicism, or to glide ghostlike through the empty rationality of time as constructed in the capitalist market. Emerson writes in "Circles":

> It is the highest power of divine moments that they abolish our contritions also. I accuse myself of sloth and unprofitableness day by day; but when these waves of God flow into me, I no longer reckon lost time. I no longer poorly compute my possible achievement by what remains to me of the month or the year; for these moments confer a sort of omnipresence and omnipotence which asks nothing of duration, but sees that the energy of the mind is commensurate with the work to be done, without time.[77]

Emerson's social imagination, his sense of the power and contingency of the relays linking persons to one another in perpetually shifting networks, was woven out of the endless possibility he found in a past and future extending millions of years. "The same law of eternal procession ranges all that we call the virtues, and extinguishes each in the light of a better," he writes in "Circles." And, in "The Over-Soul": "Our faith comes in moments; our vice is habitual. Yet there is a depth in those brief moments which constrains us to ascribe more reality to them than to all other experiences."[78] In these deep moments, flux on the surface of the abyss of time, Emerson began to imagine the most astounding possibilities of American democracy.

CONCLUSION

The Ends of Time

I have focused the last full chapter of this book on Emerson because his work exemplifies two ideas central to my argument. The first of these major ideas is that the phenomenon we experience as *time* emerges out of the efforts of human beings to make productive use of the nonhuman world. We might think of temporal modes such as deep time or clock time as facts of nature or technological imperatives, aspects of the world to which we must adapt ourselves. However, while time may be anchored in the nonhuman world, always partly beyond reach, Emerson's writings demonstrate how we bring time within human culture through our labor. As we perform work with time, as we strive to shape our selves and our social worlds into new forms, we create the temporal modes that we inhabit.

Time is thus a product of human activity, but a product whose form is not wholly within the control of any individual or group. Emerging out of the competing interests and desires of myriad actors, time as we experience it is inherently political. This is the second of the key ideas illustrated so well by Emerson's work. Emerson's effort to employ time to transform the social world reminds us that time is defined in relation to the purposes it serves. Hence, we can never say what time is. Instead, we can only ask what kinds of worlds different forms of time make possible, and what interests are served by the creation of such worlds. Indeed, Emerson poses the most central question of American politics: what are the ends of time?

A Republic in Time has been structured to provide examples of important ways that select individuals have employed time for particular ends of social (that is, greater than individual) consequence. All of these figures worked within the conceptual world described in Chapter 1—the Jeffersonian paradigm of a nation extending itself through time, seeking perpetually for a utopian horizon located somewhere in the future. Hence, collectively the subjects discussed here illustrate how the idea of the nation extends beyond territoriality and into temporality. From there, I have sought to identify some of the temporal modes that were available for use by social thinkers in creating different visions of this republic in time, and also to look closely at the detailed maps of American time that the more intentional of such thinkers laid out. In this respect, the just-concluded chapter on Emerson's use of deep time is similar to Chapter 3, which analyzes how Catharine Beecher and Henry Thoreau employed ideas about mechanical time to make arguments in support of different kinds of social reform. Chapter 2, on mechanical time, and Chapter 4, on deep time, illustrate the heterogeneity of these temporal modes as they were produced and reproduced by many individuals interacting with technology and nature. Chapters 3 and 5 focus on more systematic efforts by particular individuals, who might be described as "theorists," to make use of these temporal modes in the service of their competing social and political programs. In Chapter 3, I identify several thinkers who appropriated mechanical time in such a way and analyze two of the most successful of these thinkers in detail, while in Chapter 5, I focus only on Emerson. Does this mean that deep time was less important than mechanical time for American efforts to create imaginative visions of modern nationhood? Quite the contrary: the subsequent centrality of Emerson's ideas to American concepts of freedom and the good life suggests that deep time was an equally powerful concept in the long run. Both technology and nature provided significant resources for the creation of national time.

National time can best be thought of as the meeting place of the diverse ends sought after by the actors employing such resources. That is, the special form of time in which the people imagine their collective life, which we call national time, takes shape as a result of the struggles of different individuals and groups to create a nation that reflects their interests and aspirations. The abstraction of the nation provides a venue not only for political solidarity but also for conflict. Our emotional commitment to the nation, our sense of patriotism and affiliation with something larger than ourselves, is tempered by the understanding that the nation is the one place where our imaginative lives are most likely to encounter those who differ from us, even those who would oppose our ends. Because constructions of time reflect our diverse subject positions and interests, national time can never be homogeneous. Diverse forms of temporality are not marginal or subversive; rather, it is precisely the heterogeneity of time, the character of time as it emerges from struggle, that makes it national, because this heterogeneity is what makes it political. Benedict Anderson is quite right to say that our experience of national belonging is based upon our shared imaginings of a collective movement within time. However, this time is not a unity; it is multifarious and protean, riven with conflict.

In defining national time in this way, I do not wish to ignore the fact that the actors in such conflicts are not always equals and that the outcomes are not always just. Time can often be employed by one group of people in order to exercise power over another group. Such groups often possess different amounts of power to define time, different levels of access to the national political culture. Such issues come to the fore in a story told by Philip Morgan about a postbellum Lowcountry conflict over time between newly liberated African Americans, who wished to continue working in the task system to which they were accustomed, and officials of the Freedmen's Bureau, who wished to teach the freedmen and freedwomen to measure and sell their labor by units of time. Morgan notes that the African Americans' resistance to adopting this practice reflected their understanding of autonomy. Within slavery, the task system (which operated primarily in the Lowcountry) typically left workers with part of the day to call their own. Once the allotted tasks were completed, the obligation to work for the master was done. Each enslaved person was then free, in a relative sense, to choose how to spend the remaining time of the day. While the white northerners who sought to reform this practice viewed these African Americans as obtuse for their resistance to a supposedly more modern way of organizing labor, the workers were in fact simply employing time in a way that reflected their interests as they understood them.[1] There are multiple intergroup conflicts at play here — not only white versus black, but northerner versus southerner, manager versus laborer, and so forth. Clearly there is more at stake in this conflict than a difference of opinion, or even a difference of values or of an ethical sense of the good. Hence, the anecdote reveals the complexity of assessing such conflicts in terms of justice. While the Freedmen's Bureau agents possessed more power than the newly freed African Americans, their actions can be seen as both emancipatory and oppressive. They wished to aid the laborers in bettering their situation, and yet they attempted to do so by bringing them within a paradigm of labor that was, as E. P. Thompson has illustrated, itself a form of class domination.[2]

While remaining aware of the ways in which, as this episode reveals, particular forms of time can become instruments of exploitation or domination, I have sought to contest the view that the nation's dominant temporal mode simply reflects the interests and ideological predispositions of the ruling class. Although much of my analysis of culture is ultimately grounded in a Marxist point of view, I am most sympathetic to revisionist Marxists such as Antonio Gramsci and Louis Althusser, whose analyses of hegemony and ideology have provided us with ways of thinking about cultural power that do not reduce class interests to monoliths. While it is certainly the case that many aspects of our culture work to persuade the disenfranchised that their interests are the same as those of the ruling class, it is not at all a settled matter what those ruling-class interests are. Thoreau's friends and readers might have thought of him as an eccentric, but Thoreau nevertheless shared with Catharine Beecher a position of great privilege. Individuals such as these used their literacy and their access to publication to spread their ideas and contest each other's visions of America. The ideas that the powerful sent into circulation through the nation were heterogeneous.

Furthermore, a number of the figures I discuss in this work possessed highly ambiguous class status. A very successful artisan such as Simon Willard was financially prosperous but still made a living working with his hands. However, Willard's clocks were relatively expensive, and therefore the ideas about time that Willard created circulated mostly among the middling and upper classes. Chauncey Jerome was for a few years one of the most successful businessmen in America, but his autobiography reveals more than a trace of a working-class outlook on life. In contrast to Willard, Jerome created products that were affordable for many working-class and farming families. Hence, at the period of his greatest personal wealth, Jerome's products linked him firmly to the less affluent. Such contradictions and ironies make it difficult to say how these men's class identity ought to be defined, and I have not attempted to fix their position within one category or another. In general, then, I have focused on the ways in which the temporal productions of such individuals interacted with one another creatively. Such a focus does not deny the importance of an analysis of class, race, region, or any other category of group domination and resistance that might operate within the nation. There is certainly more to say on the topic of how temporality can become an instrument of such domination, but in this book I have chosen to emphasize the more positive and even utopian possibilities of the nation. This is a useful perspective to offer now in response to the current academic movement to consider culture in global terms, which has led some to attack the nation as an obstacle to liberation and others to dismiss the relevance of the nation altogether.

Why write a book about national time in the era of globalization and post-nationalism? To put the case plainly, I believe that the movement among some intellectuals and scholars to denationalize culture and politics is both ahistorical and, unintentionally, politically regressive. To cite just one example, Wai Chee Dimock, an influential scholar whose insights I have long admired, has recently argued that a global perspective requires us to readjust our temporal horizons as scholars toward what she calls, in some places, deep time, and in others — drawing on the work of Fernand Braudel — *longue durée*. Dimock's call for scholars to frame their analyses within "a duration antedating the birth of any nation and outlasting the demise of all" resonates well with contemporary efforts to internationalize or denationalize American studies, some of which I discussed in Chapter 1 of this book.[3] Where Benedict Anderson uses "empty, homogeneous time" to make nationhood the central fact of modern imaginative and political life, Dimock would, in contrast, use *longue durée* to minimize the historical significance of the nation. Dimock's readings of individual works are lucid and persuasive, but the theoretical foundation of these readings is troubling. Just as Anderson has assumed too natural and essential a relationship between the nation and what is really only one particular form of time, so does Dimock move too radically to detach time from all ties to nationhood. Dimock sees nation-states as mere epiphenomena floating on the surface of deep time, inconsequential in comparison to centuries-long historical movements such as (to cite one of her main examples) the development of Islam. Dimock represents time itself as transhistorical in order to represent the rise of the modern nation-state as a minor event in history. Representing time as prior to, and more fundamental than, nationhood leaves time itself just as homogeneous and abstract as it is in Anderson's theory.

There are important consequences to this practice of dehistoricizing certain conceptions of time. Both deep time and *longue durée* are ways of thinking about time that are made possible by the cultural and intellectual activities of the age of nationalism. These conceptions cannot be detached from their origins and treated as transhistorical phenomena. I have shown in this book how closely the development of deep time has been tied to the imaginative invention of national history. Similarly, Braudel's concept of *longue durée* crosses national boundaries, but it is nevertheless closely tied to the history of modern nation formation. Braudel argues that temporality is historical and shifts in relation to both national and global economics, politics, and culture. Thus, while Dimock uses the *Bhagavad Gita* as an example of a text representing *longue durée*, Braudel explicitly excludes most of India (outside of major commercial centers) from "world time" due to its historical lack of global trade relations.[4] For Braudel, the local only comes into world time when it is linked to the national and international via commerce. Thus, Braudel seems to exclude an ancient text like the *Bhagavad Gita* from any discussion of *longue durée*. Dimock dismisses the importance of national territory and history alike because such constructs are not "natural" but instead "no more than a fiction."[5] However, Braudel makes clear that his concept of *longue durée* is, if not precisely a fiction, at least something invented—for it is a construction of temporality arising from the economic conditions of a global system, a vast creation of the activities of millions if not billions of individuals. The fact that the activities of those individuals cross national boundaries makes them international, or perhaps transnational, rather than nonnational or postnational. Dimock posits that if we think about history in very long terms, we will recognize that the nation is merely an artifact of a particular era, and we will therefore disavow its importance. However, this hypothesis not only disregards the importance of the historically constructed nature of transnational temporal spans such as geological deep time and Braudel's *longue durée*, but it also eschews Emerson's most important insight: it is precisely when we become aware that national time is not natural, but something we produce, that we can begin to use that time as an instrument to create the social and political worlds that we would like to inhabit.

Relying on this insight of Emerson's, *A Republic in Time* argues for the ongoing relevance of the nation, not simply to scholarly accounts of the past but to political culture in the age of globalization. If the nation can extend through time as well as space, then the attenuation of territorial borders and the globalization of commerce and culture need not mean the death of the nation. The nation may continue to exist as an imaginative venue for real political discourse and for the meeting of parties with conflicting interests. To be sure, the nation can be, and often is, used as an instrument of domination or exploitation by certain powerful groups. However, such negative possibilities have to be evaluated in the context of the many positive outcomes of rights-based, constitutional democracy. Given that global capitalism would like to reduce all interests to the same desire for unfettered consumption, the nation is a crucial tool for keeping alive our consciousness of the fact that human beings do in fact have interests that conflict. It was through the idea of the nation that writers like Beecher and Thoreau were able to infuse the ominously shallow market-oriented culture of their time with more critical values. Once we understand the nation not merely as a homogenizing force but also as a locus of healthy dispute, ethical conflict, and philosophical faith, we can begin to employ its resources against the transformation of human culture into a homogeneous commodity.

Remaining committed to the nation does not mean that we ought to dismiss the recent movement toward cosmopolitanism. However, we should strive to achieve a cosmopolitanism that is international rather than antinational.[6] Some of the most cosmopolitan political dissenters in America have understood that the temporal character of the national state makes it available as an instrument for reform and revolution. Thomas Paine begins *Common Sense* by urging his readers to consider that governments were formed by human beings, within history. Human beings first form societies, Paine argues, and only subsequently political states. Initially these states are very simple, meeting beneath a "convenient tree"; only later do they become more complex and corrupt.[7] Paine uses the fact that governments are created by the people within historical time to argue for the legitimacy of revolution. When the people remember that they created the state, Paine suggests, then they will realize that they can also make revolutionary changes. Similarly, Emerson opens his essay "Politics" by pointing out that the state's "institutions are not aboriginal, though they existed before we were born." Since these institutions were created within historical time, they are "all imitable, all alterable."[8]

Assertions such as these do not mean that Paine and Emerson wished to do away with the state altogether. Rather, they recognized that the state's desirability as an institution for organizing political power resides precisely in its temporal limitations — that is, in the fact that it is temporary and therefore always limited in its dominion. Some forms of social and political organization strive to make themselves unchallengeable by representing themselves as natural and therefore eternal. Since we understand the state to be unnatural and therefore temporary, we can make use of the state as an instrument for circumscribing power. This does not mean that the state will always play such a positive role, only that it has that potential. As citizens, we are responsible for ensuring that the state provides a provisional balancing of the interests among the people of a nation. If the balance proves unsuitable as time passes, then the state can be changed. It is only when people organize themselves nationally that they acquire access to such an instrument for managing conflict. Both religious fundamentalism and global capitalism are totalizing institutions that would supercede the nation and replace the temporal, and hence democratic, institutions of the state with ideologies professing themselves beyond the reach of history.

There are, then, two reasons we need to keep talking about the nation in American studies. The first reason is given to us by circumstance: globalization does not mean the death of the nation. The nation will continue to travel forward through time as institution and ideal regardless of what happens to the borders and territory of the United States. The second reason we ought to grasp by choice: the nation is an instrument of political health. In its heterogeneous, multifarious nature, the nation enables us to resist more totalizing, less exorable forms of social organization and political control. We will continue to live within national time, and we should embrace this fate, for in it we may find our salvation.

NOTES

Introduction

1. Peabody, "The American Almanac," 28–30. *The American Almanac and Repository of Useful Knowledge*, published in Boston from 1830 to 1862, was begun by Jared Sparks, but by 1835 J. E. Worcester had taken over as editor.

2. See, for example, Channing, "The Present Age," in *Works*, 159–72; and Emerson, "The Present Age," vol. 2 of *Early Lectures*, 157–72.

3. Peabody, "The American Almanac," 29, 36.

4. Today, most people are no longer aware of a difference between mean and apparent solar time. If one were to measure the length of a day from solar noon to solar noon—that is, from one instance of the sun's passage directly over a given point on the earth's surface to the next—then the length of each day would vary considerably over the course of the year. This phenomenon occurs because of the earth's rotation on its own axis as it orbits the sun, because of eccentricities in the earth's motion, and because its orbit around the sun is an ellipsis rather than a circle. Clock time, or mean solar time, is simply an average of the time that would be told on all the days of the year by marking local noon at the time of the sun's passage directly overhead. The difference between apparent and mean solar time, known as the "equation of time," can be as much as eighteen minutes on some days of the year; four times a year, it is zero. For a more in-depth discussion of this issue, see, for example, Milham, *Time and Timekeepers*, 1–20, an accessible account written by a professional astronomer; and the National Maritime Museum, "The Equation of Time."

5. Worcester, ed., *The American Almanac*, 50.

6. For a summary of the debates surrounding the dating of the emergence of the modern nation-state, see Anthony D. Smith, *The Nation in History*, 27–51.

7. Pocock, *The Machiavellian Moment*, 32. It should be noted that Pocock's treatment of medieval temporal experience does not do justice to that complex subject.

8. David Noble describes Pocock's treatment of time and space in terms of a "dualism" that "related republican virtue to timeless space and monarchical corruption to time as the environment of ephemeral tradition." While I agree with Noble that Pocock characterizes republican philosophers as concerned about the possibility of corruption within time, it is crucial to Pocock's account that the republic only emerges once modern humanist time has super-

ceded medieval eschatological time. Hence, fantasies of a "timeless" republic are simply one strategy for dealing with the recognition that the republic exists within time. Noble, *Death of a Nation*, xxxv.

9. Locke, *Two Treatises of Government*, 301. Locke uses "America" to exemplify a state of nature several times in the text of the *Second Treatise*.

10. My argument here focuses on "Western" theories of time and nationhood. There is a great deal of fascinating scholarship, in anthropology and related fields, describing how other cultures have conceptualized time. See, for example, Hirsch and Stewart, "Introduction: Ethnographies of Historicity," and the other essays included in this special issue of *History and Anthropology* devoted to the topic of how historical time is constructed in different cultures around the world.

11. For two different views of the Lockean influence on the Declaration, see Bailyn, *Ideological Origins*, and Wills, *Inventing America*; for a more general exploration of Locke's influence on American culture, see Brown, *The Consent of the Governed*. For a detailed analysis of the role played by temporality in the thought of the Revolutionary generation, see Lienesch, *New Order of the Ages*.

12. Anderson, *Imagined Communities*, xiii, 47–65, 67.

13. Benjamin, *Illuminations*, 261; Anderson, *Imagined Communities*, 24.

14. Anthony D. Smith, *Nationalism and Modernism*, 136.

15. Gellner, *Nationalism*, 20, 28–29.

16. Simmel, *Simmel on Culture*, 177.

17. Mumford, *Technics and Civilization*, 14.

18. Thompson, "Time, Work-Discipline, and Industrial Capitalism," 56–57; Simmel, *Simmel on Culture*; Mumford, *Technics and Civilization*.

19. Landes, *Revolution in Time*.

20. Social and economic historians have produced a vast literature attempting to define the nature of capitalism in general and free-market capitalism in particular. In a practical sense, I rely most directly upon Charles Sellers's description of "the market" as an "intricate network of production for exchange" whose "irresistible commodities drew people into producing the commodities it demanded." Sellers, *The Market Revolution*, 4. Lying more deeply behind my understanding of the market economy is the magisterial analysis of Braudel, *Civilization and Capitalism*.

21. Mumford, *Technics and Civilization*, 15.

22. Bhabha, *The Location of Culture*, 139–70.

23. Pease, "Doing Justice to C. L. R. James's *Mariners, Renegades, and Castaways*," 18. See also James, *Mariners, Renegades, and Castaways*.

24. Pease and Wiegman, "Futures," 16, 17.

25. Stephens, *On Time*, 21.

26. Dohrn-van Rossum, *History of the Hour*, 14–15.

27. See Hensley, "Time, Work, and Social Context in New England"; McCrossen, *Holy Day, Holiday* and "'Conventions of Simultaneity'"; Mark M. Smith, *Mastered by the Clock*; Bruegel, "Time That Can Be Relied Upon" and *Farm, Shop, Landing*; and O'Malley, *Keeping Watch*. Note that although Bruegel's article "Time That Can Be Relied Upon" is in some respects an earlier version of the same material developed in the later monograph *Farm, Shop, Landing*, the article presents a lengthier and more detailed discussion of temporality than does the subsequent book.

28. McCrossen, "By the Clock," 558.

29. Elias, *Time*, 145.

30. McCoy, *The Elusive Republic*, 200–201.

31. Latour, "On Technical Mediation," 29–64. It should be noted that Latour's purpose in this essay is to argue against Heidegger's view of technology as part of the process of "becoming" of human beings, a "revealing" of something essential to human nature. See Heidegger, "The Question Concerning Technology."

32. Emerson, *Essays and Lectures*, 119.

33. Strasser, "Making Consumption Conspicuous," 770.

34. Prown, *Art as Evidence*, 93.

Chapter One

1. O'Sullivan, "The Great Nation of Futurity," 429.

2. Ibid., 427.

3. Ibid.

4. As Peter Onuf explains, "Jefferson looked forward to the proliferation of free republican states" that would constitute a "benign imperial order, predicated on the reciprocity of benefits and the security of natural rights." Onuf, *Jefferson's Empire*, 53.

5. Henry Nash Smith, *Virgin Land*, 3.

6. I discuss several examples of "revisionist" scholarship that focuses on the land, at the expense of time, over the course of the next few pages; in addition, I have in mind influential works challenging mid-twentieth-century understandings of gender, race, and class, such as Kolodny, *The Lay of the Land*; Anzaldúa, *Borderlands/La Frontera*; and Gilroy, *The Black Atlantic*. While these works, especially Anzaldúa's, pay some attention to time, they all focus their analysis of North American political culture primarily upon space and the land (or, in

Gilroy's case, the land and sea). These themes also often come together in the so-called new western history, exemplified by Limerick, Milner, and Rankin, eds., *Trails*.

7. Jefferson, Letter to James Monroe, October 24, 1823, in *Writings*, ed. Peterson, 1481.

8. Jehlen, *American Incarnation*, 17–18.

9. Noble, *Death of a Nation*, 1.

10. Rowe, *The New American Studies*, 12.

11. Pease, "Postnational Politics and American Studies."

12. In addition to the work of Rowe and Pease, other recent influential work by such figures as Amy Kaplan, Stephanie Lamenager, and Paul Giles has contributed to the consensus narrative of the United States as a nation initially defining itself through territorial integrity and then moving toward postnationality as this claim to integral space becomes untenable. See Kaplan, "Where Is Guantánamo?" and *The Anarchy of Empire*; Lamenager, *Manifest and Other Destinies*; and Giles, *Virtual Americas*.

13. Buell, "American Literary Emergence as a Postcolonial Phenomenon."

14. Pocock, *The Machiavellian Moment*, 462, 510.

15. The warning against imperialism comes from Jefferson, Letter to William Short, July 28, 1791, in *Papers*, 20:688. The phrase "Empire of liberty" appears in a letter from Jefferson to George Rogers Clark dated December 25, 1780, in *Papers*, 4:237–38. Jefferson also used the very similar phrase "empire for liberty" almost twenty years later; see Letter to James Madison, April 27, 1809, in *Writings*, ed. Lipscomb and Bergh, 12:277.

16. Martin Brückner has recently observed that we may be suffering from "a certain thematic exhaustion with the subject of Empire" that stems from the fact that "when addressing imperial practices the slippage into making doctrinal arguments is made easy by the sheer volume of primary and secondary sources." Brückner, "The Critical Place of Empire in Early American Studies," 811.

17. For an important dissenting view, see Onuf, *Jefferson's Empire*, which argues that Jefferson and his contemporaries did not associate the concept of empire with tyranny at all. While I admire Onuf's command of Jefferson's writings and of intellectual history in general, I am less sanguine than he that Jefferson perceived no paradox in the idea of an American empire. As I hope my discussion of Jefferson's ideas throughout this chapter will make clear, I certainly agree with Onuf that it would be simplistic and misleading to label Jefferson an "imperialist" in the twenty-first-century sense.

18. Jefferson, Letter to Aaron Burr, June 17, 1797, in *Papers*, 29:439.

19. Simms, *Poetry and the Practical*, 8–9.

20. Schoolcraft, "The Rise of the West," 494.

21. O'Sullivan, "Great Nation," 427.

22. O'Sullivan, "Annexation," 9, 10.

23. Dimock, *Empire for Liberty*, 26.

24. During, "Literature — Nationalism's Other? The Case for Revision," 138.

25. Anthony D. Smith, *The Nation in History*, 57.

26. On the immense influence of German romanticism on the development of American attitudes toward history, see Firda, "German Philosophy of History"; and O'Brien, *Conjectures of Order*, 1:125–45, 2:691–99.

27. Levin, *History as Romantic Art*, 6–7.

28. Nina Baym finds that in America "establishment hostility to the novel per se began to evaporate only with the success of Walter Scott's *Waverley* in 1814. This suggests that the novel, demonized as history's other, escaped its pariah status by becoming historical itself." Baym, *American Women Writers and the Work of History*, 23.

29. There are, as one would expect, some important exceptions to this generalization. For example, William Prescott twice cautions readers of his *Conquest of Mexico* against judging the actions of people in the past by the standards of the nineteenth-century present. Such a caution is more typical of post-nineteenth-century American academic historical writing than it is of the writings of Prescott's contemporaries. See Prescott, *History of the Conquest of Mexico and History of the Conquest of Peru*, 6, 685–86. It is noteworthy that Prescott's work seems to have been interpreted by his contemporaries in Romantic terms despite the author's own cautions.

30. Levin, *History as Romantic Art*, 8–9.

31. Channing, "On the Elevation of the Laboring Classes," in *Works*, 47.

32. Simms, *Views and Reviews*, 189.

33. Harvey, *American Geographics*, 249.

34. Sigourney refers to Charles Rollin's *Ancient History*, a very well-known text available in nineteenth-century America in a variety of more or less radically abridged editions. Sigourney, *Letters of Life*, 203–4.

35. Quoted in England, "The Democratic Faith in American Schoolbooks," 197.

36. Willard, *An Address to the Public*, 28.

37. On republican motherhood in the Revolutionary era, see Kerber, *Women of the Republic*; on Emma Willard as an example of nineteenth-century republican motherhood, see Baym, "Women and the Republic: Emma Willard's Rhetoric of History," in *Feminism and American Literary History*, 121–35.

38. Scott, "What, Then, Is the American? This New Woman?," 690, 696–97.

39. The edition of Willard's *Universal History* that I read at the Library of Virginia was inscribed by a student at the Washington Male School in 1871.

40. Willard states in the explanatory text that a larger and more detailed version of this pedagogical tool was available for teachers to use in classrooms, but I have not seen an extant copy of this larger chart. It is also advertised in the back of the book.

41. Anonymous, "Willard's System of Universal History," 262.

42. Willard, *Universal History in Perspective*, 301.

43. On the influence of contemporary pedagogical theory on Willard's choice of this image of the tree, see Calhoun, "Eyes for the Jacksonian World," esp. 16, 19.

44. O'Sullivan, "Annexation," 5.

45. Malthus, *On Population*, 9.

46. Jefferson, Letter to Jean-Baptiste Say, February 1, 1804, in *Writings*, ed. Peterson, 1144.

47. McCoy, *The Elusive Republic*, 195.

48. Ibid., 131.

49. Lienesch, *New Order of the Ages*, 83.

50. Jefferson, Letter to Joseph Priestley, March 21, 1801, in *Writings*, ed. Peterson, 1086.

51. Jefferson's remarks to Priestley bring to mind John Demos's discussion of the change in meaning of the word "revolution" in the late eighteenth century: "From now on, revolution would signify not a turning back into old paths but the creation of entirely new ones." Demos, *Circles and Lines*, 47.

52. Jefferson, Letter to Samuel Kercheval, July 12, 1816, in *Writings*, ed. Peterson, 1402.

53. Jefferson, who was in France during the Constitutional Convention of 1787, grew increasingly critical of the U.S. Constitution as he aged, eventually coming to view it as a failed document. In the passage quoted, he seems to employ the "constitution" (note the lack of capitalization) in a somewhat abstract way as embodying the political ideals of the people; this would not obviate his developing criticisms of particular aspects of the document that his peers had drawn up in the 1787 Convention.

54. Jefferson, Letter to John C. Breckenridge, August 12, 1803, in *Writings*, ed. Peterson, 1138.

55. Jefferson, Letter to Joseph Priestley, January 29, 1804, in *Writings*, ed. Ford, 8:295.

56. Fisher, "Democratic Social Space," 64.

57. Jefferson, Letter to William Ludlow, September 6, 1824, in *Writings*, ed. Peterson, 1496–97.

58. John Quincy Adams, "Society and Civilization," 81. The essay is credited to Adams in the journal.

59. In addition to McCoy, sources for this explanation of stadialism include Dekker, *James Fenimore Cooper the Novelist* and *The American Historical Romance*; Levin, *History as Romantic Art*; and Pocock, *The Machiavellian Moment*.

60. Bancroft, *History of the United States*, 4:457, 462.

61. Willard, *History of the United States, or, Republic of America*, 469.

62. Willard, *An Address to the Public*, 35.

63. McCoy, *The Elusive Republic*, 32.

64. Willard, *Universal History in Perspective*, 3.

65. Willard, *Last Periods of Universal History*, 528.

66. Baym, *American Women Writers and the Work of History*, 53.

67. Nye, *The Almost Chosen People*, 68.

68. Schoolcraft, "The Rise of the West," 495.

69. Bancroft, *Literary and Historical Miscellanies*, 287, 291, 292, 297, 302, 317.

70. Daniels, *Fields of Vision*, 160.

71. Wilton and Barringer, *American Sublime*, 102.

72. Dekker, *American Historical Romance*, 98.

73. Cole, *The Collected Essays and Prose Sketches*, 16–17.

74. Peckham, *Gotham Yankee*, 68; Charles H. Brown, *William Cullen Bryant*, 100–101.

75. Bryant, "The Ages," in *Poetical Works*, 11–21.

76. Berkeley, *Works*, 4:366.

77. Willard, *Journals and Letters, from France and Great-Britain*, 66, 71.

78. Michael Lienesch discusses these contradictory themes of decline and progress from a somewhat different perspective in *New Order of the Ages*, 38–60.

79. Jefferson, Letter to William Ludlow, in *Writings*, ed. Peterson, 1497.

80. On Jefferson and clocks, see Bedini, "Thomas Jefferson, Clock Designer"; and McLoughlin, *Jefferson and Monticello*, 371–72.

81. The meaning of such a distinction might lie in anthropologist Johannes Fabian's argument that Western civilization has used the control of time as a marker of civilized status: "The other is constructed as a system of coordinates . . . in which given societies of all times and places may be plotted in terms of relative distance from the present." Fabian criticizes this practice, while historians such as David Landes and Daniel Boorstin have celebrated the very similar notion that Europe achieved its economic success by using time with more

discipline than people in any other region of the world. See Fabian, *Time and the Other*, 26; Boorstin, *The Discoverers*, chapters 1–3; Landes, Introduction, *Revolution in Time*.

82. Kelsall, *Jefferson and the Iconography of Romanticism*, 131.

83. Jefferson, Letter to Joseph Priestley, March 21, 1801, in *Writings*, ed. Peterson, 1086.

84. Kimball, *Thomas Jefferson, Architect*, 169.

85. Jefferson, Letter to John Adams, August 1, 1816, in *The Adams-Jefferson Letters*, 485.

Chapter Two

1. See, for example, William Paley's use of the watch as an emblem of design in *Natural Theology* (1802). For a general survey of the use of mechanical time-keepers as metaphors during the Englightenment, see Macey, *Clocks and the Cosmos*, 65–120.

2. A full-page reproduction of this label can be seen in Palmer, *A Treasury of American Clocks*, 169.

3. On the English clock industry and international trade, see Bird, *English House Clocks*, 295–306; and Landes, *Revolution in Time*, 231–47, 293–346.

4. The American clocks competed not primarily on quality but on price. As Jerome explains in his autobiography, his first shipment of brass-movement clocks was priced so much lower than similar English-made clocks that the British customs officers thought he was trying to avoid paying import duties. The officials therefore exercised their right to buy the entire shipment for the declared valuation. After Jerome sent two more such shipments, the customs officers finally allowed the American-made clocks to enter the London market, where they achieved great success. Jerome, *History of the American Clock Business*, 60–62.

5. The system of mass-produced, interchangeable parts seems to have emerged initially in France during the 1880s but became known as the American System, even in Europe, by the early nineteenth century. I thank Charles Hummel for pointing this out to me.

6. Landes, *Revolution in Time*, 336–37; O'Malley, *Keeping Watch*, 31–32; Stephens, *On Time*, 85–86.

7. Jerome, *History of the American Clock Business*, 134.

8. Many examples of the wide variety of clock designs available in the 1840s can be seen in the Decorative Arts Photographic Collection (DAPC) at the Winterthur Museum and Library in Wilmington, Delaware. The DAPC archives multiple images of objects of historic value in public and private collections.

For complex objects such as clocks, the DAPC provides both interior and exterior images from front, side, and back. It is thus a superior resource to other image collections, such as guidebooks for collectors of antiques, which typically feature only a single, exterior image of each object. In the DAPC, see the following files for models of clocks that would have been for sale in the 1840s: Seth Thomas, Silas Hoadley, Joseph Ives, Chauncey Jerome, and Forestville Manufacturing Company. See also the Eli Terry file, which includes some relevant examples from "Eli Terry and Sons," though Terry himself had left the mass production of clocks by that time. For additional images, see the following books: Bailey, *Two Hundred Years of American Clocks and Watches*; Palmer, *A Treasury of American Clocks*; and Schorsch, *The Warner Collector's Guide to American Clocks*.

9. On the use of clocks in Shaker communities, see Swank, *Shaker Life, Art, and Architecture*, 138–39; and Sprig and Larkin, *Shaker Life, Work, and Art*, 43–44. See also the DAPC file for Shaker clockmaker Benjamin Youngs of Watervliet, New York.

10. Historians have been able to use data such as probate records to determine a general rise in clock ownership, and to a lesser extent watch ownership, over the course of the nineteenth century. However, such efforts must always be constrained by the limitations of the available data. Hence, it is impossible to make definitive statements about the extent of mechanical timepiece ownership; we can only trace the general trend of increase. See, for example, Mark M. Smith, *Mastered by the Clock*, 29–37.

11. On the emergence of the American watch industry in the 1850s, see O'Malley, *Keeping Watch*, 172–77; Stephens, *On Time*, 92–97; and Landes, *Revolution in Time*, 339–46.

12. This interpretation of the interaction between human and nonhuman is derived from Latour, "On Technical Mediation."

13. Prown, *Art as Evidence*, 87.

14. In addition to Prown, my analysis here is indebted to James V. Kavanaugh's treatment of objects as "the sensuously perceptible form of culture" by means of which "individuals in a society 'create themselves' or define themselves culturally" by objectifying their ideas in "culturally prescribed phenomenal forms." Kavanaugh, "The Artifact in American Culture," 67.

15. On the relative rates of clock and watch ownership, see, for example, the statistics compiled from probate records by Mark M. Smith in *Mastered by the Clock*, 34.

16. The term "grandfather clock" did not come into use until 1878, when Henry Clay Work's song "My Grandfather's Clock" became popular. See Gloag, *A*

Complete Dictionary of Furniture, 372. The song's complete lyrics are available on several websites.

17. On the complexities of clock making in the preindustrial era, see Dreppard, *American Clocks and Clockmakers*, 42–56; and Zea and Cheney, *Clock Making in New England, 1725–1825*.

18. For more detailed discussions of the watch trade in the late eighteenth and early nineteenth centuries, see Stephens, *On Time*, 51–55; and Landes, *Revolution in Time*, 264–92.

19. None of the studies of quantitative data on clock and watch ownership in nineteenth-century America have, as of yet, separated out tall case clocks made in the eighteenth century. Hence, indirect evidence such as images and descriptions of clocks is the best available at this time.

20. The poem is titled "The Old Clock on the Stairs." Longfellow, *Poems and Other Writings*, 51.

21. Elizabeth O'Leary goes so far as to say that in this painting "the roles of mistress and servant are not only indistinct but nearly indecipherable." O'Leary, *At Beck and Call*, 48.

22. My reading of the family's economic status is indebted to that of Anneliese Harding, who concludes that this family "enjoys a measure of prosperity but is not wealthy." Harding, *John Lewis Krimmel*, 43. On this painting, see also Naeve, *John Lewis Krimmel*, 69–71.

23. Oscar P. Fitzgerald's *Four Centuries of American Furniture* provides useful descriptions and photographs of tall case clocks in the Chippendale and Federal styles on pages 69 and 94, respectively.

24. For another representation of such a clock, see Krimmel's painting *The Country Wedding* (1820).

25. This painting was a great hit when initially exhibited in New York and made Mount's reputation. See Frankenstein, *Painter of Rural America*, 14–15.

26. On the tendency of clocks made in rural areas to depart from metropolitan design standards, see Bailey, *Two Hundred Years of American Clocks and Watches*, 25; and Drepperd, *American Clocks and Clock-Makers*, 46.

27. This clock's case is thought to come from the shop of the famous Newport furniture maker Job Townsend. The clock is located in the Newport Room of the Winterthur Museum (Winterthur object catalog number 1951.0028). The clock measures ninety-eight inches in height, nineteen inches in width, and ten inches in depth. The dial and works are brass, while the cabinet is constructed of pine, poplar, walnut, and ash. See the curatorial notes in the Winterthur object catalog.

28. Stuart Sherman provides a fascinating account of the significant differences in

how we hear the sound of a clock: as "tick, tick, tick" or as "tick, tock." According to Sherman, the first implies an endless chain of identical moments, while the latter suggests a beginning and a conclusion. Sherman, *Telling Time*, 1–25.

29. While there was no reason most people in the eighteenth century would have needed to know time to the second, Dreppard notes that the seconds dials on tall case clocks did serve a useful function as "telltales to indicate at a glance that the clock was running." Drepperd, *American Clocks and Clockmakers*, 36.

30. According to Longfellow's poem, the clock possesses a "voice" that not only "says" things but also "sighs," "echoes," "repeats," "is heard," "makes reply," and "sayeth incessantly." In other words, the attribution of voice to the clock is a major conceit of the poem. Longfellow, *Poems and Other Writings*, 51–53.

31. Museum curator Donald Fennimore, intimately familiar with the workings of the Wady clock, explains that this small dial "registers tidal reverses every six hours and twelve minutes, the hand making a complete revolution once every fifteen days." Fennimore, *Metalwork in Early America*, 301.

32. As with my analysis of all of the clocks discussed in this chapter that are in Winterthur's collections, my analysis of the Wady clock is based on first-hand observation of the object. This analysis necessarily combines objective description with more subjective interpretation of the meaning of the phenomena observed. For example, the description of the dial face and the time tracks is based on my personal observation. My comment that one can easily tell time to the quarter hour using the hour hand alone is based on my own experience of doing this, using the quarter-hour marks on the time track. I heard the ticking sound of the seconds hand myself; it is distinctly audible from several feet away (at least). My comment that the clock "combines an allusion to old-fashioned methods of telling time in its inner time track with a more precise and modern time track for the minute hand" is, of course, more of a subjective interpretation of the clock's design. The comment at the end of the same paragraph, in which I suggest that the clock must have signified "the origin of clock time in cultural traditions," is also an interpretive judgment. My analysis of the "lunette" on the clock face is based on my personal observation of the feature, along with my reading in Fennimore's book about the function of the small dial for tracking tidal changes. My concluding point, that the mechanism for tracking the tides "reflects local needs and interests," is an interpretation of the significance of the clock's physical features. Throughout this chapter, readers should remain aware that material culture studies always involve a combination of objective observation and subjective judgment.

33. Garrett, "*Novus Ordo Seclorum*," 16.

34. Wendy A. Cooper has documented the significance of such forms in *Classical Taste in America*.

35. Evans, "The Christian M. Nestell Drawing Book," 133–40.

36. See, for example, the Lemuel Curtis banjo wall clock at the Winterthur Museum (object catalog number 67.1449), which features lyre-shaped arms and an eagle finial along with paintings of figures in classical garb on both the throat and the bottom panel of the clock; the tall clock by Griffith Owen of Philadelphia (object catalog number 57.1026), dated 1800–1815, which features an eagle inlay on the case along with eagle and urn finials; and the Elnathan Taber banjo wall clock (object catalog number 57.978), dated ca. 1815, which features lyre side arms and a painting of the figure of Aurora from classical mythology in the glass panel at the base. See also the file for Spencer Nolen in the DAPC for examples of neoclassical illustrations.

37. Priddy, Flanigan, and Weidman, "The Genesis of Neoclassical Style in Baltimore Furniture."

38. The Dubuc clock is in the Empire Parlor of the Winterthur Museum (object catalog number 1957.0744). It is eighteen inches high and twenty-two inches wide, constructed with bronze enamel and iron in the dial. The Mallet clock is in the Empire Hall at Winterthur (object catalog number 1989.0060). It is twenty-two inches high and nineteen inches wide, constructed of bronze-plated lead, glass, and steel. For comparison, see also the French neoclassical shelf clock with a bust of Washington in Winterthur's Dining Room Cross Hall (object catalog number 1957.0795) and the Arsandaux Washington shelf clock in the Baltimore Drawing Room (object catalog number 57.0782).

39. Katherine Grier explains that "In a world where artificial light was precious, and was provided for most families by kerosene lamps rather than municipal systems, parlor center tables were the location of the brightest pool of light in the room and the most decorative lamps." A clock on a side table or mantel would be on the fringes of the room's illumination. Grier, *Culture and Comfort*, 97.

40. The way that the outer dial ring glows in dim light first became apparent to me when the lights in the Empire Parlor were dimmed as I left the room with a member of the museum's curatorial staff. Subsequent experimentation proved that this soft luminescence is quite distinct and remarkable.

41. This tall clock is in the Pennsylvania Dutch Room on the first floor of the Winterthur Museum (object catalog number 1958.2874). It is constructed of several kinds of wood, including maple and mahogany, along with iron and brass.

42. This clock is located in the Music Room of the Winterthur Museum (object catalog number 1965.2275). It stands twenty-eight inches in height and is eleven inches wide and five inches in depth. It is constructed of mahogany and pine with metal parts of brass and lead.

43. The technical analysis of this clock's operation is to be found in LaFond, Collection of Research Notes, box 397. In regard to the missing disk, Lafond writes, "A comparison of the Winterthur clock and a Simon Willard calendar shelf clock in the collection of the Dedham, Massachusetts, Historical Society reveals that the clock originally had a wheel illustrating the phases of the moon and possibly other lunar and solar computations." Lafond goes on to explain the mechanics by which this disk would revolve once every fifty-nine days. The rest of my description of the physical characteristics of the clock comes from firsthand study of the object in the Winterthur Museum.

44. The clock pictured here is located in the Gold and White Room of the Winterthur Museum (object catalog number 1957.0952A–B). It stands forty-one inches high and is ten inches wide and almost four inches in depth. It is constructed of mahogany, pine, brass, and glass.

45. For other examples of "banjo" wall clocks, including some with various "Patent" indications, see the Lemuel Curtis timepiece, Winterthur Museum (object catalog number 67.1449); the Jabex Baldwin "diamond head" banjo timepiece, Winterthur Museum (object catalog number 57.645); the New Hampshire country painted banjo timepiece, Winterthur Museum (object catalog number 59.2716); the anonymous banjo timepiece, Winterthur Museum (object catalog number 57.1062); the Elnathan Taber neoclassical banjo timepiece, Winterthur Museum (object catalog number 57.0978); and the DAPC files for Simon Willard and Aaron Willard.

46. Foley, *Willard's Patent Time Pieces*, 7.

47. The advertisement is reproduced as an illustration in ibid., 9.

48. Carolyn C. Cooper, "Social Construction of Invention through Patent Management," 960.

49. The descriptive portion of Willard's patent application is reproduced as an appendix in Foley, *Willard's Patent Time Pieces*, 341.

50. The advantages of Willard's design, and its appropriation by other clockmakers, are discussed in Zea, "Clockmaking and Society at the River and the Bay," 56.

51. The example of a lighthouse clock pictured here is located at Old Sturbridge Village, Massachusetts (collection number 57.1.16). For other examples of lighthouse clocks, see the DAPC file for Simon Willard at Winterthur. See also the two meticulous reproductions at Winterthur by the later master crafts-

man James Conlon (object catalog number 1958.0590A–B and object catalog number 1957.1011A–C).

52. Stilgoe, *Common Landscape of America*, 111.

53. Melville, *Moby-Dick*, 63; Jefferson, *Writings*, ed. Peterson, 49.

54. Kris Fresonke has demonstrated how the narratives of American explorers from Lewis and Clark to Zebulon Pike rendered landscape in picturesque terms in order to bring it within the national imaginary, and Rebecca Bedell has made a related argument about the work of painters such as Thomas Moran. See Fresonke, *West of Emerson*; and Bedell, *The Anatomy of Nature*.

55. Quoted in Foley, *Willard's Patent Time Pieces*, 346.

56. Stephens, *On Time*, 85.

57. Eli Terry's DAPC file includes multiple images of a large number of his pillar-and-scroll clocks, including images of the interiors, patent labels, and other features that would not normally be portrayed in published guides for collectors. Although these clocks were mass-produced, Terry created a wide variety of design elements that he combined in different ways to create different versions of the general design. Thus, everything from the finials to the images on the glass panels tends to vary from clock to clock. In my research in the DAPC and in guides for collectors, I found that the design features that I have described here are among the most common.

58. For photographs of clocks featuring painted images of Mount Vernon, see the DAPC files not only for Eli Terry but also for his onetime employee and then competitor, Seth Thomas.

59. Jennifer Clark notes that for many Americans in the early decades of the nineteenth century, machinery was "believed to be the vehicle of American success and the best expression of her rapid advance." John F. Kasson has also called attention to the link between technological advancement and republican ideals. Jennifer Clark, "The American Image of Technology," 432; Kasson, *Civilizing the Machine*. For an elegant statement of dissent from the scholarly consensus, see Steven Lubar's argument that, before about 1830, the majority of Americans "evinced neither love for technological ingenuity nor a belief that technological advance was essential for economic growth." Lubar, "The Transformation of Antebellum Patent Law," 937.

60. Jerome, "Introduction," 8.

61. The DAPC file for Silas Hoadley contains multiple images of the exteriors and interiors of two of these Franklin clocks. I have based my analysis of the clock's general design, and of the Franklin label in particular, upon these images in the DAPC. Other examples of this clock can be found at the National Associa-

tion of Watch and Clock Collectors Museum in Columbia, Pennsylvania, and the Henry Ford Museum in Dearborn, Michigan.

62. Alcott, *The Young Man's Guide*, 43.

63. The Waterbury ad is reproduced in Stephens, *On Time*, 96.

64. McCabe, *The Illustrated History of the Centennial Exhibition*, 488.

65. Anonymous, "On Time," 690.

66. Curtis, "My Friend the Watch," 75.

67. As business historian John Joseph Murphy notes, "Quantity production and transient merchandising quickly became the twin pillars upon which the clock industry was firmly established." See Murphy, "Entrepreneurship," 183.

68. Featherstonehaugh, *Excursion through the Slave States*, 92.

69. Fisher, "Democratic Social Space," 62.

70. Biographical information about Edmonds can be found in two books: H. Nichols B. Clark, *Francis W. Edmonds*; and Mann, *Francis William Edmonds*.

71. On railroad travel and timekeeping in New England, see Stephens, "'The Most Reliable Time.'" Nationally, see Bartky, *Selling the True Time*.

72. Mann, *Francis William Edmonds*, 29.

73. Drepperd, *American Clocks and Clock-Makers*, 95–96.

74. Jerome, *History of the American Clock Business*, 137. Subsequent parenthetical references are to this edition.

75. McCabe, *Great Fortunes*, 316.

76. Clock parts had been made of brass before. In fact, higher quality clocks had always used brass. However, the development of new techniques to produce large quantities of sheet brass in the 1830s made the metal much cheaper and paved the way for Jerome's new product. Roberts, *Eli Terry and the Connecticut Shelf Clock*, 149.

77. Hawthorne, *The Scarlet Letter*, 35.

78. Bill Brown, *A Sense of Things*, 27.

79. See the DAPC file for Chauncey Jerome for multiple images of the Gothic Revival clock model. This was a common design for clocks from many different makers.

80. Barnum, *Struggles and Triumphs*, 404.

81. The most thorough account of the bankruptcy is in A. H. Saxon's academic biography of Barnum. Saxon is notably partisan and describes Jerome's entire autobiography as "a disquieting litany of complaints from start to finish" and Jerome as a "whining author." However, despite his more sympathetic attitude toward Barnum, Saxon still concludes that "between these two claims of bliss-

ful ignorance, one may be pardoned for hesitating to take sides." Saxon, *P. T. Barnum*, 196–97.

Chapter Three

1. Gillian Brown, *Domestic Individualism*; Sklansky, *The Soul's Economy*.
2. Marxist sociologist Val Burris provides a wonderfully concise and lucid definition of reification:

   It describes a situation of isolated individual producers whose relation to one another is indirect and realized only through the mediation of things (the circulation of commodities), such that the social character of each producer's labor becomes obscured and human relationships are veiled behind the relations among things and apprehended as relations among things. In this manner a particular (historical) set of social relations comes to be identified with the natural properties of physical objects, thereby acquiring an appearance of naturalness or inevitability — a fact which contributes, in turn, to the reproduction of existing social relations. (Burris, "Reification," 23–24)

3. Lukács, *History and Class Consciousness*, 93.
4. Blumin, *The Emergence of the Middle Class*, 187–88. See also Ryan, *Cradle of the Middle Class*; Grier, *Culture and Comfort*; and Halttunen, *Confidence Men and Painted Women* and "From Parlor to Living Room."
5. Merish, *Sentimental Materialism*, 92.
6. Brantlinger, *Fictions of State*, 140.
7. Gillian Brown, *Domestic Individualism*; Romero, *Home Fronts*.
8. In employing the term "personhood," I draw upon Benedict Anderson's definition of individual identity as a phenomenon that "must be narrated" in terms that are always particular to a historical moment, and upon Priscilla Wald's analysis of how the "reformulation of personhood" that Anderson describes inevitably "accompanies the constitution of a new community," such as the United States self-consciously felt itself to be in the early to mid-nineteenth century. Anderson, *Imagined Communities*, 204; Wald, *Constituting Americans*, 4.
9. Sedgwick, *Home*, 9–10. Subsequent parenthetical references are to this edition.
10. Merish, *Sentimental Materialism*, 120, 121, 126.
11. Sigourney, *Letters to Mothers*, 80–81.
12. Ibid., 153–54.
13. Howland, *The American Economical Housekeeper*, 43. It is interesting that the word "American" in the 1845 title was changed to "New England" in 1847.

The two editions are identical in other respects. This change would seem to indicate a degree of uncertainty regarding the extent to which the domestic practices of any region or local area could be construed as truly national.

14. Howland, *The American Economical Housekeeper*, 45.

15. Zea and Cheney, *Clock Making in New England, 1725–1825*, 132.

16. Similarly, Mark M. Smith's recent revisionist study of the importance of clock time in the South, for example, does not contest the assumption that the clock first became important in factories:

> As the changes wrought by the nineteenth century began to usher in separate spheres . . . housework and domestic chores came to acquire a clock-regulated quality that women had sometimes experienced in the public world of eighteenth-century work. In some ways, middle- and working-class northern women were united by a familiarity with either the factory or the domestic clock. But southern women, the mistresses most obviously, did not go to the factory. Instead, the factory and its attendant time discipline came to them, first in the form of the household clock that joined white women's traditional task orientation and, second, in instances when mistresses had to manage household labor. . . . Clocks, for example, were important for cooking and recipes. (Smith, *Mastered by the Clock*, 60)

17. Gardner, "Labor," 85. Subsequent parenthetical references are to this text.

18. Halttunen, *Confidence Men and Painted Women*, 106.

19. Hale, *Keeping House and House Keeping*, 108. Subsequent parenthetical references are to this edition.

20. Blumin, *The Emergence of the Middle Class*, 185.

21. Stowe, *The Minister's Wooing*, 13.

22. Tichi, "Domesticity on Walden Pond," 99, 101.

23. Beecher, *A Treatise on Domestic Economy*, 157. Subsequent parenthetical references are to this edition. Although Beecher made some revisions between the many editions of this book issued throughout the nineteenth century, all of the passages quoted in this essay are identical in the first edition and the 1851 edition cited here.

24. Thoreau, *Walden*, 111. Subsequent parenthetical references are to this edition.

25. Michael O'Malley also comments on Beecher's strategy of using time in the domestic realm to promote Christian virtue and produce "good citizens." However, O'Malley argues that Beecher "rooted her conception of time in nature, rather than in clocks"—a dichotomy I view as unnecessary—and concludes that she "specifically rejected clock time in favor of a virtuous temporal rigor

drawn from the Bible." While my analysis shares much of O'Malley's sense of the productive power Beecher located in the employment of time, I depart from O'Malley in that I characterize not only Beecher but also Thoreau as working *with* clock time, rather than against it. See O'Malley, *Keeping Watch*, 50–52.

26. Beecher, *The Evils Suffered by American Women*, 7–8.

27. Ibid., 8.

28. Ibid., 9. This interpretation of Beecher's text accords with Nancy Armstrong's more general argument that the normative modern subject is established as female in nineteenth-century literary texts; see Armstrong, *Desire and Domestic Fiction*.

29. De Certeau, *The Practice of Everyday Life*, 201.

30. Ibid., xii.

31. Sklar, *Catharine Beecher*.

32. Gillian Brown, *Domestic Individualism*, 20–21; see also Kaplan, "Manifest Domesticity."

33. Tonkovich, *Domesticity with a Difference*, 103.

34. Ryan, *The Empire of the Mother*.

35. Gross, "Culture and Cultivation," 54.

36. Fisher, "Democratic Social Space," 65; see also Michael T. Gilmore's characterization of *Walden* as a retreat from the world of market capitalism in *American Romanticism in the Marketplace*.

37. Cavell, *Conditions Handsome and Unhandsome*, 19.

38. Douglas, *The Feminization of American Culture*.

39. Richardson, *Henry Thoreau*, 168.

40. For an extended treatment of the relationship between Thoreau's economic ideas and those of his contemporaries, see Neufeldt, *The Economist*.

41. The aphorism "Get your work done up in the forenoon" is quoted in Beecher and Stowe, *The American Woman's Home*, 311.

42. Richardson, *Henry Thoreau*, 139.

Chapter Four

1. Twain, *Letters from the Earth*, 16. Subsequent parenthetical references are to this edition.

2. On Jerome, Ussher, and other attempts to date the origin of the world biblically, see Toulmin and Goodfield, *The Discovery of Time*, 75–77; and Blackburn and Holford-Strevens, *The Oxford Companion to the Year*, 425.

3. Willard, *Universal History in Perspective*.

4. [A. L.], "Scripture Geology and Scripture Astronomy," 353, 359.

5. On the mostly friendly relationship between natural history and theology before the nineteenth century, see Porter, *The Making of Geology*, especially chapter 8 on the friction that developed in the late eighteenth century as geologists began to turn away from their former careful avoidance of topics within the purview of religion.

6. Chambers, *Vestiges of the Natural History of Creation*, 5.

7. Cummings, *Mark Twain and Science*, 27–30; Dean, "Geology in American Literature and Thought," 295–96.

8. Anonymous, "The State of the World before Adam's Time," 754. This piece was reprinted from *Sharpe's London Magazine*. *Harper's* quickly became notorious for reprinting material from the British press without respect to copyright, but it was hardly the only American magazine to engage in this practice.

9. See Levin, *History as Romantic Art*, 6–7; and Fisher, "Democratic Social Space," 60–61.

10. A number of scholars have noted that exponents of U.S. national identity in the nineteenth century attempted to appropriate American Indian history into the national history of the United States. This effort was inherently problematic since the U.S. government was engaged in an official campaign of "Indian Removal" during most of the century, and since white settlers were engaged in their own unofficial efforts to appropriate Indian lands. Imagining time in the land itself was less paradoxical than arrogating the histories of aboriginal peoples still viewed by most white Americans as alien to the nation.

11. Hutton had read a paper titled "Concerning the System of the Earth, Its Duration and Stability" before the Royal Society of Edinburgh in 1785; a version of this paper, called simply "Theory of the Earth," was published in the *Transactions* of that society in 1788. The monograph *Theory of the Earth*, extensively revised and expanded, appeared in 1795.

12. On Hutton, Playfair, and the reception of uniformitarianism, see Dean, *James Hutton and the History of Geology*; and Porter, *The Making of Geology*.

13. Agassiz did not invent glacial theory by himself, but his *Études sur les Glaciers* (1840) was the most influential exposition. See Merrill, *The First One Hundred Years of American Geology*, 211.

14. Henry Adams, review of *Principles of Geology*, 471; and *The Education of Henry Adams*, 227.

15. Henry Adams, review of *Principles of Geology*, 467, 470.

16. Eisley, *Darwin's Century*, 58. The same comparison to the Copernican Revolution is made by Toulmin and Goodfield in *The Discovery of Time*, 142.

17. The London advertisement and Church's broadside are reproduced as illustrations in Harvey, *The Voyage of the Icebergs*, 14, fig. 4; and 28–29, fig. 16.

18. McPhee, *Basin and Range*; the phrase "deep time" is used throughout the book.

19. Gould, *Time's Arrow, Time's Cycle*, 3.

20. Anonymous, review of *The Bridgewater Treatises*, 552.

21. Lyon, "The Search for Fossil Man," 69.

22. Anonymous, "Editor's Table," 130.

23. Anonymous, "Geology System Makers," 29.

24. S. L. Dana, review of *Elementary Geology*, 104.

25. Hitchcock, *Elementary Geology*, 285.

26. For a more detailed account of Hitchcock's natural theology, see Lawrence, "Edward Hitchcock: The Christian Geologist."

27. Anonymous, "Lyell's Geological Tour," 200.

28. On clepsydrae, see Dohrn–van Rossum, *History of the Hour*, 21–25; and Landes, *Revolution in Time*, 6–10.

29. Schoolcraft, "The Rise of the West," 490.

30. Thoreau, *The Maine Woods*, 81. Subsequent parenthetical references to "Ktaadn" are to this edition. "Ktaadn, and the Maine Woods" was originally published in the important *Union Magazine of Literature and Art* in 1848; a heavily revised version called simply "Ktaadn" was left as a section of the unfinished book *The Maine Woods* at Thoreau's death. For the difficult textual issues surrounding "Ktaadn," see Moldenhauer's appendix to the Princeton edition cited here.

31. James D. Dana, *Manual of Geology*, vii.

32. Gray, review of *Manual of Geology*, 379.

33. Anonymous, "Earth and Man," 205.

34. Orra White married Edward Hitchcock in 1821. She was a gifted artist and illustrated many of the geological features Edward studied and wrote about. The two illustrations included here are from *Plates Illustrating the Geology and Scenery of Massachusetts*, a book whose authorship is usually attributed to Edward despite the fact that it consists almost entirely of lithographs made from Orra's illustrations.

35. Harris, *The Pre-Adamite Earth*, 67. Subsequent parenthetical references are to this edition.

36. Bedell, *The Anatomy of Nature*, 29–41.

37. Ibid., 33.

38. James D. Dana, *Manual of Geology*, 588.

39. Willis, *Summer Cruise in the Mediterranean*, 67–68.

40. Levin, *History as Romantic Art*, 7.

41. Silliman, "Supplement by the Editor," 435. For a discussion of this edition of

Bakewell, including Silliman's additions, see Merrill, *The First One Hundred Years of American Geology*, 154–58.

42. Freud, *Civilization and Its Discontents*, 19.
43. Parry, "Acts of God, Acts of Man," 61. The fragment from Cole's notes is excerpted from a longer section quoted by Parry.
44. Cole, "Sicilian Scenery and Antiquities: Number Two," in *Collected Essays and Prose Sketches*, 43.
45. Miller, *The Empire of the Eye*, 10–11.
46. Fresonke, *West of Emerson*, 69.
47. Novak, *Nature and Culture*, 38.
48. Thoreau, *A Week*, 71.
49. Ibid., 29.

Chapter Five

1. Emerson, *The Journals and Miscellaneous Notebooks*, 14:60.
2. This attribute of kitchen clocks was first pointed out to me by Carlene Stephens; my own subsequent study of nineteenth-century representations of kitchen clocks has confirmed the accuracy of Stephens's observation.
3. Emerson, *The Journals and Miscellaneous Notebooks*, 4:200.
4. Walls, *Emerson's Life in Science*, 223.
5. Kateb, *Emerson and Self-Reliance*, 21.
6. Cameron, *Emerson's Reading*. See also Whicher, *Freedom and Fate*, 145; Saucerman, "A Note on Emerson's Use of Lyell," 50–52; and Wilson, *Emerson's Sublime Science*, 37–38.
7. Harry Hayden Clark, "Emerson and Science," 225–26.
8. Emerson, *The Early Lectures*, 1:29.
9. Ibid., 2:32.
10. Emerson, *The Journals and Miscellaneous Notebooks*, 5:106.
11. Richardson, *Emerson: The Mind on Fire*, 215.
12. Emerson, *Collected Works*, 1:36.
13. Ibid., 1:14.
14. Guthrie, *Above Time*, 19.
15. Emerson, *The Journals and Miscellaneous Notebooks*, 5:333.
16. Packer, *Emerson's Fall*, 99.
17. Emerson, *The Journals and Miscellaneous Notebooks*, 5:444.
18. Emerson, *Collected Works*, 1:64.
19. Ibid., 1:89.
20. This book was not given the title *Essays: First Series*, by which it is now known, until it was reissued in 1847. In my discussion I will refer to it simply as *Essays*,

since this more accurately captures Emerson's original sense of this work as a completed whole, not a collection of miscellaneous pieces already calling out for supplementation or sequel. One qualification to this way of thinking about *Essays* must be noted, however: Emerson did plan to include the essay "Nature" in the volume but could not bring it to a satisfactory state in time. Emerson noted that this essay would balance the essay on "Art." The fact that Emerson thought of the individual pieces complementing each other suggests the wholeness of the book, but the deferred publication of "Nature" in the 1844 *Essays: Second Series* compromises this wholeness. See Robinson, "The Method of Nature and Emerson's Period of Crisis," 74–92, 201 (n. 2).

21. Emerson, *Collected Works*, 2:6. The passage to which the line was added appears in *The Journals and Miscellaneous Notebooks*, 7:33. This source for the passage is noted by Ferguson and Carr in their appendix to *Collected Works*, "Parallel Passages." Throughout this chapter, I have relied upon the scholarship of Ferguson and Carr in locating the unpublished sources of various passages in the published *Essays*.

22. Emerson, *Collected Works*, 2:14, 20.

23. Ibid., 2:20.

24. According to the *Oxford English Dictionary*, in the nineteenth century the term "compend" could indicate either a concise version of something or a part of something that represents the whole. In contrast, "correlative" was used to indicate the reciprocal relationship or mutual obligation of disparate things, such as right and obligation or father and son.

25. Emerson, *Collected Works*, 2:237.

26. Lee Rust Brown, *The Emerson Museum*, 2.

27. Emerson, *Early Lectures*, 2:15.

28. Emerson, *Collected Works*, 2:27.

29. George Stack traces numerous continuities in the treatment of nature from Emerson to Nietzsche but portrays most of Emerson's ideas about nature as coming from Kantian idealism. Stack contrasts Nietzsche to Emerson by describing Nietzsche's ideas as less abstract and more firmly rooted in natural science. Of course, Stack's excellent book was published before the many recent studies on Emerson and science. See Stack, *Nietzsche and Emerson*, especially chapter 2, "Nature: The Riddle of the Sphinx." On the Emerson-Nietzsche connection, see also Lopez, "Emerson and Nietzsche: An Introduction," as well as the rest of the special issue of *ESQ* edited by Lopez and devoted to the topic.

30. Nietzsche, *The Portable Nietzsche*, 42.

31. Nietzsche, *Human, All Too Human*, 16–17 (part 1, section 2).

32. Nietzsche, *Beyond Good and Evil*, 11 (section 3).

33. Emerson, *Collected Works*, 2:22–23.

34. Emerson, *The Journals and Miscellaneous Notebooks*, 7:544.

35. Emerson, *Collected Works*, 2:37.

36. Ibid., 2:34.

37. Ibid., 2:35.

38. Guthrie, *Above Time*, 98.

39. Nietzsche, *Thus Spoke Zarathustra*, 161.

40. Emerson, *Collected Works*, 2:53.

41. Ibid., 2:72.

42. Ibid., 2:73.

43. Ibid., 2:38.

44. Ibid., 2:40–41.

45. Ibid., 2:49, 48.

46. Kateb, *Emerson and Self-Reliance*, 15. On the common challenge mounted by both Emerson and Nietzsche to liberalism's assumptions of self-contained autonomy, in which each "takes otherness seriously in a way that liberal individualism generally does not," see Mikics, *The Romance of Individualism in Emerson and Nietzsche*, 9.

47. Emerson, *Collected Works*, 2:72.

48. Carlyle, *Sartor Resartus*, 198.

49. Emerson, *Collected Works*, 2:175.

50. Ibid., 2:159.

51. Cary Wolfe argues that Emerson's reliance on "possession" as a crucial metaphor of selfhood inevitably results in isolation and an illusory freedom that is only "imaginary." Wolfe treats Emerson's concept of possession as equivalent to the possession of private property within market capitalism, and thus argues that when we possess ourselves we are, ironically, alienated from ourselves as well as from others. I maintain, however, that Emerson means to oppose the kind of possession Wolfe describes with a different, more philosophically viable form of possession. Wolfe cites Emerson's description in "Self-Reliance" of a "cultivated man" who acquires "living property" in himself by rejecting the materialism of the capitalist world. In my view, it seems clear that Emerson employs the term "property" here precisely in order to critique the poverty of the concept as held by most of his contemporaries and to assert a richer way of thinking about what we might possess in the world. See Wolfe, "Alone with America," esp. 150.

52. Emerson, *Collected Works*, 1:124. Robinson, "The Method of Nature and Emerson's Period of Crisis," describes the crucial place of this lecture in

Emerson's thinking about nature. The lecture was delivered at Waterville College, now known as Colby College.

53. Emerson, *Collected Works*, 3:104.

54. Ibid., 1:125.

55. Kateb, *The Inner Ocean*, 77.

56. Emerson, *Collected Works*, 2:161.

57. Newfield, *The Emerson Effect*, 24.

58. Cameron, "The Way of Life by Abandonment," 4, 31.

59. Kateb, *Emerson and Self-Reliance*, 97–98.

60. Emerson, *Collected Works*, 3:104–5.

61. Ibid., 5:15. James Saucerman points out the similarity between this passage and Lyell's analysis in the *Principles of Geology*. Saucerman, "The Influence of Sir Charles Lyell on Emerson's Use of Geologic Imagery," 138–40.

62. Irving, *The Sketch-Book of Geoffrey Crayon*, 224–29.

63. Emerson, *Collected Works*, 3:112.

64. The distinction here is similar to the one philosophers make between "a noun" and "a thing named by a noun"—the word versus the thing itself. I thank Russell Goodman for schooling me in this fascinating concept during a game of "twenty questions" in the New Mexico desert.

65. Emerson, *Collected Works*, 1:18.

66. Ibid., 3:33.

67. Emerson, *Essays and Lectures*, 713. This line is from *Representative Men*, first given as a series of lectures in 1845–46 and then published as a book in 1850.

68. Emerson, *Collected Works*, 3:13.

69. As Walls explains, "In using metaphors from science, Emerson was not importing exotic figures from some remote zone beyond literature, but operating in a shared middle ground." Walls, *Emerson's Life in Science*, 24.

70. Nietzsche, *On the Advantage and Disadvantage of History for Life*, 10 (section 1). Emerson's phrase "practical power" comes from the famous final line of "Experience": "Never mind the ridicule, never mind the defeat: up again, old heart!—it seems to say,—there is victory yet for all justice; and the true romance which the world exists to realize, will be the transformation of genius into practical power." Emerson, *Collected Works*, 3:49.

71. Emerson, *Essays and Lectures*, 709.

72. Ibid., 698–99.

73. Emerson, *Collected Works*, 1:125.

74. Ibid., 3:110.

75. Toulmin, *Cosmopolis*, 13. It might well be asked what it means to attribute historical agency to an abstract concept such as modernity. T. J. Clark has shown

that "modern" is a term that people have employed to describe a whole variety of related phenomena that are intangible yet produce powerful transformative effects in everyday life. Individuals require a concept such as modernity to crystallize these changes, to bring them into focus. Thus far, it would seem that people create modernity; modernity does not give itself definitions. However, to view a historical category such as the modern as purely the sum of a series of voluntary acts of representations on the part of atomized individuals would be simplistic. Such acts of representation possess a social existence that transcends individuals. Just as the psychology of a crowd takes on a life of its own that is not reducible to the individuals amongst the crowd, an idea such as the modern cannot be reduced to discrete acts of representation on the part of individuals. In this way, modernity can be said to act as a historical agent, not merely a representation but representing itself in certain ways. See T. J. Clark, *The Painting of Modern Life*.

76. Toulmin, *Cosmopolis*, 41.
77. Emerson, *Collected Works*, 2:187–88.
78. Ibid., 159.

Conclusion

1. Morgan, "The Task System and the World of Lowcountry Blacks," 594–96.
2. On class differences and time, see not only Thompson, "Time, Work-Discipline, and Industrial Capitalism," but also Gutman, *Work, Culture, and Society*; Roediger and Foner, *Our Own Time*; O'Malley, *Keeping Watch*; and McCrossen, *Holy Day, Holiday*.
3. Dimock, "Planetary Time and Global Translation," 490.
4. Braudel, *The Perspective of the World*, 17.
5. Dimock, "Deep Time," 756, 757.
6. Bruce Robbins observed in the late 1990s that postcolonial critics had begun divesting the concept of cosmopolitanism of its linguistically implicit claim to universality in favor of a new formulation of the concept that included difference and diversity: "Like nations, cosmopolitanisms are now plural and particular." Hence, according to Robbins at the time, "there is a growing consensus that cosmopolitanism sometimes works together with nationalism rather than against it." This interest in a paradoxically local cosmopolitanism has only grown in the years since Robbins made these comments. Robbins, "Introduction Part I," 2.
7. Paine, *Common Sense*, 48.
8. Emerson, *Collected Works*, 3:117.

BIBLIOGRAPHY

[A. L.] "Scripture Geology and Scripture Astronomy." Review of *The Epoch of Creation: The Scripture Doctrine Contrasted with the Geological Theory*, by Eleazar Lord. *United States Magazine and Democratic Review* 29 (October 1851): 353–60.

Adams, Henry. Review of *Principles of Geology; or, The Modern Changes of the Earth and Its Inhabitants, Considered as Illustrative of Geology*, by Sir Charles Lyell. *North American Review* 107 (October 1868): 465–501.

———. *The Education of Henry Adams*. New York: Houghton Mifflin, 1973.

Adams, John Quincy. "Society and Civilization." *American Review: A Whig Journal* 2 (July 1845): 80–90.

Alcott, William. *The Young Man's Guide*. Boston: Lilly, 1834.

Anderson, Benedict. *Imagined Communities: Reflections on the Origin and Spread of Nationalism*. Rev. ed. New York: Verso, 1991.

Anonymous. "Earth and Man." Review of *The Earth and Man: Lectures on Comparative Physical Geography, in Its Relation to the History of Mankind*, by Arnold Guyot. *American Whig Review* 14 (September 1851): 195–208.

———. "Editor's Table." *Harper's New Monthly Magazine* 4 (December 1851): 128–31.

———. "Geology System Makers." *Scientific American*, 25 September 1847, 29.

———. "Lyell's Geological Tour." *United States Democratic Review* 17 (September 1845): 199–202.

———. "On Time." *Putnam's Magazine* 15 (June 1870): 686–93.

———. Review of *The Bridgewater Treatises*, vol. 5: *Geology and Mineralogy*, by Rev. William Buckland. *Southern Literary Messenger* 5 (August 1839): 548–58.

———. "The State of the World before Adam's Time." *Harper's New Monthly Magazine* (November 1850): 754–58.

———. "Willard's System of Universal History." *North American Review* 43 (July 1836): 262–63.

Anzaldúa, Gloria. *Borderlands/La Frontera: The New Mestiza*. San Francisco: Aunt Lute, 1987.

Armstrong, Nancy. *Desire and Domestic Fiction: A Political History of the Novel*. New York: Oxford University Press, 1987.

Bailey, Chris H. *Two Hundred Years of American Clocks and Watches*. Englewood Cliffs: Prentice-Hall, 1975.

Bailyn, Bernard. *The Ideological Origins of the American Revolution*. Cambridge, Mass.: The Belknap Press of Harvard University Press, 1967.

Bakewell, Robert. *An Introduction to Geology*. 2nd American ed. Edited by Benjamin Silliman. New Haven: Hezekiah Howe, 1833.

Bancroft, George. *History of the United States*. 10 vols. Boston: Little, Brown, 1874–78.

———. *Literary and Historical Miscellanies*. New York: Harper, 1855.

Barnum, Phineas T. *Struggles and Triumphs*. New York: Arno, 1970.

Bartky, Ian R. *Selling the True Time: Nineteenth-Century Timekeeping in America*. Stanford: Stanford University Press, 2000.

Baym, Nina. *American Women Writers and the Work of History, 1790–1860*. New Brunswick: Rutgers University Press, 1995.

———. *Feminism and American Literary History*. New Brunswick: Rutgers University Press, 1992.

Bedell, Rebecca. *The Anatomy of Nature: Geology and American Landscape Painting, 1825–1875*. Princeton: Princeton University Press, 2002.

Bedini, Silvio A. "Thomas Jefferson, Clock Designer." *Proceedings of the American Philosophical Society* 108 (June 1964): 163–80.

Beecher, Catharine E. *A Treatise on Domestic Economy*. New York: Harper, 1851.

———. *The Evils Suffered by American Women and American Children: The Causes and the Remedy*. New York: Harper, 1846.

Beecher, Catharine E., and Harriet Beecher Stowe. *The American Woman's Home; or, Principles of Domestic Science*. New York: Arno, 1971.

Benjamin, Walter. *Illuminations*. Edited by Hannah Arendt. Translated by Harry Zohn. New York: Schocken, 1969.

Berkeley, George. *Works*. 4 vols. Edited by A. C. Fraser. Oxford: Clarendon Press, 1901.

Bhabha, Homi K. *The Location of Culture*. London: Routledge, 1994.

Bird, Anthony. *English House Clocks, 1600–1850: An Historical Survey and Guide for Collectors and Dealers*. Newton Abbot, UK: David and Charles, 1973.

Blackburn, Bonnie, and Leofranc Holford-Strevens. *The Oxford Companion to the Year*. New York: Oxford University Press, 1999.

Blumin, Stuart. *The Emergence of the Middle Class: Social Experience in the American City, 1760–1900*. Cambridge: Cambridge University Press, 1989.

Boorstin, Daniel. *The Discoverers: A History of Man's Search to Know His World and Himself*. New York: Random House–Vintage Books, 1985.

Brantlinger, Patrick. *Fictions of State: Culture and Credit in Britain, 1694–1994*. Ithaca: Cornell University Press, 1996.

Braudel, Fernand. *Civilization and Capitalism: 15th–18th Century*. 3 vols. Translated by Siân Reynolds. New York: Harper and Row, 1981–84.

Brown, Bill. *A Sense of Things: The Object Matter of American Literature*. Chicago: University of Chicago Press, 2003.

Brown, Charles H. *William Cullen Bryant*. New York: Scribner's, 1971.

Brown, Gillian. *Domestic Individualism: Imagining Self in Nineteenth-Century America*. Berkeley: University of California Press, 1990.

———. *The Consent of the Governed: The Lockean Legacy in Early American Culture*. Cambridge, Mass.: Harvard University Press, 2001.

Brown, Lee Rust. *The Emerson Museum: Practical Romanticism and the Pursuit of the Whole*. Cambridge, Mass.: Harvard University Press, 1997.

Brückner, Martin. "The Critical Place of Empire in Early American Studies." *American Literary History* 15 (Winter 2003): 809–21.

Bruegel, Martin. *Farm, Shop, Landing: The Rise of a Market Society in the Hudson Valley, 1780–1860*. Durham, N.C.: Duke University Press, 2002.

———. "'Time That Can Be Relied Upon': The Evolution of Time Consciousness in the Mid-Hudson Valley, 1790–1860." *Journal of Social History* 28 (Spring 1995): 547–64.

Bryant, William Cullen. *Poetical Works*. New York: AMS, 1971.

Buell, Lawrence. "American Literary Emergence as a Postcolonial Phenomenon." *American Literary History* 4 (1992): 411–42.

Burris, Val. "Reification: A Marxist Perspective." *California Sociologist* 10, no. 1 (1988): 22–43.

Calhoun, Daniel H. "Eyes for the Jacksonian World: William C. Woodbridge and Emma Willard." *Journal of the Early Republic* 4 (Spring 1984): 1–26.

Cameron, Kenneth Walter. *Emerson's Reading*. Hartford: Transcendental, 1962.

Cameron, Sharon. "The Way of Life by Abandonment: Emerson's Impersonal." *Critical Inquiry* 25 (Autumn 1998): 1–31.

Carlyle, Thomas. *Sartor Resartus*. Edited by Kerry McSweeney and Peter Sabor. New York: Oxford University Press, 1999.

Cavell, Stanley. *Conditions Handsome and Unhandsome: The Constitution of Emersonian Perfectionism*. Chicago: University of Chicago Press, 1990.

Chambers, Robert. *Vestiges of the Natural History of Creation, with a Sequel*. New York: Harper, 1857.

Channing, William Ellery. *Works*. Boston: American Unitarian Association, 1878.

Clark, H. Nichols B. *Francis W. Edmonds: American Master in the Dutch Tradition*. Washington, D.C.: Smithsonian Institution Press, 1988.

Clark, Harry Hayden. "Emerson and Science." *Philological Quarterly* 10 (July 1931): 225–60.

Clark, Jennifer. "The American Image of Technology from the Revolution to 1840." *American Quarterly* 39 (Autumn 1987): 431–49.

Clark, T. J. *The Painting of Modern Life: Paris in the Art of Manet and His Followers*. New York: Knopf, 1985.

Cole, Thomas. *The Collected Essays and Prose Sketches*. Edited by Marshall Tymn. St. Paul: John Colet Press, 1980.

Cooper, Carolyn C. "Social Construction of Invention through Patent Management: Thomas Blanchard's Woodworking Machinery." *Technology and Culture* 32 (October 1991): 960–98.

Cooper, Wendy A. *Classical Taste in America, 1800–1840*. New York: Abbeville Press and the Baltimore Museum of Art, 1993.

Cummings, Sherwood. *Mark Twain and Science: Adventures of a Mind*. Baton Rouge: Louisiana State University Press, 1988.

Curtis, George Wm. "My Friend the Watch." *Atlantic Monthly* 11 (January 1863): 70–79.

Dana, James D. *Manual of Geology*. Philadelphia: Bliss, 1863.

Dana, S. L. Review of *Elementary Geology*, by Edward Hitchcock. *North American Review* 52 (January 1841): 103–9.

Daniels, Stephen. *Fields of Vision: Landscape Imagery and National Identity in England and the United States*. Princeton: Princeton University Press, 1993.

Dean, Dennis R. "Geology in American Literature and Thought." In *Two Hundred Years of American Geology: Proceedings of the New Hampshire Bicentennial Conference on the History of Geology*, edited by Cecil J. Schneer. Hanover, N.H.: University Press of New England, 1979.

———. *James Hutton and the History of Geology*. Ithaca: Cornell University Press, 1992.

De Certeau, Michel. *The Practice of Everyday Life*. Berkeley: University of California Press, 1988.

Dekker, George. *James Fenimore Cooper the Novelist*. London: Routledge, 1967.

———. *The American Historical Romance*. New York: Cambridge University Press, 1987.

Demos, John. *Circles and Lines: The Shape of Life in Early America*. Cambridge, Mass.: Harvard University Press, 2004.

Dimock, Wai Chee. "Deep Time: American Literature and World History." *American Literary History* 13 (Winter 2001): 755–75.

———. *Empire for Liberty: Melville and the Poetics of Individualism*. Princeton: Princeton University Press, 1989.

————. "Planetary Time and Global Translation: 'Context' in Literary Studies." *Common Knowledge* 9 (Fall 2003): 488–507.

Dohrn-van Rossum, Gerhard. *History of the Hour: Clocks and Modern Temporal Orders*. Translated by Thomas Dunlap. Chicago: University of Chicago Press, 1996.

Douglas, Ann. *The Feminization of American Culture*. New York: Knopf, 1977.

Drepperd, Carl W. *American Clocks and Clock-Makers*. Enlarged ed. Boston: Charles T. Branford, 1958.

During, Simon. "Literature—Nationalism's Other? The Case for Revision." In *Nation and Narration*, edited by Homi K. Bhabha, 139–53. London: Routledge, 1990.

Elias, Norbert. *Time: An Essay*. Translated by Edmund Jephcott. Oxford: Blackwell, 1992.

Eisley, Loren. *Darwin's Century: Evolution and the Men Who Discovered It*. New York: Anchor-Doubleday, 1961.

Emerson, Ralph Waldo. *Collected Works*. 6 vols. Edited by Robert E. Spiller, Alfred R. Ferguson, Joseph Slater, Jean Ferguson Carr, Douglas Emory Wilson, Wallace E. Williams, Philip Nicoloff, Robert E. Burkholder, and Barbara L. Packer. Cambridge, Mass.: The Belknap Press of Harvard University Press, 1971–2003.

————. *The Early Lectures*. 3 vols. Edited by Stephen E. Whicher, Robert E. Spiller, and Wallace E. Williams. Cambridge, Mass.: The Belknap Press of Harvard University Press, 1959–72.

————. *Essays and Lectures*. Edited by Joel Porte. New York: Library of America, 1983.

————. *The Journals and Miscellaneous Notebooks*. 16 vols. Edited by William H. Gilman, Alfred R. Ferguson, George P. Clark, Merrell R. Davis, Merton M. Sealts Jr., Ralph H. Orth, A. W. Plumstead, Harrison Hayford, J. E. Parsons, Ruth H. Bennett, Linda Allardt, Susan Sutton Smith, David W. Hill, Ronald A. Bosco, and Glen M. Johnson. Cambridge, Mass.: Harvard University Press, 1960–1982.

England, J. Merton. "The Democratic Faith in American Schoolbooks, 1783–1860." *American Quarterly* 15 (Summer 1963): 191–99.

Evans, Nancy Goyne. "The Christian M. Nestell Drawing Book: A Focus on the Ornamental Painter and His Craft in Early Nineteenth-Century America." *American Furniture* (1998): 99–163.

Fabian, Johannes. *Time and the Other: How Anthropology Makes Its Object*. New York: Columbia University Press, 1983.

Featherstonehaugh, G. W. *Excursion through the Slave States, from Washington on the Potomac to the Frontier of Mexico; With Sketches of Popular Manners and Geological Notices.* New York: Harper, 1844.

Fennimore, Donald. *Metalwork in Early America: Copper and Its Alloys from the Winterthur Collection.* Winterthur, Del.: Henry Francis du Pont Winterthur Museum, 1996.

Firda, Richard Arthur. "German Philosophy of History and Literature in the *North American Review*, 1815–1860." *Journal of the History of Ideas* 32 (January–March 1971): 133–42.

Fisher, Philip. "Democratic Social Space: Whitman, Melville, and the Promise of American Transparency." *Representations* 24 (Autumn 1988): 60–101.

Fitzgerald, Oscar P. *Four Centuries of American Furniture.* Radnor: Wallace-Homestead Book Company, 1995.

Foley, Paul J. *Willard's Patent Time Pieces: A History of the Weight-Driven Banjo Clock, 1800–1900.* Norwell: Roxbury Village Publishing, 2002.

Frankenstein, Alfred. *Painter of Rural America: William Sidney Mount, 1807–1868.* Washington, D.C.: Printed by H. K. Press, 1968.

Fresonke, Kris. *West of Emerson: The Design of Manifest Destiny.* Berkeley: University of California Press, 2003.

Freud, Sigmund. *Civilization and Its Discontents.* Translated by James Strachey. New York: Norton, 1989.

Gardner, H. C. "Labor; or, Striking for Higher Wages." *Ladies' Repository* 19 (January 1859): 7–11; (February 1859): 82–85.

Garrett, Wendell. "Novus Ordo Seclorum: A New Order of the Ages." Introduction to *Neo-Classicism in America: Inspiration and Innovation, 1810–1840.* An exhibition catalog. New York: Hirschl and Adler Galleries, 1991.

Gellner, Ernest. *Nationalism.* New York: New York University Press, 1997.

Giles, Paul. *Virtual Americas: Transnational Fictions and Transatlantic Imaginary.* Durham, N.C.: Duke University Press, 2002.

Gilmore, Michael T. *American Romanticism in the Marketplace.* Chicago: University of Chicago Press, 1985.

Gilroy, Paul. *The Black Atlantic: Modernity and Double Consciousness.* Cambridge, Mass.: Harvard University Press, 1993.

Gloag, John. *A Complete Dictionary of Furniture.* Revised and expanded by Clive Edwards. Woodstock: Overlook Press, 1991.

Gould, Stephen Jay. *Time's Arrow, Time's Cycle: Myth and Metaphor in the Discovery of Geological Time.* Cambridge, Mass.: Harvard University Press, 1987.

Gray, Asa. Review of *Manual of Geology*, by James D. Dana. *North American Review* 97 (October 1863): 372–87.

Grier, Katherine C. *Culture and Comfort: Parlor Making and Middle-Class Identity, 1850–1930*. Washington, D.C.: Smithsonian Institution Press, 1997.

Gross, Robert A. "Culture and Cultivation: Agriculture and Society in Thoreau's Concord." *Journal of American History* 69 (June 1982): 42–61.

Guthrie, James K. *Above Time: Emerson's and Thoreau's Temporal Revolutions*. Columbia: University of Missouri Press, 2001.

Gutman, Herbert. *Work, Culture, and Society*. New York: Viking, 1976.

Hale, Sarah J. *Keeping House and House Keeping: A Story of Domestic Life*. New York: Harper, 1845.

Halttunen, Karen. *Confidence Men and Painted Women: A Study of Middle-Class Culture in America, 1830–1870*. New Haven: Yale University Press, 1982.

———. "From Parlor to Living Room: Domestic Space, Interior Decoration, and the Culture of Personality." In *Consuming Visions: Accumulation and Display of Goods in America, 1880–1920*, edited by Simon J. Bronner, 157–89. New York: Norton, 1989.

Harding, Anneliese. *John Lewis Krimmel: Genre Artist of the Early Republic*. Winterthur, Del.: Winterthur Museum, 1994.

Harris, John. *The Pre-Adamite Earth: Contributions to Theological Science*. Rev. ed. Boston: Gould and Lincoln, 1854.

Harvey, Bruce A. *American Geographics: U.S. National Narratives and the Representation of the Non-European World, 1830–1865*. Stanford: Stanford University Press, 2001.

Harvey, Eleanor Jones. *The Voyage of the Icebergs: Frederic Church's Arctic Masterpiece*. New Haven: Yale University Press for the Dallas Museum of Art, 2002.

Hawthorne, Nathaniel. *The Scarlet Letter*. Centenary ed., vol. 1. Edited by Fredson Bowers. Columbus: Ohio State University Press, 1962.

Heidegger, Martin. "The Question Concerning Technology." In *Basic Writings*, edited by David Farrell Krell, 287–317. New York: Harper and Row, 1977.

Hensley, Paul B. "Time, Work, and Social Context in New England." *New England Quarterly* 65 (December 1992): 531–59.

Hirsch, Eric, and Charles Stewart. "Introduction: Ethnographies of Historicity." *History and Anthropology* 16 (September 2005): 261–74.

Hitchcock, Edward. *Elementary Geology*. 8th ed. New York: Newman and Ivison, 1852.

Hitchcock, Edward, and Orra White Hitchcock. *Plates Illustrating the Geology and Scenery of Massachusetts*. Boston: Pendleton's Lithography, 1832.

Howland, E. A. *The American Economical Housekeeper and Family Receipt Book*. Worcester, Mass.: William Allen, 1845.

Irving, Washington. *The Sketch-Book of Geoffrey Crayon, Gent.* Edited by Susan
Manning. New York: Oxford University Press, 1998.

James, C. L. R. *Mariners, Renegades, and Castaways: The Story of Herman
Melville and the World We Live In.* Edited by Donald Pease. Hanover, N.H.:
University Press of New England, 2001.

Jefferson, Thomas. *The Papers of Thomas Jefferson.* 33 vols. Edited by Julian P.
Boyd, Charles T. Cullen, John Catanzariti, and Barbara B. Oberg. Princeton:
Princeton University Press, 1950–2006.

———. *The Writings of Thomas Jefferson.* 20 vols. Edited by Andrew A.
Lipscomb and Albert Ellery Bergh. Washington, D.C.: Issued under the
auspices of the Thomas Jefferson Memorial Association of the United States,
1903–4.

———. *The Writings of Thomas Jefferson.* 10 vols. Edited by Paul Leicester
Ford. New York: Putnam, 1892–99.

———. *Writings.* Edited by Merrill D. Peterson. New York: Library of
America, 1984.

Jefferson, Thomas, and John Adams. *The Adams-Jefferson Letters.* 2 vols. Edited
by Lester J. Capon. Chapel Hill: University of North Carolina Press, 1959.

Jehlen, Myra. *American Incarnation: The Individual, the Nation, and the
Continent.* Cambridge, Mass.: Harvard University Press, 1986.

Jerome, Chauncey. *History of the American Clock Business for the Past Sixty
Years, and Life of Chauncey Jerome.* New Haven: F. C. Dayton Jr., 1860.

———. "Introduction." *Chauncey Jerome, Manufacturer of Brass Clocks: A
Trade Catalog.* Bristol, Conn.: American Clock and Watch Museum, 1971.

Kaplan, Amy. *The Anarchy of Empire in the Making of U.S. Culture.* Cambridge,
Mass.: Harvard University Press, 2002.

———. "Where Is Guantánamo?," *American Quarterly* 57 (September 2005):
831–58.

———. "Manifest Domesticity." *American Literature* 70 (September 1998):
581–606.

Kasson, John F. *Civilizing the Machine: Technology and Republican Values in
America, 1776–1900.* New York: Grossman, 1976.

Kateb, George. *Emerson and Self-Reliance.* Thousand Oaks, Calif.: Sage, 1995.

———. *The Inner Ocean: Individualism and Democratic Culture.* Ithaca:
Cornell University Press, 1992.

Kavanaugh, James V. "The Artifact in American Culture: Development of an
Undergraduate Program in American Studies." In *Material Culture and the
Study of American Life,* edited by Ian M. G. Quimby, 64–75. New York: W. W.
Norton for the Henry Francis du Pont Winterthur Museum, 1978.

Kelsall, Malcolm. *Jefferson and the Iconography of Romanticism: Folk, Land, Culture, and the Romantic Nation*. New York: St. Martin's, 1999.

Kerber, Linda. *Women of the Republic: Intellect and Ideology in Revolutionary America*. Chapel Hill: University of North Carolina Press, 1980.

Kimball, Fiske. *Thomas Jefferson, Architect*. New York: Da Capo Press, 1968.

Kolodny, Annette. *The Lay of the Land: Metaphor as Experience and History in American Life and Letters*. Chapel Hill: University of North Carolina Press, 1975.

LaFond, Edward. Collection of Research Notes. Winterthur Archives (Archives 16).

Lamenager, Stephanie. *Manifest and Other Destinies: Territorial Fictions of the Nineteenth-Century United States*. Lincoln: University of Nebraska Press, 2004.

Landes, David S. *Revolution in Time: Clocks and the Making of the Modern World*. Rev. ed. Cambridge, Mass.: The Belknap Press of Harvard University Press, 2000.

Latour, Bruno. "On Technical Mediation—Philosophy, Sociology, Genealogy." *Common Knowledge* 3, no. 2 (Spring 1994): 29–64.

Lawrence, Philip J. "Edward Hitchcock: The Christian Geologist." *Proceedings of the American Philosophical Society* 116 (February 1972): 21–34.

Levin, David. *History as Romantic Art: Bancroft, Prescott, Motley, and Parkman*. Stanford: Stanford University Press, 1959.

Lienesch, Michael. *New Order of the Ages: Time, the Constitution, and the Making of Modern American Political Thought*. Princeton: Princeton University Press, 1988.

Limerick, Patricia Nelson, Clyde Milner, and Charles Rankin, eds. *Trails: Toward a New Western History*. Lawrence: University Press of Kansas, 1991.

Locke, John. *Two Treatises of Government*. Edited by Peter Laslett. New York: Cambridge University Press, 1988.

Longfellow, Henry Wadsworth. *Poems and Other Writings*. Edited by J. D. McClatchy. New York: Library of America, 2000.

Lopez, Michael. "Emerson and Nietzsche: An Introduction." *ESQ* 43, nos. 1–4 (1997): 1–35.

Lubar, Steven. "The Transformation of Antebellum Patent Law." *Technology and Culture* 32 (October 1991): 932–59.

Lukács, Georg. *History and Class Consciousness: Studies in Marxist Dialectics*. Translated by Rodney Livingstone. Cambridge, Mass.: MIT Press, 1971.

Lyon, John. "The Search for Fossil Man: Cinq Personnages a la Recherche du Temps Perdu." *Isis* 61 (Spring 1970): 68–84.

Macey, Samuel. *Clocks and the Cosmos: Time in Western Life and Thought.* Hamden, Conn.: Archon, 1980.

Malthus, Thomas Robert. *On Population.* Edited by Gertrude Himmelfarb. New York: Modern Library, 1960.

Mann, Maybell. *Francis William Edmonds: Mammon and Art.* New York: Garland, 1977.

McCabe, James D. *The Illustrated History of the Centennial Exhibition.* Philadelphia: The National Publishing Company, 1876.

——. *Great Fortunes, and How They Were Made; or, The Struggles and Triumphs of Our Self-Made Men.* Cincinnati and Chicago: E. Hannaford; San Francisco: F. Dewing, 1872.

McCoy, Drew R. *The Elusive Republic: Political Economy in Jeffersonian America.* Chapel Hill: University of North Carolina Press, 1980.

McCrossen, Alexis. "By the Clock." Review of *Selling the True Time: Nineteenth-Century Timekeeping in America,* by Ian R. Bartky. *Reviews in American History* 28 (December 2000): 553–59.

——. "'Conventions of Simultaneity': Time Standards, Public Clocks, and Nationalism in American Cities and Towns, 1871–1905." *Journal of Urban History* 33 (January 2007): 217–53.

——. *Holy Day, Holiday: The American Sunday.* Ithaca: Cornell University Press, 2000.

McLoughlin, Jack. *Jefferson and Monticello: The Biography of a Builder.* New York: Holt, 1988.

McPhee, John. *Basin and Range.* New York: Farrar, Straus & Giroux, 1982.

Melville, Herman. *Moby-Dick; or, The Whale.* Edited by Harrison Hayford, Hershel Parker, and G. Thomas Tanselle. Evanston and Chicago: Northwestern University Press and the Newberry Library, 1988.

Merish, Lori. *Sentimental Materialism: Gender, Commodity Culture, and Nineteenth-Century American Literature.* Durham, N.C.: Duke University Press, 2000.

Merrill, George P. *The First One Hundred Years of American Geology.* New Haven: Yale University Press, 1924.

Mikics, David. *The Romance of Individualism in Emerson and Nietzsche.* Athens: Ohio University Press, 2003.

Milham, Willis I. *Time and Timekeepers: Including the History, Construction, Care, and Accuracy of Clocks and Watches.* New York: Macmillan, 1941.

Miller, Angela. *The Empire of the Eye: Landscape Representation and American Cultural Politics, 1825–1875.* Ithaca: Cornell University Press, 1993.

Morgan, Philip D. "Work and Culture: The Task System and the World of

Lowcountry Blacks, 1700–1880." *William and Mary Quarterly*. 3rd series. 39 (October 1982): 563–99.

Mumford, Lewis. *Technics and Civilization*. New York: Harcourt, 1934.

Murphy, John Joseph. "Entrepreneurship in the Establishment of the American Clock Industry." *Journal of Economic History* 26 (June 1966): 169–86.

Naeve, Milo M. *John Lewis Krimmel: An Artist in Federal America*. Newark: University of Delaware Press, 1987.

National Maritime Museum. "The Equation of Time." <http://www.nmm.ac.uk/server/show/conWebDoc.351>.

Neufeldt, Leonard N. *The Economist: Henry Thoreau and Enterprise*. New York: Oxford University Press, 1989.

Newfield, Christopher. *The Emerson Effect: Individualism and Submission in America*. Chicago: University of Chicago Press, 1996.

Nietzsche, Friedrich. *Beyond Good and Evil: Prelude to a Philosophy of the Future*. Translated by Walter Kaufmann. New York: Random House–Vintage Books, 1989.

———. *Human, All Too Human*. Translated by Gary Handwerk. Stanford: Stanford University Press, 1995.

———. *On the Advantage and Disadvantage of History for Life*. Translated by Peter Preuss. Indianapolis: Hackett, 1980.

———. *The Portable Nietzsche*. Translated by Walter Kaufman. New York: Penguin, 1976.

———. *Thus Spoke Zarathustra*. Translated by R. J. Hollingdale. New York: Penguin, 1969.

Noble, David W. *Death of a Nation: American Culture and the End of Exceptionalism*. Minneapolis: University of Minnesota Press, 2002.

Novak, Barbara. *Nature and Culture: American Landscape and Painting, 1825–1875*. New York: Oxford University Press, 1995.

Nye, Russel B. *The Almost Chosen People: Essays in the History of American Ideas*. East Lansing: Michigan State University Press, 1966.

O'Brien, Michael. *Conjectures of Order: Intellectual Life and the American South, 1810–1860*. 2 vols. Chapel Hill: University of North Carolina Press, 2004.

O'Leary, Elizabeth L. *At Beck and Call: The Representation of Domestic Servants in Nineteenth-Century American Painting*. Washington, D.C.: Smithsonian Institution Press, 1996.

O'Malley, Michael. *Keeping Watch: A History of American Time*. Washington, D.C.: Smithsonian Institution Press, 1990.

Onuf, Peter. *Jefferson's Empire: The Language of American Nationhood*. Charlottesville: University Press of Virginia, 2000.

O'Sullivan, John. "Annexation." *United States Democratic Review* 17 (July–August 1845): 5–10.

———. "The Great Nation of Futurity." *United States Democratic Review* 6 (November 1839): 426–30.

Packer, B. L. *Emerson's Fall: A New Interpretation of the Major Essays*. New York: Continuum, 1982.

Paine, Thomas. *Common Sense*. Edited by Edward Larkin. Peterborough, Ontario: Broadview, 2004.

Paley, William. *Natural Theology*. London: Faulder, 1802.

Parry, Elwood C., III. "Acts of God, Acts of Man: Geological Ideas and the Imaginary Landscapes of Thomas Cole." In *Two Hundred Years of Geology in America*, edited by Cecil J. Schneer, 53–71. Hanover, N.H.: University Press of New England, 1979.

Peabody, William Bourne Oliver. "The American Almanac." *North American Review* 41 (July 1835): 28–46.

Pease, Donald E. "Doing Justice to C. L. R. James's *Mariners, Renegades, and Castaways*." *Boundary 2* 27, no. 2 (Summer 2000): 1–19.

———. "Postnational Politics and American Studies." *49th Parallel* 8 (Summer 2001). <http://www.49thparallel.bham.ac.uk/back/issue8/pease.htm>.

Pease, Donald E., and Robyn Wiegman. "Futures." In *The Futures of American Studies*, edited by Donald E. Pease and Robyn Wiegman, 1–42. Durham, N.C.: Duke University Press, 2002.

Peckham, H. H. *Gotham Yankee: A Biography of William Cullen Bryant*. New York: Russell and Russell, 1971.

Pocock, J. G. A. *The Machiavellian Moment: Florentine Political Thought and the Atlantic Republican Tradition*. Princeton: Princeton University Press, 1975.

Porter, Roy. *The Making of Geology: Earth Science in Britain, 1660–1815*. Cambridge: Cambridge University Press, 1977.

Prescott, William H. *History of the Conquest of Mexico and History of the Conquest of Peru*. New York: Modern Library, n.d.

Priddy, Sumpter, III, J. Michael Flanigan, and Gregory R. Weidman. "The Genesis of Neoclassical Style in Baltimore Furniture." *American Furniture* (2000): 59–99.

Prown, Jules David. *Art as Evidence: Writings on Art and Material Culture*. New Haven: Yale University Press, 2001.

Richardson, Robert D. *Emerson: The Mind on Fire*. Berkeley: University of California Press, 1995.

―――――. *Henry Thoreau: A Life of the Mind*. Berkeley: University of California Press, 1986.

Robbins, Bruce. "Introduction Part I: Actually Existing Cosmopolitanism." In *Cosmopolitics: Thinking and Feeling Beyond the Nation*, edited by Pheng Cheah and Bruce Robbins, 1–19. Minneapolis: University of Minnesota Press, 1998.

Robinson, David. "The Method of Nature and Emerson's Period of Crisis." In *Emerson Centenary Essays*, edited by Joel Myerson, 74–92. Carbondale: Southern Illinois University Press, 1982.

Roberts, Kenneth D. *Eli Terry and the Connecticut Shelf Clock*. Bristol: Ken Roberts Publishing, 1973.

Roediger, David, and Philip S. Foner. *Our Own Time: A History of American Labor and the Working Day*. New York: Greenwood, 1987.

Rollin, Charles. *The Ancient History of the Egyptians, Carthaginians, Assyrians, Babylonians, Medes and Persians, Macedonians, and Grecians*. 10 vols. London: Knapton, 1738.

Romero, Lora. *Home Fronts: Domesticity and Its Critics in the Antebellum United States*. Durham, N.C.: Duke University Press, 1997.

Rowe, John Carlos. *The New American Studies*. Minneapolis: University of Minnesota Press, 2002.

Ryan, Mary P. *Cradle of the Middle Class: The Family in Oneida County, New York, 1790–1865*. Cambridge: Cambridge University Press, 1981.

―――――. *The Empire of the Mother: American Writing about Domesticity, 1830–1860*. New York: Haworth Press, 1982.

Saucerman, James. "A Note on Emerson's Use of Lyell." *American Notes and Queries* 20, nos. 3–4 (November–December 1981): 50–52.

―――――. "The Influence of Sir Charles Lyell on Emerson's Use of Geologic Imagery." Ph.D. diss., University of Missouri, 1977.

Saxon, A. H. *P. T. Barnum: The Legend and the Man*. New York: Columbia University Press, 1989.

Schoolcraft, Henry Rowe. "The Rise of the West: A Prospect of the Mississippi Valley." In *The First West: Writing from the American Frontier, 1776–1860*, edited by Edward Watts and David Rachels, 487–94. New York: Oxford University Press, 2002.

Schorsch, Anita. *The Warner Collector's Guide to American Clocks*. New York: Warner, 1981.

Scott, Anne Firor. "What, Then, Is the American? This New Woman?," *Journal of American History* 65 (December 1978): 679–703.

Sedgwick, Catharine M. *Home*. Boston: Munroe, 1835.

Sellers, Charles. *The Market Revolution: Jacksonian America, 1815–1846.* New York: Oxford University Press, 1991.

Sherman, Stuart. *Telling Time: Clocks, Diaries, and English Diurnal Form, 1660–1785.* Chicago: University of Chicago Press, 1996.

Sigourney, Lydia. *Letters of Life.* New York: Appleton, 1861.

———. *Letters to Mothers.* Hartford: Hudson & Skinner, 1838.

Silliman, Benjamin. "Supplement by the Editor." In *An Introduction to Geology,* by Robert Bakewell. 2nd American ed. Edited by Benjamin Silliman, 389–466. New Haven: Hezekiah Howe, 1833.

Simmel, Georg. *Simmel on Culture: Selected Writings.* Edited by David Frisby and Mike Featherstone. London: Sage, 1997.

Simms, William Gilmore. *Poetry and the Practical.* Fayetteville: University of Arkansas Press, 1996.

———. *Views and Reviews in American Literature, History and Fiction: First Series.* Cambridge, Mass.: The Belknap Press of Harvard University Press, 1962.

Sklansky, Jeffrey. *The Soul's Economy: Market Society and Selfhood in American Thought, 1820–1920.* Chapel Hill: University of North Carolina Press, 2002.

Sklar, Kathryn Kish. *Catharine Beecher: A Study in American Domesticity.* New Haven: Yale University Press, 1973.

Smith, Anthony D. *Nationalism and Modernism: A Critical Survey of Recent Theories of Nations and Nationalism.* New York: Routledge, 1998.

———. *The Nation in History: Historiographical Debates about Ethnicity and Nationalism.* Hanover, N.H.: University Press of New England, 2000.

Smith, Henry Nash. *Virgin Land: The American West as Symbol and Myth.* New York: Random House–Vintage Books, 1950.

Smith, Mark M. *Mastered by the Clock: Time, Slavery, and Freedom in the American South.* Chapel Hill: University of North Carolina Press, 1997.

Sprig, June, and David Larkin. *Shaker Life, Work, and Art.* New York: Stewart, Tabori, and Chang, 1987.

Stack, George. *Nietzsche and Emerson: An Elective Affinity.* Athens: Ohio University Press, 1992.

Stephens, Carlene. *On Time: How America Has Learned to Live by the Clock.* Boston: Little, Brown–Bulfinch Press, 2002.

———. "'The Most Reliable Time': William Bond, the New England Railroads, and Time Awareness in 19th-Century America." *Technology and Culture* 30 (January 1989): 1–24.

Stilgoe, John. *Common Landscape of America, 1580 to 1845.* New Haven: Yale University Press, 1982.

Stowe, Harriet Beecher. *The Minister's Wooing*. New York: Penguin, 1999.

Strasser, Susan. "Making Consumption Conspicuous: Transgressive Topics Go Mainstream." *Technology and Culture* 43 (October 2002): 755–70.

Swank, Scott T. *Shaker Life, Art, and Architecture: Hands to Work, Hearts to God*. New York: Abbeville Press, 1999.

Thompson, E. P. "Time, Work-Discipline, and Industrial Capitalism." *Past and Present* 38 (December 1967): 56–97.

Thoreau, Henry David. *A Week on the Concord and Merrimack Rivers; Walden, or, Life in the Woods; The Maine Woods; Cape Cod*. Edited by Robert F. Sayre. New York: The Library of America, 1985.

———. *The Maine Woods*. Edited by Joseph J. Moldenhauer. Princeton: Princeton University Press, 1972.

———. *Walden*. Edited by J. Lyndon Shanley. Princeton: Princeton University Press, 1971.

Tichi, Cecelia. "Domesticity on Walden Pond." In *A Historical Guide to Henry David Thoreau*, edited by William E. Cain, 95–122. New York: Oxford University Press, 2000.

Tonkovich, Nicole. *Domesticity with a Difference: The Nonfiction of Catharine Beecher, Sarah J. Hale, Fanny Fern, and Margaret Fuller*. Jackson: University Press of Mississippi, 1997.

Toulmin, Stephen. *Cosmopolis: The Hidden Agenda of Modernity*. Chicago: University of Chicago Press, 1992.

Toulmin, Stephen, and June Goodfield. *The Discovery of Time*. Chicago: University of Chicago Press, 1977.

Twain, Mark. *Letters from the Earth*. Edited by Bernard Devoto. New York: Harper and Row, 1962.

Wald, Priscilla. *Constituting Americans: Cultural Anxiety and Narrative Form*. Durham, N.C.: Duke University Press, 1995.

Walls, Laura Dassow. *Emerson's Life in Science: The Culture of Truth*. Ithaca: Cornell University Press, 2003.

Whicher, Stephen. *Freedom and Fate: An Inner Life of Ralph Waldo Emerson*. 2nd ed. Philadelphia: University of Pennsylvania Press, 1971.

Willard, Emma. *Abridged History of the United States, or, Republic of America*. New York: Barnes, 1843.

———. *An Address to the Public, Particularly the Members of the Legislature of New York, Proposing a Plan for Improving Female Education*. Middlebury, Conn.: Copeland, 1819.

———. *History of the United States, or, Republic of America*. New York: Barnes, 1855.

———. *Journals and Letters, from France and Great-Britain*. Troy, N.Y.: Tuttle, 1833.

———. *Last Periods of Universal History*. New York: Barnes, 1855.

———. *Universal History in Perspective*. New York: Barnes, 1866.

Willis, N. Parker. *Summer Cruise in the Mediterranean*. New York: Scribner, 1853.

Wills, Garry. *Inventing America: Jefferson's Declaration of Independence*. Garden City, N.J.: Doubleday, 1978.

Wilson, Eric. *Emerson's Sublime Science*. New York: St. Martin's, 1999.

Wilton, Andrew, and Tim Barringer. *American Sublime: Landscape Painting in the United States, 1820–1880*. Princeton: Princeton University Press, 2002.

Wolfe, Cary. "Alone with America: Cavell, Emerson, and the Politics of Individualism." *New Literary History* 25 (Winter 1994): 137–57.

Worcester, J. E., ed. *The American Almanac and Repository of Useful Knowledge*. Boston: Charles Bowen, 1834.

Zea, Philip. "Clockmaking and Society at the River and the Bay: Jedidiah and Jabez Baldwin, 1790–1820." In *The Bay and the River: 1600–1900*, edited by Peter Benes and Jane M. Benes, 46–58. Dublin Seminar for New England Folklife: Annual Proceedings, 1981. Boston: Boston University, 1981.

Zea, Philip, and Robert C. Cheney. *Clock Making in New England, 1725–1825: An Interpretation of the Old Sturbridge Village Collection*. Edited by Caroline F. Sloat. Sturbridge, Mass.: Old Sturbridge Village, 1992.

INDEX

Abridged History of the United States (Willard), 34, 43–46

Adams, Henry, 15, 153–54

Adams, John, 58

Adams, John Quincy, 42

Address to the Public, An (Willard), 30–31, 42–44, 46

"Advice to a Young Tradesman, Written by an Old One" (Franklin), 94

Agassiz, Louis, 14, 153–54, 158, 173, 209

"Ages, The" (Bryant), 51–52

Alcott, William, 94

Althusser, Louis, 15, 28, 220

American Almanac, 1–3

American Economical Housekeeper and Family Receipt Book, The (Howland), 120–23

American Incarnation (Jehlen), 20–21

American Journal of Science and the Arts ("Silliman's Journal"), 158

American Review, 42

"American Scholar, The" (Emerson), 189, 194–95

American Whig Review, 164–65

Anderson, Benedict, 6–8, 26, 219, 221, 240 (n. 8)

Annals of the History of the World (Ussher), 147

"Annexation" (O'Sullivan), 25–26, 34, 36

Atlantic Monthly, 96

Augustine, Saint, 5, 191, 210

Autobiography (Franklin), 103

Autobiography (Jefferson), 88

Bakewell, Robert, 160–61

Bancroft, George, 19, 28, 42, 48, 53

"Banjo clock" (Willard), 83–86

Bankson, John, 75

Barnum, P. T., 105, 108, 110

Barringer, Tim, 49

"Bartleby, the Scrivener" (Melville), 117

Baym, Nina, 44, 47

Beals, J. J. & W.: clock label of, 59–62

Bedell, Rebecca, 173–75

Beecher, Catharine, 4, 74, 127, 218, 220, 223; and Christian salvation, 14, 132, 135–36; and market economy, 14, 134, 136; on economy of time, 130–31; theory of temporal economy, 130–37; on productivity of domestic sphere, 132–34; critique of factory timetables, 133–34; on domestic consumption as a form of production, 134; on maternal power, 135–36; compared to Thoreau, 139–42, 144–45; compared to Emerson, 205

Benjamin, Walter, 6, 59

Berkeley, George, 52–53, 164

Beyond Good and Evil (Nietzsche), 199

Bhabha, Homi, 8

Bhagavad Gita, 222

Bible, 128, 137, 146–50, 154, 156–57, 159–60, 173, 175, 186, 190–91, 193, 195, 212, 241–42 (n. 25)

Blair, Hugh, 28–29

Blumin, Stuart, 115

Brantlinger, Patrick, 116–17

Braudel, Fernand, 221–22

Breckenridge, John C., 39

Bridgewater Treatises (Buckland), 157

Brown, Bill, 107–8

Brown, Gillian, 114, 117, 135

Brown, Lee Rust, 197

Bruegel, Martin, 10

Bryant, William Cullen, 19, 53; "The Ages," 51–52; "The Prairies," 52

Buckland, William, 157

Buell, Lawrence, 22

Buffon, Comte de (Georges-Louis Leclerc), 14

Burke, Edmund, 28

Byron, George Gordon, Lord, 29

Cabinet-Maker and Upholsterer's Guide (Hepplewhite), 75

Calendar shelf clock (Willard), 81–83

Cameron, Sharon, 211–12

Carlyle, Thomas, 29, 207–8

Cavell, Stanley, 139, 188

Chambers, Robert, 148, 153

Channing, William Ellery, 29

Cheney, Robert C., 122–23

Child, Lydia Maria, 30

Church, Frederic Edwin, 154–56, 173

"Circles" (Emerson), 216

Clark, Harry Hayden, 189

Clepsydra, 161

Clocks and clock time: and modernity, 1–3, 7–9, 13, 14, 59, 62, 112; and national identity, 4, 60–62, 65, 80–81, 90, 98–101, 111–12; heterogeneous nature of, 10, 13, 14, 16, 62–65, 74, 101, 112–13; as commodity, 14, 59–62, 63–65, 91, 96–98, 102–8, 110, 111, 114–17, 220; in domestic fiction, 14, 117–18, 120–23, 126; in Beecher, 14, 131, 132–34, 145; in Thoreau, 14, 131, 137, 140, 143–45, 170, 172; and material culture studies, 16, 65–66; and historical time, 34, 64, 80, 91–94; at Monticello, 55–58; construction of, 66–67, 70; in genre paintings, 67–69, 73–74, 96–101, 102, 137; and natural time, 70–74, 81–83, 85, 88; and neo-

classicism, 73–78; compared to deep time, 156, 170, 172, 186, 190, 205, 209; in Emerson, 186, 190, 192, 205, 209, 217. *See also* Hoadley, Seth; Jerome, Chauncey; Paul, John; Terry, Eli; Wady, James; Willard, Simon

Clonney, James Goodwyn, 137

Cole, Thomas, 19, 50, 53, 54, 182; *The Course of Empire*, 48–51, 53, 173–78, 182–83; *The Subsiding of the Waters of the Deluge*, 174–75

Common Sense (Paine), 223

"Compensation" (Emerson), 204–8, 212, 215

"Connection between Geology and Natural Religion, The" (Hitchcock), 159

Conquest of Mexico (Prescott), 29

Cooper, Carolyn, 85, 93

Course of Empire, The (Cole), 48–51, 53, 173–78, 182–83

Crèvecoeur, J. Hector St. John de, 144

Curtis, George William, 96

Cuvier, Georges, 157

Dana, James D., 158, 162–65, 178, 180, 190

Daniels, Stephen, 48–49

Darwin, Charles, 14

Death of a Nation (Noble), 20–21

De Certeau, Michel, 134

Declaration of Independence, 6

Declaration of Independence of the United States of America (Trumbull), 56

Dekker, George, 49, 51

Democratic Review, 17, 147, 161

Descartes, René, 215

Dickinson, Emily, 159

Dimock, Wai Chee, 26, 221–22

"Divinity School Address" (Emerson), 189

Dohrn–van Rossum, Gerhard, 10
Douglas, Ann, 139
Dubuc, Jean-Baptiste, 75–78
During, Simon, 26

Earth and Man, The (Guyot), 164
Eaton, Amos, 158
Edmonds, Francis William, 98–102, 120
Education of Henry Adams, The (Adams), 153–54
Ehninger, John, 96–98, 102
Eisley, Loren, 154
Elementary Geology (Hitchcock), 158–59, 178
Elias, Norbert, 10–11
Elgin National Watch Company, 94
Elusive Republic, The (McCoy), 12
Emerson, Ralph Waldo, 4, 15, 20, 51, 185, 217, 218, 222, 223
— theories and ideas of: early ideas about natural history, 186, 187, 188–89, 191–92; and deep time, 186, 187, 190, 194–98, 200–201, 208–9, 212, 216; on biblical chronology, 186, 190, 191, 208; on mechanical time, 186, 190, 205; and science, 186–89; and American democracy, 187, 189, 205–6, 209–16; and antihumanism, 187, 198, 211–12, 215–16; and liberal democratic politics, 187, 210–12, 215–216; and Nietzsche, 188, 198–200, 203; and natural theology, 189–90, 197; and geological theory, 193–95, 209, 211; on mastery of time, 202–3, 208, 212; transformation and being within time, 203–6, 215–16; on individualism and social belonging, 205–6, 208–9, 215–16; and Carlyle, 207–8; use of figurative language, 212–14; and Toulmin, 215

— works of: "Experience," 20, 213, 214; journals, 186, 187, 190, 191, 192–94, 200–201; "The Divinity School Address," 189; *Nature* (1836 book), 189, 191–93, 194, 195, 203, 213; "The American Scholar," 189, 194–95; "The Relation of Man to the Globe," 189–90, 194; "The Humanity of Science," 190, 197; "History," 195–98, 200–201, 205, 208; *Essays*, 195–98, 200–211; "The Philosophy of History," 197; "Self-Reliance," 201–6, 208, 210, 215–16; "Compensation," 204–8, 212, 215; "The Over-Soul," 208–9, 210, 216; "The Method of Nature," 209–10, 214; "Nature" (1844 essay), 210–12, 214–16; *English Traits*, 211–12; "The Poet," 213; "Shakespeare," 213; *Representative Men*, 213, 214–15; "Montaigne," 214–15; "Circles," 216
English Traits (Emerson), 211–12
Essay on Population (Malthus), 36–38
Essays (Emerson), 195–98, 200–211
"Experience" (Emerson), 20, 213, 214

Featherstonehaugh, George, 97
Fichte, Johann Gottlieb, 29
Fisher, David Hackett, 27
Fisher, Philip, 40, 98, 137
Foley, Paul, 83
Franklin, Benjamin, 88, 93–94, 103–4
"Franklin" clock (Hoadley), 93–94
Fresonke, Kris, 183
Freud, Sigmund, 181
Futures of American Studies, The (Pease and Wiegman), 9

Gardner, Mrs. H. C., 123–27, 129–30, 132
Garret, Wendell, 74

Gellner, Ernest, 7

Geology, 14–15, 222; and Twain, 146, 149–50; and American conceptions of history, 151–52, 162–65; history of, 152–54; and Church, 154–56; and natural theology, 157–60; of Niagara Falls, 160–61; and American conceptions of the land, 165–70; and Thoreau, 170–73; and Cole, 173–78; and ruins, 178–83; and aesthetics, 183–85; and Emerson, 186–87, 189–95, 198, 209, 211–12, 213; and Nietzsche, 198

Geology and Mineralogy (Buckland), 157

Geology of Massachusetts (Hitchcock), 159

Gibbon, Edward, 47, 48

Gilmore, Michael, 137

Goodman, Russell, 188

Gould, Stephen Jay, 156

Gramsci, Antonio, 220

Gray, Asa, 162–65

"Great Nation of Futurity, The" (O'Sullivan), 17–19, 23, 25–28, 40, 151

Greenough, Horatio, 47

Gross, Robert, 137

Guthrie, James K., 192–93, 203

Guyot, Arnold, 158, 164, 190

Hale, Sarah Josepha, 14, 126–29

Hall, James, 158

Halliburton, Thomas Chandler, 96

Halttunen, Karen, 125

Harper's New Monthly Magazine, 151, 157–58

Harris, John, 168–70, 172, 183

Harvey, Bruce, 30

Hawthorne, Nathaniel, 106

Hensley, Paul, 10

Hepplewhite, George, 75

Herder, Johann Gottfried, 29

"History" (Emerson), 195–98, 200–201, 205, 208

History of the American Clock Business for the Past Sixty Years, and Life of Chauncey Jerome (Jerome), 61, 102–12, 220

History of the Anglo-Saxons (Turner), 191

History of the United States (Bancroft), 42

History of the United States (Willard), 32, 43

Hitchcock, Edward, 15, 158–60, 165–68, 178, 183, 189

Hitchcock, Orra White, 165–68

Hoadley, Silas, 91, 93–96, 107

Home (Sedgwick), 117–20, 124

Howland, E. A., 120–22

"Humanity of Science, The" (Emerson), 190, 197

Hutton, James, 14, 152–53, 195

Icebergs, The (Church), 154–56, 173

Iliad (Homer), 161

Illustrated History of the Centennial Exhibition (McCabe), 94

Illustrations of the Huttonian Theory of the Earth (Playfair), 152

"Imagined community": theory of nation as, 6–7, 9, 11, 26, 32, 74, 218

Introduction to Geology (Bakewell), 160, 180

Irving, Washington, 151, 212

James, C. L. R., 9

Jefferson, Thomas: and Declaration of Independence, 6; and Locke, 6; on westward expansion, 12, 18, 36–37, 39–41; on "empire of liberty," 12, 23, 36, 40; on American development through time, 19, 20, 23, 25, 28, 37–41, 54, 218; on tyranny as corruption,

24, 39, 54–55; and Malthus, 36–37; on heterogeneous time, 40–41; and civic humanism, 46; and Cole, 49; and Monticello, 54–58; and clocks, 55–56; *Autobiography*, 88; on Eddystone Lighthouse, 88; and Thoreau, 144, 170; and geology, 162, 165

Jehlen, Myra, 20–21, 27, 53

Jerome, Chauncey: opens export trade to England, 60, 105–7; *History of the American Clock Business for the Past Sixty Years, and Life of Chauncey Jerome*, 61, 102–12, 220; on clocks and civilization, 61, 111–12; "Introduction" to trade catalog, 93; on clock-making process, 93, 106–7; as businessman, 96, 102–3, 106–7, 220; and clocks as commodities, 96, 103, 104, 107; and market capitalism, 102–12, 114, 117, 220; and Franklin, 103, 104; and clocks as currency, 105, 108; and Barnum, 105, 108, 110

Jerome, Saint, 147

Journals and Letters from France and Great Britain (Willard), 52–53

Joy of Cooking, The, 122

Kammen, Michael, 27

Kant, Immanuel, 191, 207–8

Kateb, George, 15, 188, 205–6, 210–11, 215

Keeping House and House Keeping (Hale), 126–29

Kelsall, Malcolm, 54, 56

Kercheval, Samuel, 38

Kimball, Fiske, 57

Knickerbocker magazine, 182

Krimmel, John Lewis, 67–70, 73–74

"Ktaadn" (Thoreau), 161, 170–73, 177, 184

Kuhn, Thomas, 154

"Labor; Or, Striking for Higher Wages" (Gardner), 123–26

Ladies' Repository, 123

Landes, David, 8

Last Periods of Universal History (Willard), 46

Latour, Bruno, 13–14

Lawson, Richard, 75

Lectures on Rhetoric and Belles Lettres (Blair), 28–29

Leslie, Robert, 55

Letters from the Earth (Twain), 146–50, 156–58

Letters to Mothers (Sigourney), 119

Levin, David, 29, 180

Life on the Mississippi (Twain), 150

Lighthouse alarm clock (Willard), 86–90

Listening to Father's Watch (Spencer), 70

Locke, John: *Two Treatises of Government*, 5, 6

Longfellow, Henry Wadsworth, 67, 73

Lopez, Michael, 188

Ludlow, William, 41, 54, 165

Lukács, Georg, 115, 120

Lyell, Charles, 14, 152–53, 158, 160–61, 173, 178, 180, 182, 189, 193, 195, 209, 211

Lyon, John, 157

Maclure, William, 158

Madison, James, 37, 38, 57

Mallet, Louis, 75–78

Malthus, Thomas, 36–38, 40, 49

Mann, Maybell, 100

Manual of Geology (Dana), 162, 178

Marx, Karl, 28, 114–15, 220

Maynard, Barksdale, 131

McCabe, James, 94, 96, 103–4

McCoy, Drew: *The Elusive Republic*, 12, 37, 38, 46

McCrossen, Alexis, 10

McPhee, John, 156

Melville, Herman, 88, 117

Merish, Lori, 115, 118

"Method of Nature, The" (Emerson), 209–210, 214

Miller, Angela, 183

Minister's Wooing, The (Stowe), 130

Moby-Dick (Melville), 88

Monroe, James, 19

Montaigne, Michel de, 214–15

"Montaigne" (Emerson), 214–15

Monticello, 54–58

Morgan, Philip, 219

Mother's Watch (Clonney), 137

Mount, William Sidney, 67–70

Mumford, Lewis, 7–8

Muséum d'Histoire Naturelle, Paris, 187

"My Friend the Watch" (Curtis), 96

Natural theology, 15, 59, 156–61, 183, 187, 189–90, 191, 197, 232 (n. 1)

Nature (1836 book by Emerson), 189, 191–93, 194, 195, 203, 213

"Nature" (1844 essay by Emerson), 210–12, 214–16

New England Economical Housekeeper and Family Receipt Book, The (Howland), 120–23

Newfield, Christopher, 210–212

New York Times, 158

Nietzsche, Friedrich, 198–200, 203, 214

Noble, David: *Death of a Nation*, 20, 27, 53

Nolen, Spencer, 86

North American Review, 1, 32, 153, 158, 163

Novak, Barbara, 183

Nye, Russell, 47

Olney, Jesse, 30

O'Malley, Michael, 10

"On Truth and Lie in an Extra-Moral Sense" (Nietzsche), 198–99

Origin of Species (Darwin), 198

O'Sullivan, John: "The Great Nation of Futurity," 17–19, 23, 25–28, 40, 151; on American expansion through time, 17–19, 26, 27, 28, 34, 36, 40; and Jefferson, 18, 23, 25, 28, 54; views on tyranny, 23, 25–26; "Annexation," 25–26, 34, 36; and Malthus, 34, 36; and romantic history, 53

"Over-Soul, The" (Emerson), 208–9, 210, 216

Owen, Robert, 158

Packer, Barbara, 193

Paine, Thomas, 223

Paley, William, 157, 189

Patent timepiece (Willard), 83–86

Paul, John, 78–80

Peabody, William O. B., 1–3

Pease, Donald, 22, 27; *The Futures of American Studies*, 9

Perry, Ellwood C., III, 182

"Philosophy of History, The" (Emerson), 197

Pillar-and-scroll shelf clock (Terry), 91–93

Plates Illustrating the Geology and Scenery of Massachusetts (Hitchcock and Hitchcock), 165–68

Playfair, John, 14, 152, 189, 195

Pocock, J. G. A., 5, 7, 22, 23, 46–47

"Poet, The" (Emerson), 213

"Politics" (Emerson), 223

Postnational American studies, 9, 20–22, 221–24, 228 (n. 12), 249 (n. 6)

"Prairies, The" (Bryant), 52

Pratt, Mary Louise, 22

Pre-Adamite Earth, The (Harris), 169–70, 183

Prescott, William, 28; *Conquest of Mexico*, 29
Priestley, Joseph, 38, 39, 40, 57
Principles of Geology (Lyell), 152–53, 160, 173, 178, 182, 189
Prown, Jules, 16, 65

Quilting Frolic (Krimmel), 67–70

Raymond, Henry, 157–58
Reification, 14, 114–16, 118, 120, 134
"Relation of Man to the Globe, The" (Emerson), 189–90, 194
Religion of Geology, The (Hitchcock), 159
Representative Men (Emerson), 213, 214–215
Ricardo, David, 140
Richardson, Robert D., 140, 143, 191
Roberts, Ken, 106
Rollin, Charles, 30
Romero, Lora, 117
Roughing It (Twain), 150
Rowe, John Carlos, 22
Ruins, or the Effects of Time (Cole), 182
Rustic Dance after a Sleigh Ride (Mount), 67–70
Ryan, Mary, 136

"Sam Slick" (Halliburton), 96
Sartor Resartus (Carlyle), 207–8
Say, Jean-Baptiste, 36
Schoolcraft, Henry Rowe: "The Rise of the West," 24–25, 48, 161
Scientific American, 158
Scott, Anne Firor, 31
Scott, Sir Walter, 29
Sedgwick, Catharine, 30, 117–20, 124–27, 129–30, 132–33
"Self-Reliance" (Emerson), 201–6, 208, 210, 215–16

Shakespeare, William, 151, 212, 213
"Shakespeare" (Emerson), 213
Sigourney, Lydia, 30, 119, 127
Silliman, Benjamin, 158, 160, 180–82
Simmel, Georg, 7, 8, 10
Simms, William Gilmore, 19, 24, 25, 29, 47, 48, 53, 54
Sketch-Book, The (Irving), 151, 212
Sklansky, Jeffrey, 114
Smith, Anthony D., 6, 27
Smith, Henry Nash, 18, 25
Smith, Mark M., 10, 133
"Society and Civilization" (Adams), 42
Southern Literary Messenger, 157
Speculator, The (Edmonds), 98–99, 102
Spencer, Lilly Martin, 70
Spruck, Peter, 55
Stadialism, 41–53, 56, 162–64, 173–78, 194
Stephens, Carlene, 10
Stilgoe, John, 88
Stowe, Harriet Beecher, 117, 130
Strasser, Susan, 16
Struggles and Triumphs (Barnum), 110
Subsiding of the Waters of the Deluge, The (Cole), 174–75
Sugar Loaf Mountain, Deerfield (Hitchcock), 165

Taking the Census (Edmonds), 98–102, 120
Temple of Jupiter Serapis, 178–80
Terry, Eli, 4, 60, 91–93, 96, 102–5, 107–8
Terry, Theodore, 108
Theory of the Earth (Hutton), 152
Thomas, Seth, 91, 107
Thompson, E. P., 8, 133, 219
Thoreau, Henry: and Beecher, 4, 14, 74, 130–31, 137–42, 144–45, 205, 218, 220, 223; and national narrative, 4, 74, 223; and masculinity, 14, 139, 144;

representation of market economy as natural, 14, 139–40, 142–45; as domestic writer, 130–31, 139–42, 145; and representative personhood, 137, 141–42; and productive time, 137–39, 141–42, 144–45; *Walden,* 137–45; as public voice, 139, 220, 223; and labor theory of value, 140; "Ktaadn," 161–62, 170–73, 177, 184; on American territory, 161–62, 172–73, 184–85; and deep time, 170–73, 177, 183, 184–85; and Cole, 177, 183; *A Week on the Concord and Merrimack Rivers,* 184–85; and Emerson, 205, 212

Tichi, Cecelia, 130

Time: mechanical (clock time), 1–3, 7–8, 10, 13–14, 55–57, 59–66, 70, 73–74, 78, 85–86, 88–90, 102, 111–24, 128, 132–35, 137, 140, 143–44, 145, 156, 161, 170, 172, 187, 190, 192, 205, 217, 218, 220; and nature, 1–4, 7, 10, 11, 14, 15, 34–38, 52–53, 56, 59, 62–63, 68, 73–74, 83, 85–86, 88, 90, 137–45, 150–56, 161–78, 182–85, 186–87, 190–95, 196–98, 199, 200–201, 202–3, 205, 208, 212–13, 217, 218, 222; as heterogeneous, 2–4, 8–11, 13–14, 40–41, 59, 62, 63–65, 74, 101, 113, 116–17, 130, 144–45, 177–78, 187, 206–8, 218–19; as homogeneous, 4, 6–9, 59, 218–19, 221; and political theory, 5–9, 13–14, 17–22, 26–28, 36–42, 44–47, 54–58, 59–62, 80–81, 111–13, 114–17, 130–45, 151–52, 163–65, 183–85, 188–89, 209–16, 218–19, 220, 221–24; deep time, 15, 151, 156, 165, 168, 169–73, 175, 177, 180–85, 186–87, 189–90, 193–95, 198, 201, 205, 209–12, 214–16, 217–18, 221–22

"Time, Work Discipline, and Industrial Capitalism" (Thompson), 8

Timing (theory of Elias), 10–11

Tonkovich, Nicole, 136

Toulmin, Stephen, 215

Transcendentalist Club, 189

Treatise on Domestic Economy, A (Beecher), 130–36, 141, 145

Trumbull, John, 56

Turner, Frederick Jackson, 18

Turner, Sharon, 191

Twain, Mark, 146–51, 153–54, 156–58

Two Treatises of Government (Locke), 5–6

Uncle Tom's Cabin (Stowe), 117

Universal History in Perspective (Willard), 32, 46

Ussher, James, 147

Vestiges of the Natural History of Creation (Chambers), 148, 153

Wady, James, 70–74, 122

Walden (Thoreau), 137–45

Walls, Laura Dassow, 188, 193

Waltham Watch Company, 94, 96

Washington, George, 3, 75–78, 91, 99–100

Washington (Greenough), 47

Watches: and modernity, 7, 10, 94, 96, 102, 205; as commodities, 13–14, 59, 62, 63–64, 65, 66, 67, 80, 112; in Jefferson, 57; in genre painting, 69–70, 137; and neoclassicism, 75; in domestic fiction, 128

Waterbury Watch Company, 94

Week on the Concord and Merrimack Rivers, A (Thoreau), 184–85

West, Cornel, 15, 188

Wiegman, Robyn, 9

Willard, Emma: and education reform, 19, 30–32, 44–46; history textbooks,

32–34, 43–47, 147; *An Address to the Public*, 30–31, 42–46; *History of the United States*, 32, 43; *Universal History in Perspective*, 32, 46; *Abridged History of the United States*, 34, 43, 44–46; and stadialism, 42–47, 52–53; *Last Periods of Universal History*, 46; *Journals and Letters from France and Great Britain*, 52–53; on Versailles, 52–53; and Jefferson, 54

Willard, Simon: and national narrative, 4; calendar shelf clock, 81–83; and artisanal ideal, 83, 85–86, 90–91, 103, 104, 112, 220; and patents, 83–85; patent timepiece ("banjo clock"), 83–86; lighthouse alarm clock, 86–90; and Terry, 91; and Jerome, 103, 104

Willard brothers (Aaron, Benjamin, Ephraim), 81, 112

Willis, Nathaniel Parker, 178–80, 182

Wilton, Andrew, 49

Winthrop, John, 135

Wordsworth, William, 29

Yankee Peddler (Ehninger), 96–98, 102

Young Man's Guide, The (Alcott), 94

Zea, Philip, 122–23